Moving from COBOL to C

Moving from COBOL to C

Mo Budlong

A Division of Prentice Hall Computer Publishing
11711 North College, Carmel, Indiana 46302 USA

FIRST EDITION

International Standard Book Number: 0-672-30327-2

Library of Congress Catalog Card Number: 93-83595

96 95 94 93 4 3 2 1

Interpretation of the printing code: the rightmost double-digit number is the year of the book's printing; the rightmost single-digit, the number of the book's printing. For example, a printing code of 93-1 shows that the first printing of the book occurred in 1993.

Composed in Palatino and MCPdigital by Prentice Hall Computer Publishing

Printed in the United States of America

Trademarks

Publisher
Richard K. Swadley

Acquisitions Manager
Jordan Gold

Acquisitions Editor
Stacy Hiquet

Development Editor
Philip Paxton

Senior Editor
Tad Ringo

Manuscript Editor
Howard Peirce

Editorial Coordinators
Rebecca S. Freeman
Bill Whitmer

Editorial Assistants
Rosemarie Graham
Sharon Cox

Technical Reviewer
Wendy Clark

Marketing Manager
Greg Wiegand

Cover Designer
Dan Armstrong

Director of Production and Manufacturing
Jeff Valler

Production Manager
Corinne Walls

Imprint Manager
Kelli Widdifield

Book Designer
Michele Laseau

Production Analyst
Mary Beth Wakefield

Proofreading/Indexing Coordinator
Joelynn Gifford

Production
Julie Brown
Mitzi F. Gianakos
Howard Jones
John Kane
Heather Kaufman
Wendy Ott
Juli Pavey
Angela Pozdol
Linda Quigley
Michelle Self
Donna Winter
Alyssa Yesh

Indexers
John Sleeva
Suzanne Snyder

OVERVIEW

CONTENTS

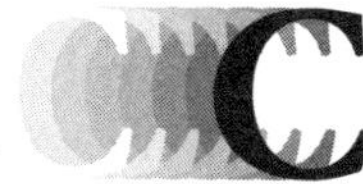

ACKNOWLEDGMENTS

This is my first project for Sams Publishing and Prentice Hall, and I want to thank Stacy Hiquet and Phil Paxton for the work they put in on the project and for their consistent support and encouragement. Howard Peirce and Wendy Clark did a terrific job and had some great ideas for the finished book.

I want to thank Heather Mlodinow, an accomplished COBOL programmer who struggled with my approach to the move to C, and her husband, Len, an accomplished screenwriter, who struggled with my approach to English.

Mostly I want to thank my wife, Helen. She has always been my first line editor and my first line of defense against becoming pompous or pedantic. She always seems to know just when to laugh at me. Helen, Heather, and Len all enthusiastically supported the project, offering real help when I needed it, so thanks guys (or rather, gals and guy).

About the Author

Mo Budlong has been a programmer and hardware engineer for 20 years. He started his computer career in England, designing the hardware for a computer-controlled camera fader for BBC Television.

He has taught and lectured about computers for 15 years. Mo is currently a software consultant with several software packages on the market, including BASIC and C compilers, and an assembler written for special-purpose computers.

Mo is the author of many computer books, including the *COBOL Cookbook Volume 1,* the *VS COBOL Cookbooks Volumes 1, 2 and 3,* and the *C100 Manual.* He has regular columns in two national computer magazines and has been published in *Portable 100, The Programmer's Journal,* and *The C Gazette.*

INTRODUCTION

Welcome to C

C created a revolution in programming. It is fast, relatively easy to implement on different computers, and can be used either for quick and dirty programming tasks or for involved data processing problems. It started as a language used to develop operating systems, compilers, and programming tools.

C is far more powerful than this limited area suggests, and it has become the language of choice for just about every type of processing except business-oriented programming.

C is a very rudimentary language. The actual kernel of C is a very small, but extendible, set of commands. For example, C contains no input and output commands. Input and output are handled by extending the language with a library of routines that write to the screen or accept data from the keyboard.

Early C compilers sometimes came with a very small companion set of library routines. I/O and data formatting were left to the programmer. Moving C to a new machine meant creating routines from scratch. The C kernel language does not have an `ACCEPT` or `DISPLAY` verb, or anything like them. In those days, the idea of taking on an accounting project was unthinkable. You had to start by writing a screen handler, a keyboard handler, printer formatting, and a host of support logic, as well as file I/O. These exist as an integral part of COBOL, but do not exist for C.

Slowly, the C library has become standardized, and it is more and more possible to think of C as a complete language, because the parts that were missing are now supplied as a library with any new compiler that you buy.

ANSI C

The American National Standards Institute has created a definition for a standardized C and support library which has been adopted by most writers of C compilers. This standard dramatically impacts what you can expect from the language.

C++ started as an extension of C, although it has since achieved the status of a separate language. C++ uses a more rigid approach to C, which before had been fairly relaxed. The influence of C++ on C compilers is just becoming noticeable.

The Future of C

C is gradually working its way across the boundaries that previously limited its use to utilities and text processing. C is now used to code database languages and spreadsheets, and is working its way into business computing as an applications and systems language.

Understanding C is crucial for the future. The popularity of C has spawned new languages such as Ada and C++, and a foundation in C will make those languages more accessible to you.

About This Book

Many COBOL programmers have attempted to learn C with little or no success. I was one such programmer, and I came to C with a solid background in hardware design, assembly language programming, BASIC, and COBOL. I tried the basic text on C, *The C Programming Language,* by Kernighan and Ritchie, the authors of the language. My first effort was a bust. I later tried a book about C for BASIC programmers and another about C for COBOL programmers. Both of them helped me get a foot in the door, but I found that after the first couple of chapters, I was left in the dust.

So I studied the problem. I discovered the answer in the *Basic Study Manual,* by L. Ron Hubbard. This gem of a book includes the principal reasons that a person has trouble studying a subject, including why *I* was having trouble, and how to remedy those problems. Every book or course I had seen on C took a quantum leap from teaching you C to assuming that you knew C and teaching you some tricks. This is described in the *Basic Study Manual* as a "skipped gradient."

I went back, worked out where things had been skipped for me, and found a patient C expert. I bought him dinner and got myself straightened out over coffee by asking questions in the right area. This kind of research lead to this book.

This book uses an untraditional approach to C. The parts of C are introduced in a completely different order than the average C text or curriculum (which obviously doesn't work). This book compares C to what you know and slowly builds up to the rest of the language.

C professionals might laugh at this book. In fact, one such professional to whom I described this project looked at me aghast and said, "I didn't know that COBOL programmers *could* be taught C!"

I don't think the problem lies with COBOL programmers, but with the texts and courses.

Who Should Use This Book

This book is aimed at intermediate and advanced COBOL programmers. Beginners will also benefit from the book, but if you begin to feel that you have skipped a gradient (feel confused or reeling), back away and nail down COBOL first.

What I Expect from You

You are expected to be familiar with the basic steps of editing, compiling, and linking. If you are not, review Appendix A, "Program Development," which covers the basics. I also expect that you will code, compile, link, and run the examples in the book, and experiment with the concepts.

Working with Your Compiler

Up through Chapter 8, "Scope, Storage, and Prototyping," this book uses the original "laid back" style of C coding. If you are using a modern C compiler, you may find that your compiler issues many warnings about functions that are not declared or functions that don't return values, and generally nags you about syntactic conventions that have come into existence in recent years. Unfortunately, a lot of this syntax interferes with learning the basics of C. In order to shut your compiler up, there should be an option that allows you to reduce the warning levels issued by the compiler. A warning level of 1 is all you usually need.

Target Compilers

All of the COBOL in this book was compiled and tested using the MS-DOS version of Acu-COBOL, and/or the SCO UNIX Acu-COBOL and Microfocus COBOL compilers. Some of it was also tested on the VAX COBOL compiler.

The C compilers used for most of the book were Microsoft's C/C++ 7.0 and Microsoft's Visual C++ (which includes C). Some testing was also done on an SCO UNIX C compiler and the VAX C compiler. All examples should be portable across most C compilers.

Microsoft's C/C++ 7.0 C and C++ package was replaced by Microsoft Visual C++ (which includes a C compiler) in March 1993. All references to Microsoft C/C++ 7.0 or Microsoft Visual C++ refer to both compilers unless the text explicitly differentiates between the two.

Plan of the Book

The book is illustrated with many comparisons between COBOL and C, both simple and complex.

The book is in roughly three sections (though this division is not formal):

- The early chapters are COBOL programs with C versions for comparison. This keeps the material on familiar ground.
- The middle chapters deal with C concepts and are partially explained with examples in COBOL.
- The final chapters are new concepts in C sometimes explained with COBOL, and end with some very advanced C techniques.

I have avoided coding C utility examples. Many books and courses are illustrated with examples of how to build a compiler or create simple language interpreters. Although you will eventually be able to do this, and may even want to, I have tackled C in COBOL terms, dealing with user input, screen display, maintaining files, and building record structures for storing data. This is the world you know, and C can deal with these problems. If you study C as a data processing language rather than a language you can use to write operating systems, you will gain a much greater understanding of the language.

By the time you reach the end of the book, you should be able to code professionally in C and ready to explore all of the language.

Supporting Material

The book also includes several appendixes designed to supplement areas touched on in the book.

- Appendix A, "Program Development," covers the basics of editing, compiling, and linking under MS-DOS, UNIX, and VAX.
- Appendix B, "COBOL to C Cross-Reference," is a useful cross-reference of C and COBOL programming syntax where comparisons exist.
- Appendix C, "The Standard C Library," is a listing of some of the most popular functions from a standard C library. It is provided so that you can quickly look up a library function used in the book. For a detailed description of a library function, you should refer to your compiler documentation.
- Appendix D, "Filters, Pipes, and Redirection," describes redirection. This is a technique used in C programs that is not available to COBOL programmers.
- There are two things that C does not contain that it desperately needs. A solid screen/keyboard interface, and a good indexed file handling system. There are commercial packages (libraries) designed to address these shortcomings, and Appendix E, "Screen Handling and Indexed Files," discusses some of the alternatives available.

This book concludes with a glossary of unusual terms used in the book. I have attempted to explain new terms as I introduce them, but if you find yourself puzzling over a word, check for it in the glossary. If you don't find it there, ask around, look it up, or define it somehow. One misunderstood word can make the rest of the text confusing.

Companion Disk

A low-cost companion disk is available through the order form at the back of this book. The disk will save you a lot of typing. If you choose to order the disk, it will be sent to you quickly so that you can begin work as soon as possible.

A Final Note

If you are interested in the *Basic Study Manual,* it is available from the Bookstore Officer at (818) 957-1500. This book sure straightened me out about studying, and I have to recommend it.

1

Elements of C

Glance briefly at a COBOL program and an equivalent C program, and you might get the impression that you're looking at programming languages from alternate realities. In one reality, judicious sobriety and logical progression have yielded the practical COBOL language. In the other, chaos and unreason are a way of life, and one of its mad inhabitants threw C together after having tea with Alice.

In spite of appearances, C is an orderly language, but one that is very different from COBOL. In this chapter, I will explore the following differences:

- C free-form source versus COBOL structured source
- C `#include` compared to COBOL `COPY`
- C variables versus COBOL `DATA DIVISION`
- C functions versus COBOL paragraphs
- C versus COBOL program entry and exit points
- C and COBOL identifiers (variable names, function names and paragraph names)
- C punctuation
- An initial look at C arithmetic

- A brief look at displaying data on the screen
- Comments in C

Once you understand these basic differences, you will be ready to start writing C programs.

Free-Form Source Code in C

The quickest way to get a feel for C is to compare simple C and COBOL programs. The examples in Listings 1.1 and 1.2 set up two numbers and add them together.

Listing 1.1. ADDER.COB.

```
000100 IDENTIFICATION DIVISION.
000200 PROGRAM-ID. ADDER.
000300 ENVIRONMENT DIVISION.
000400
000500 DATA DIVISION.
000550 WORKING-STORAGE SECTION.
000600 01  VAR-A     PIC 99.
000700 01  VAR-B     PIC 99.
000800
000900 PROCEDURE DIVISION.
001000 MAIN-LOGIC SECTION.
001100 PROGRAM-BEGIN.
001200    MOVE 1 TO VAR-A.
001300    MOVE 2 TO VAR-B.
001400    PERFORM ADD-EM-UP.
001500    DISPLAY VAR-A.
001600 EXIT-PROGRAM.
001700    EXIT PROGRAM.
001800 STOP-RUN.
001900    STOP RUN.
002000
002100 THE-OTHER SECTION.
002200 ADD-EM-UP.
002300    COMPUTE VAR-A
002400          = VAR-A + VAR-B.
002500* or ADD VAR-B TO VAR-A.
002600
```

Listing 1.2. adder.c.

```
#include <stdio.h>



int var_a;
int var_b;


main()
{
    var_a = 1;
    var_b = 2;
    add_em_up();
    printf("%d",var_a);
}





add_em_up()
{
    var_a = var_a + var_b;
}
```

The first apparent difference is that C seems to be much less formal. There are no column requirements or line numbering. C is a free-form language. The compiler starts at the beginning of the file and ignores white space, spaces, tabs, and end-of-line characters; it then compiles any non-whitespace characters that it finds. Listing 1.3 is another example of the same program using the free-form rules. Notice that in spite of the differences in layout, all of the elements are still there.

Listing 1.3. adder.c—scrambled code.

```
#include <stdio.h>
int var_a;  int var_b;
main() { var_a = 1; var_b = 2;
 add_em_up(); printf("%d",var_a);}
add_em_up() { var_a = var_a + var_b; }
```

Because C's source code structure is open-ended, it is necessary to adopt some conventions that make the source code readable. Listing 1.2 demonstrates a fairly common convention, although there are others. If you run across something that looks like Listing 1.3, the programmer may be trying to obscure the source code deliberately.

Scrambled C

Since C has become such a portable language, it is possible to develop source code that will compile on numerous machines without modification. You can create a package on one machine and expect it to run on others as well. The problem is that you must have access to each of the target machines in order to compile and link an executable. In the UNIX world this is an impossible task.

Developers have taken to distributing source code to buyers with instructions on how to compile it on their target machine. The drawback to this is that you let your source code go.

One solution is to scramble the code using bizarre source code layouts and meaningless variable names in an effort to obscure what is going on in the program.

This has become such a popular technique that there are commercial products on the market that scramble the code and generally try to make it unreadable.

C *#include* Files

As you may have guessed, the `#include` directive in Listing 1.2 is similar to the COBOL `COPY` verb. It copies the entire source code of the file named within the angle brackets (<>). An alternative syntax allows for quotes (for example, `"stdio.h"`), but for now, stick with the angle brackets.

The file stdio.h is a standard header file (hence the .h extension) needed for most programs. For now, just include it in all programs. This will cause no problems, and I will explain the file in more detail in Chapter 8, "Scope, Storage, and Prototyping." The stdio.h file should have been distributed with your C compiler and should already be installed on your system.

The `#include` directive is one of the few C position-dependent commands. An `#include` statement must start on a line of its own, and it must be the first word on the line. It doesn't have to start at column 1, but only tabs and spaces are allowed to appear on a line before it. Thus,

```
#include <stdio.h>
```

and

```
#include <stdio.h>
```

are both valid, but

```
int var_a;     #include <stdio.h>
```

is not.

Variables— Definition and Initialization

Listing 1.2 is fairly easy to follow and compare to the COBOL example. The first two lines define the global variables `var_a` and `var_b` as integers, and reserve space for them. This is the job normally taken care of by the working storage section of a COBOL program.

In C, the declaration and definition of a numeric global variable is guaranteed to set the value of the variable to zero. COBOL requires data items to be initialized or the contents are unpredictable. C does a default initialization to zero for numeric variables, but also allows initialization. Listings 1.4 and 1.5 are the COBOL and C versions of the same program, with the initialization done either in working storage or at definition.

Listing 1.4. ADDER.COB—initialization.

```
000100 IDENTIFICATION DIVISION.
000200 PROGRAM-ID. ADDER.
000300 ENVIRONMENT DIVISION.
000400
000500 DATA DIVISION.
000550 WORKING-STORAGE SECTION.
000600 01   VAR-A  PIC 99 VALUE 1.
000700 01   VAR-B  PIC 99 VALUE 2.
000800
000900 PROCEDURE DIVISION.
001000 MAIN-LOGIC SECTION.
001100 PROGRAM-BEGIN.
001300     PERFORM ADD-EM-UP.
```

continues

Listing 1.4. continued

```
001400     DISPLAY VAR-A.
001500 EXIT-PROGRAM.
001600     EXIT PROGRAM.
001700 STOP-RUN.
001800      STOP RUN.
001900
002000 THE-OTHER SECTION.
002100 ADD-EM-UP.
002200     COMPUTE VAR-A =
002300     VAR-A + VAR-B.
002400* or ADD VAR-B TO VAR-A.
002500
```

C VERSION

Listing 1.5. adder.c—initialization.

```
#include <stdio.h>




int var_a = 1;
int var_b = 2;


main()
{
     add_em_up();
     printf("%d",var_a);
}





add_em_up()
{
     var_a = var_a + var_b;
}
```

C Functions and COBOL Paragraphs

C functions are the equivalent of COBOL procedure paragraphs. Listing 1.6 shows the paragraph structure of adder.cob, while Listing 1.7 shows the equivalent functions for adder.c. This C program contains the functions `main()` and `add_em_up()`. In general, a function in C has the syntax

```
function()
{
    [body of the function]
}
```

A function can have any name that you want (other than a reserved word, or *keyword* as it is called in C).

Listing 1.6. ADDER.COB—paragraphs.

```
000100 IDENTIFICATION DIVISION.
000200 PROGRAM-ID. ADDER.
000300 ENVIRONMENT DIVISION.
000400
000500 DATA DIVISION.
000550 WORKING-STORAGE SECTION.
000600 01   VAR-A  PIC 99 VALUE 1.
000700 01   VAR-B  PIC 99 VALUE 2.
000800
000900 PROCEDURE DIVISION.
001000 MAIN-LOGIC SECTION.
001100 PROGRAM-BEGIN.
001300     PERFORM ADD-EM-UP.
001400     DISPLAY VAR-A.
001500 EXIT-PROGRAM.
001600     EXIT PROGRAM.
001700 STOP-RUN.
001800     STOP RUN.
001900
002000 THE-OTHER SECTION.
002100 ADD-EM-UP.
002200      COMPUTE VAR-A =
002300          VAR-A + VAR-B.
002400
```

Listing 1.7. adder.c—functions.

```
#include <stdio.h>



int var_a = 1;
int var_b = 2;


main()
{
     add_em_up();
     printf("%d",var_a);
}




add_em_up()
{
     var_a = var_a + var_b;
}
```

C Program Entry and Exit Points

One function is special in C: the `main()` function. Every C program must have one. When the compiler sees a function named `main()`, it sets up `main()` as the entry point to the program. All C programs begin executing at `main()`.

The `main()` function is roughly analogous to `PROCEDURE DIVISION` in COBOL, with a few differences. A COBOL `PROCEDURE DIVISION` can begin with `DECLARATIVES`. These are special routines that are executed in the event of an error in processing. They are not executed as the first steps in the program.

To be more precise, `main()` is analogous to the first non-`DECLARATIVES` paragraph in a COBOL program.

A C function exits (or returns) at the closing brace (}), just as a COBOL function exits at the end of the paragraph. In C, this exit behavior extends to the main function, and the closing brace causes a return to the operating system or level from which the program was called. Listings 2.8 and 2.9 highlight the differences in the two types of entry and exit.

Listing 1.8. ADDER.COB—program entry and exit.

```
000100 IDENTIFICATION DIVISION.
000200 PROGRAM-ID. ADDER.
000300 ENVIRONMENT DIVISION.
000400
000500 DATA DIVISION.
000550 WORKING-STORAGE SECTION.
000600 01  VAR-A    PIC 99 VALUE 1.
000700 01  VAR-B    PIC 99 VALUE 2.
000800
000900 PROCEDURE DIVISION.
001000 MAIN-LOGIC SECTION.
001100 PROGRAM-BEGIN.
001300     PERFORM ADD-EM-UP.
001400     DISPLAY VAR-A.
001500 EXIT-PROGRAM.
001600     EXIT PROGRAM.
001700 STOP-RUN.
001800     STOP RUN.
001900
002000 THE-OTHER SECTION.
002100 ADD-EM-UP.
002200     COMPUTE VAR-A =
002300          VAR-A + VAR-B.
002400* or ADD VAR-B TO VAR-A.
002500
```

Listing 1.9. adder.c—program entry and exit.

```
#include <stdio.h>




int var_a = 1;
```

continues

Listing 1.9. continued

```
int var_b = 2;



main()
{
     add_em_up();
     printf("%d",var_a);
}



add_em_up()
{
     var_a = var_a + var_b;
}
```

C requires no special `PROGRAM EXIT` syntax, although there are some special ways of exiting a C program that I will cover in Chapter 9, "Stream File I/O."

C Punctuation

Statements in C end with a semicolon (`;`) rather than the COBOL period (`.`) used to end a sentence.

Once you name your function, append parentheses to the end and enclose the body of the function in braces (`{}`). As you learn more about C, you will see that the parentheses perform an additional task—they're more than just punctuation.

C allows multiple variables to be defined on one line by separating the variable names with commas (`,`). For example,

```
int var_a, var_b;
```

defines two integer variables.

C similarly allows multiple assignment operations using the equal sign (=):

```
main()
{
    var_a =  var_b = 2;
}
```

This style of assignment is similar to the COBOL multiple `MOVE` statement, as shown below.

```
MOVE 2 TO VAR-A
          VAR-B.
```

C Identifiers

An identifier is a label for a variable name or function name or any other label that you make up for use in the program. In the sample listings `var_a`, `var_b`, `main`, and `add_em_up` are all identifiers.

Identifiers may contain the characters *A* through *Z*, *a* through *z*, 0 through 9 and the underscore (_) character. An identifier may not start with a digit (0–9).

Table 1.1. Valid and invalid C identifiers.

Valid Identifiers	*Invalid Identifiers*
`main()`	`100_main()`
`Special_Routine()`	`200_Special_Routine()`
`do_it_to_it()`	`do-it-to-it()`
`CUSTOMER_BALANCE`	`CUSTOMER-BALANCE`
`_percent_result`	`_%_result`
`three_by_5`	`3_by_5`
`total_dollars`	`total_$`

The maximum length of an identifier is dependent on the target machine, compiler, and linker. Most modern compilers limit data names to 30 or 31 characters. The Microsoft C/C++ 7.0 compiler allows up to 247 characters in an identifier!

Linkers, however, are fussier. Most linkers examine a subset of the full length of the identifier and use that as the variable name. The Microsoft linker will support a full 247 characters, but many linkers are limited to 8–30 characters. Some older, less common linkers have a limit as small as 6 letters.

The result is that a C program containing long variable names might compile correctly, but the linker would complain of multiply defined symbols. For example, if you define the following variables:

```
int this_is_the_total_for_column_a;
int this_is_the_total_for_column_b;
```

the code might compile correctly, but a linker limited to 14 significant characters will return the following:

```
Multiple definition of symbol     <this_is_the_to>
```

Check your linker and compiler documentation, use sensible variable names, and you should have little trouble.

Arithmetic in C

For numeric variables, the COBOL verbs `MOVE`, `COMPUTE`, `ADD`, `SUBTRACT`, `MULTIPLY`, and `DIVIDE`, are handled by direct assignment operations.

Table 1.2. A short comparison of COBOL and C arithmetic operators.

COBOL Arithmetic	*C Equivalents*
`MOVE VAR-A TO VAR-B.`	`var_b = var_a;`
`MOVE ZEROES TO VAR-A.`	`var_a = 0;`
`SUBTRACT 1 FROM VAR-A.`	`var_a = var_a - 1;`
`COMPUTE VAR-A = 7.`	`var_a = 7;`

In fact, a C assignment operation looks very much like a COBOL `COMPUTE` assignment without the `COMPUTE` verb:

```
COMPUTE VAR-A = 7.                  var_a = 7;
COMPUTE VAR-A = VAR-A + VAR-B.      var_a = var_a + var_b;
```

Here's one simple way to convert MULTIPLY, DIVIDE, ADD, and SUBTRACT verbs: First work out how you would execute that statement with a COMPUTE verb, and then remove the COMPUTE.

Displaying Data

Perhaps the most mysterious part of the C program in Listing 1.2 is the call to the printf() function.

```
printf("%d",var_a);
```

COBOL uses the DISPLAY verb for placing data on the screen. C has no such verb. C was designed to be a machine-independent language; you cannot maintain that independence if you attempt to handle screen I/O as a built-in part of the language.

The solution to this and other similar problems is to create a library of C functions that are specific to the target machine. The standard C library includes functions to get keyboard input, display screen output, read and write files and many other tasks. This library is linked to by the linker. (For more information about linking and library building, see Appendix A, "Program Development.")

The printf() function is one of the functions in the standard library. It prints a string of characters on the screen. printf() has no problems printing a string, but to print numeric values, it needs to know what type of numeric value it is printing. C supports several numeric types, which I will go into in more detail in Chapter 2, "Math in C."

The values within the parentheses after printf() are called arguments. If there is more than one argument, they are separated by commas. In Listing 1.2 and Listing 1.5, the arguments are "%d" and var_a. The "%d" is a format string that tells you that the next value is an integer.

In COBOL terms, think of this as

```
CALL "printf" USING FORMAT-STRING VAR-A.
```

The printf() will come up again and again in later chapters, as it is a very powerful function for formatting and displaying data on the screen. It is discussed in detail in Chapter 4, "More on Strings and Pointers."

Commenting C Code

COBOL creates comments by ignoring everything in a line of text if an asterisk appears in column 7. All ramblings to the right of the asterisk are ignored by the compiler.

The C comment mechanism, in keeping with the freewheeling style of C, is much less structured. Comments may span several lines. C comments begin with a slash and an asterisk (/*) and end with an asterisk and a slash (*/). Everything between these opening and closing marks is ignored by the compiler.

Listings 1.10 and 1.11 are modified and commented versions of the same program.

For the sake of simplicity, I will omit the line numbering from COBOL listings from this point on in the book. (This will probably save the printer a few gallons of ink.)

Listing 1.10. ADDER.COB with comments.

```
 IDENTIFICATION DIVISION.
 PROGRAM-ID. ADDER.

* THIS PROGRAM ADDS TWO INTEGERS
* AND DISPLAYS THE RESULT.

 ENVIRONMENT DIVISION.

 DATA DIVISI/ON.
 WORKING-STORAGE SECTION.
 01  VAR-A     PIC 99.
 01  VAR-B     PIC 99.

 PROCEDURE DIVISION.
 MAIN-LOGIC SECTION.
 PROGRAM-BEGIN.
     MOVE 1 TO VAR-A.
     MOVE 2 TO VAR-B.
     PERFORM ADD-EM-UP.
     DISPLAY VAR-A.
 EXIT-PROGRAM.
     EXIT PROGRAM.
```

```
 STOP-RUN.
     STOP RUN.

 THE-OTHER SECTION.
 ADD-EM-UP.
COMPUTE VAR-A
     = VAR-A + VAR-B.
```

Listing 1.11. adder.c with comments.

```
#include <stdio.h>

/*This program adds two integers
and displays the results.*/




int var_a;
int var_b;


main()
{
     var_a = 1;
     var_b = 2;
     add_em_up();
     printf("%d",var_a);
}





add_em_up()
{
     var_a = var_a + var_b;
}
```

C comments can include asterisks, slashes, or any other characters; only the `*/` combination signals the end of the comment. Listings 1.12 and 1.13 provide two more examples of commenting.

Listing 1.12. adder.c—more comment styles.

```
#include <stdio.h>

/*
 * This program adds two integers
 * and displays the result.
 */

int var_a;
int var_b;

main()
{
     var_a = 1;
     var_b = 2;
     add_em_up();
     printf("%d",var_a);
}

add_em_up()
{
     var_a = var_a + var_b;
}
```

Listing 1.13. adder.c—more comment styles.

```
#include <stdio.h>

/*------------------------------
This program adds two integers
and displays the result.
------------------------------*/

int var_a;
int var_b;

main()
{
     var_a = 1;
     var_b = 2;
     add_em_up();
     printf("%d",var_a);
}
```

```
add_em_up()
{
     var_a = var_a + var_b;
}
```

C comments may be embedded anywhere in the text of the source code file (except between quotation marks) and still be treated as comments. Listing 1.14 provides some useful and some silly examples.

Listing 1.14. adder.c—sample comments.

```
#include <stdio.h>

/*************************************
 * This program adds two integers
 * and displays the result.
*************************************/

int var_a;                    /* result will be stored here */
int var_b;

main()
{
     var_a = 1;               /* a one */
     var_b = 2;               /* a two*/
     add_em_up();
     printf("%d",var_a);
}

/*This adds the two variables */
add_em_up(/*this is a comment*/)
{
     var_a = var_a + var_b;
}
```

Some C compilers allow nested comments, but it is not a good idea to use them. Not all compilers allow this, and nested comments are confusing. Listing 1.15 shows why you might want to use nested comments, but this technique will also drive some compilers crazy.

Listing 1.15. adder.c—nested comments.

```
#include <stdio.h>

/**************************************
 * This program adds two integers
 * and displays the result.
**************************************/

int var_a;       /* result will be stored here */
int var_b;

main()
{
     var_a = 1;                         /* a one */
     var_b = 2;                         /* a two*/
     add_em_up();
     printf("%d",var_a);
}

/*This adds the two variables.
This is the original version of the routine
that added var_a to var_b instead of vice versa.
It has been commented out by the asterisk slash
at the end of the function.
add_em_up()
{
/* add var_a to var_b */
     var_b = var_b + var_a;
}
This ends the comment.
*/

/*This adds the two variables correctly.*/
add_em_up(/*this is a comment*/)
{
     var_a = var_a + var_b;
}
```

Unless the compiler allows nested comments, the opening `/*` of `/* add var_a to var_b */` will be ignored as it is already within the comment started at `/*This adds the....` The closing `*/` of `/* add var_a to var_b */` will be seen as the closing of the comment started at `/*This adds the...` and the compiler will see only half of a function.

If your compiler produces an `Unexpected end of file` error, you should suspect that you have nested comments, and the compiler has lost its place in the source code.

Summary

You now have the basic information you need to start writing and reading C programs: source code layout, naming conventions, punctuation, some simple arithmetic, entry and exit to the main logic, and information display.

One of the biggest differences between C and COBOL is in the way each handles numeric data types. Chapter 2, "C Arithmetic," will get you over this hurdle.

2

C Arithmetic

C arithmetic operators function much like COBOL operators although the syntax is different. C is also missing some useful modifiers such as `ROUNDED` and `REMAINDER IN` for division, but there are ways around these problems.

Numeric data types in C are used in the same ways that you use COBOL numeric data types, but they have a different structure.

In this chapter you will learn about:

- C operators for `COMPUTE` and `MOVE`
- C operators for `ADD`, `SUBTRACT`, `MULTIPLY`, and `DIVIDE`
- C increment and decrement operators
- C handling for `DIVIDE WITH REMAINDER`
- C integer data types
- C floating-point data types
- C floating-point arithmetic operators
- Mixing integers and floating-point types
- Notes on rounding
- Precedence of operators

The subject of representing numbers on a computer can get very technical. Rather than try to cover the whole subject technically, I want to approach it by giving you enough information that you can understand and operate with C numbers.

C Operators for *COMPUTE* and *MOVE*

You have already had a brief look at some C arithmetic. Listings 2.1 and 2.2 expand on the adder program by using `MOVE` and `COMPUTE` to sum two variables into a third.

Listing 2.1. ADDER.COB—`COMPUTE` and `MOVE`.

```
IDENTIFICATION DIVISION.
PROGRAM-ID. ADDER.
ENVIRONMENT DIVISION.

DATA DIVISION.
WORKING-STORAGE SECTION.
01   VAR-A          PIC 99.
01   VAR-B          PIC 99.
01   VAR-C          PIC 99.

PROCEDURE DIVISION.
MAIN-LOGIC SECTION.
PROGRAM-BEGIN.
    MOVE 1 TO VAR-A.
    MOVE 2 TO VAR-B.
    PERFORM ADD-EM-UP.
    DISPLAY VAR-C.
EXIT-PROGRAM.
    EXIT PROGRAM.
STOP-RUN.
    STOP RUN.

THE-OTHER SECTION.
ADD-EM-UP.
    COMPUTE VAR-C =
         VAR-A + VAR-B.
```

Listing 2.2. adder.c—arithmetic operators.

```
#include <stdio.h>

int var_a;
int var_b;
int var_c;

main()
{
     var_a = 1;
     var_b = 2;
     add_em_up();
     printf("%d",var_c);
}

add_em_up()
{
     var_c = var_a + var_b;
}
```

C Operators for *ADD, SUBTRACT, MULTIPLY,* and *DIVIDE*

C provides a set of combined operators that has the same effect as the COBOL verbs `ADD`, `SUBTRACT`, `MULTIPLY`, and `DIVIDE`. The combined operator is created by using a standard arithmetic operator, followed immediately by an equal sign (=). The operators are `+=`, `-=`, `*=`, and `/=`. The COBOL operators and their C equivalents are shown in Table 2.1.

Table 2.1. `ADD`, `SUBTRACT`, `MULTIPLY`, **and** `DIVIDE`.

COBOL Operator	*C Operator*
`ADD 2 TO VAR-A.`	`var_a += 2;`

continues

Table 2.1. continued

COBOL Operator	*C Operator*
`SUBTRACT VAR-B FROM VAR-A.`	`var_a -= var_b;`
`MULTIPLY VAR-A BY ( 1 + 2).`	`var_a *= (1 + 2);`
`DIVIDE VAR-B BY VAR-A.`	`var_b /= var_a;`

These operators resolve the expression to the right of the operator and then add to, subtract from, multiply by, or divide into the expression to left of the operator. The result is then stored in the variable on the left side. For example, if `var_a` is assigned the value `3`, and you execute `var_a += 2`, then `var_a` now has the value `5`.

It is important to remember that the combined operators are each a single operator, and no spaces should appear between the first character and the equal sign (=).

It is also good practice to insert a space before and after the combined operator, as shown in Listing 2.4. I have run across a few compilers that cannot handle a combined operator unless it is so separated. In theory, omitting the extra spaces should not be a problem, but you will see, as you use more complex C expressions, that the extra spaces improve readability.

Listings 2.3 and 2.4 compare a flurry of arithmetic in each language.

Listing 2.3. ADDER.COB—`ADD`, `SUBTRACT`, `MULTIPLY`, and `DIVIDE`.

```
IDENTIFICATION DIVISION.
PROGRAM-ID. ADDER.
ENVIRONMENT DIVISION.

DATA DIVISION.
WORKING-STORAGE SECTION.
01  VAR-A        PIC 99.
01  VAR-B        PIC 99.
01  VAR-C        PIC 99.

PROCEDURE DIVISION.
MAIN-LOGIC SECTION.
PROGRAM-BEGIN.
    MOVE 1 TO VAR-A.
    MOVE 3 TO VAR-B.
```

```
     PERFORM COMPUTE-EM-UP.
     DISPLAY VAR-C.
 EXIT-PROGRAM.
     EXIT PROGRAM.
 STOP-RUN.
     STOP RUN.

 THE-OTHER SECTION.
 COMPUTE-EM-UP.
     SUBTRACT 1 FROM VAR_B.
     MULTIPLY VAR_B BY VAR-B.
     ADD 1 TO VAR_A.
     DIVIDE VAR_A BY VAR_B.
     COMPUTE VAR-C =
          VAR-A + VAR-B.
```

Listing 2.4. adder.c—combined operators.

```
#include <stdio.h>

int var_a;
int var_b;
int var_c;

main()
{
     var_a = 1;
     var_b = 2;
     compute_em_up();
     printf("%d",var_c);
}

compute_em_up()
{
     var_b -= 1;
     var_b *= var_b;
     var_a += 1;
     var_a /= var_b;
     var_c = var_a + var_b;
}
```

C Increment and Decrement Operators

Adding and subtracting 1 from a variable is so common that C provides special operators that do this. These are ++ and --.

The operator appears just before or after the variable name. When the increment operator (++) appears before the variable name, it is called a preincrement operator. When it appears after the variable, it is called a postincrement operator. Similarly, the decrement operator (--) comes in predecrement and postdecrement varieties. Table 2.2 shows the C increment and decrement operators and their COBOL equivalent.

Table 2.2. Increment and decrement operators.

COBOL	*C Pre-Operator*	*C Post-Operator*
`ADD 1 TO VAR-A.`	`++var_a;`	`var_a++;`
`SUBTRACT 1 FROM VAR-A`	`--var_a;`	`var_a--;`

Choosing whether to use a pre- or post-increment (or decrement) operator is unimportant when using them simply to raise or lower the value of a variable, but it can be very important in combined expressions. First look at Listings 2.5 and 2.6. Both add all integers between 1 and 10 and display the result. The `while()` control logic will be covered in more detail later, but for now just know that the statement under the `while()` is executed as long as the condition in the parentheses is TRUE. The `add_em_up()` function will be performed over and over as long as `var_b` is less than or equal to 10.

Listing 2.5. ADDER.COB—adding a range of integers.

```
IDENTIFICATION DIVISION.
PROGRAM-ID. ADDER.
ENVIRONMENT DIVISION.

DATA DIVISION.
WORKING-STORAGE SECTION.
01  VAR-A        PIC 99.
01  VAR-B        PIC 99.
```

```
PROCEDURE DIVISION.
MAIN-LOGIC SECTION.
PROGRAM-BEGIN.
   MOVE 0 TO VAR-A.
   MOVE 1 TO VAR-B.
   PERFORM ADD-EM-UP
           UNTIL VAR-B > 10.
   DISPLAY VAR-A.
EXIT-PROGRAM.
   EXIT PROGRAM.
STOP-RUN.
   STOP RUN.

THE-OTHER SECTION.
ADD-EM-UP.
   ADD VAR-B TO VAR-A.
   ADD 1 TO VAR-B.
```

Listing 2.6. adder.c—adding a range of integers.

```
#include <stdio.h>

int var_a;
int var_b;

main()
{
    var_a = 0;
    var_b = 1;
    while(var_b <= 10)
        add_em_up();
    printf("%d",var_a);
}

add_em_up()
{
    var_a += var_b;
    ++var_b;
}
```

Listings 2.7 and 2.8 are two different versions of the `add_em_up` function that you should look at closely. This is the first (and not the last) example of why C can appear to be so cryptic.

Listing 2.7. Correct use of post-increment.

```
add_em_up()
{
    var_a += var_b++;
}
```

Listing 2.8. Incorrect use of pre-increment.

```
add_em_up()
{
    var_a += ++var_b;
}
```

If `var_b` stands on its own and not as part of an equation, then `++var_b;` and `var_b++;` produce the same result.

When `var_b` appears in an equation, two steps must be performed: the variable must be incremented, and the variable must be used to satisfy the rest of the equation. The post-increment operator says, "use `var_b`, then increment it." The pre-increment operator says, "increment `var_b`, then use it." For example, Listing 2.7 adds `var_b` to `var_a`, and then increments `var_b`. Listing 2.8 increments `var_b`, and then adds it to `var_a`. To duplicate the effect created in Listing 2.6 you would want the first effect: add `var_b` to `var_a`, and then increment `var_b`.

Lisings 2.9 and 2.10 produce the same result, but one uses post-increment logic, while the other uses pre-increment.

Listing 2.9. adder.c—with pre-increment.

```
#include <stdio.h>

int var_a;
int var_b;

main()
{
     var_a = 0;
     var_b = 0;
```

```
    while(var_b < 10)
        add_em_up();
    printf("%d",var_a);
}

add_em_up()
{
    var_a += ++var_b;
}
```

Listing 2.10. adder.c—with post-increment.

```
#include <stdio.h>

int var_a;
int var_b;

main()
{
    var_a = 0;
    var_b = 1;
    while(var_b <= 10)
        add_em_up();
    printf("%d",var_a);
}

add_em_up()
{
    var_a += var_b++;
}
```

Compile and run Listings 2.11 and 2.12 to get a clear picture of the effect of the operators. One note on these listings: I have added `\n` inside the quotes of the `printf()` function. This has the effect of sending a carriage return and newline to the screen after each number. This and other special formatting characters will be covered in Chapter 4, "More on Strings and Pointers." It's also worth noting that the comment is completely ignored by the compiler and the `printf()` line under the `while()` control is the line that is executed, not the comment line.

Listing 2.11. preinc.c—the effect of pre-increment.

```
#include <stdio.h>

int var_a;

main()
{
     var_a = 0;
     while(var_a <= 10)
          /* Increment var_a and
             then print it */
          printf("%d\n",++var_a);
}
```

Listing 2.12. postinc.c—the effect of post-increment.

```
#include <stdio.h>

int var_a;

main()
{
     var_a = 0;
     while(var_a <= 10)
          /* Print var_a and then
             increment it */
          printf("%d\n",var_a++);
}
```

Listing 2.11 outputs the numbers 1 through 10, each on a separate line. Listing 2.12 outputs the numbers 0 through 10, each on a separate line.

The pre-decrement and post-decrement operators work in the same way.

C Handling for *DIVIDE* with *REMAINDER*

C provides an operator that is not available in COBOL. It is the percent sign (`%`), but is not used for calculating percentages. This is the remainder operator. The result of the remainder operator is the remainder after the left operand is divided by the right operand, as shown in Listings 2.13 and 2.14.

Listing 2.13. `DIVIDE` with `REMAINDER`.

```
DIVIDE-EM-UP.

     DIVIDE VAR-A INTO VAR-B
          GIVING VAR_C
               REMAINDER VAR-D.
```

Listing 2.14. C remainder operator.

```
divide_em_up()
{
    var_c = var_b / var_a;
    var_d = var_b % var_a;
}
```

Notice that C requires two complete statements to execute what is one statement in COBOL. The remainder operator also has a combined version (`%=`), as shown below.

```
var_a %= var_b;
```

In English, this becomes "Divide `var_a` by `var_b` and place the remainder of the division in `var_a`."

This is frequently useful for adjusting variables to ensure that they are within a certain range. For example a cursor positioning routine expects a row of 0–23 and a column of 0–79. In order to ensure that something invalid isn't used for the cursor position, you could use the remainder operator to force the row and column into range.

```
row_pos %= 24;
col_pos %= 80;
```

If `row_pos` is in the range 0–23, it is unaffected by the remainder operator. If it is over 23, it is adjusted to 0–23. 24 becomes 0, 25 becomes 1, and so on. The `col_pos` variable is similarly forced into the range of 0–79.

The `%` operator was called the modulus operator by Kernighan and Ritchie, who designed the language, probably because of some similarities to a mathematical modulus operation. A mathematical modulus is slightly different, and there has been a tendency to move away from calling the `%` a modulus operator. A lot of C programmers still call it that, and BASIC includes a similar operator. I suppose by usage you could say that a new additional definition for modulus has come into existence—an operator that produces the remainder of an integer division.

C Integer Data Types

C does not support the numeric data types that you are familiar with in COBOL. C numeric data types fall into two broad categories, integers (whole numbers) and floating-point numbers (numbers with a decimal portion).

The primary integer types are `short` and `long`, as shown in Table 2.3.

Table 2.3. Sizes of `short` and `long` integers.

C Name	*Description*	*Range*
`short`	Two-byte integer	–32768 to 32767
`long`	Four-byte integer	–2147482648 to 2147483647

So far you have used only an `int` type; where does it fit in? Some machines work naturally with a two-byte integer, while others work naturally with four bytes. An `int` declaration indicates to the compiler to use the format with which the machine is most comfortable. An `int` could be a `long` or a `short`, but it will never be smaller than a `short` (see Table 2.4).

Table 2.4. Sizes of all signed integer types.

C Name	*Description*	*Range*
`short`	Two-byte integer	–32768 to 32767
`long`	Four-byte integer	–2147482648 to 2147483647
`int`	Best fit for the machine (a two- or four-byte integer)	Machine-dependent, but at least –32768 to 32767

The `int` data type is the default data type for the compiler. This means that if a variable is defined without a data type, an implied `int` is inserted by the compiler as in Listings 2.15 and 2.16.

Listing 2.15. Variable defined without a data type.

```
#include <stdio.h>

var_a;

main()
{
     var_a = 0;
     while(var_a <= 10)
          /* Increment var_a and
               then print it */
          printf("%d\n",++var_a);
}
```

Listing 2.16. Default int added by the compiler.

```
#include <stdio.h>

int var_a;

main()
{
     var_a = 0;
```

continues

Listing 2.16. continued

```
    while(var_a <= 10)
         /* Increment var_a and
              then print it */
         printf("%d\n",++var_a);
}
```

It is good practice to always specify your variable data types as it improves readability, and C needs all the help it can get when it comes to readability. You will most frequently use `int`, and there is no need to explicitly define a `short` or a `long` unless you need to guarantee the size or range of the values. There are also unsigned versions of the above integer types for storing positive numbers.

Table 2.5. Sizes of all unsigned integer types.

C Name	*Description*	*Range*
unsigned `short`	Two-byte positive integer	0 to 65535
unsigned `long`	Four-byte positive integer	0 to 4294967295
unsigned `int`	Best fit for the machine (a two- or four-byte positive integer)	Machine-dependent, but at least 0 to 65535

Some COBOL compilers support data types that are equivalent to C integers. For example, Wang VS COBOL and LPI COBOL both use a BINARY data type that is a short signed integer.

Micro Focus COBOL and AcuCOBOL support the same integer types as COMP-5, with the size varying depending on the picture. Table 2.6 contains some examples of COBOL integers.

Table 2.6. COBOL integer types.

COBOL	*PICTURE*	*C Equivalent*
Wang VS	`BINARY`	`short int`
LPI	`BINARY`	`short int`

COBOL	PICTURE	C Equivalent
Micro Focus	`PIC 9(4) COMP-5`	`short int`
Micro Focus	`PIC 9(9) COMP-5`	`long int`
AcuCOBOL	`PIC 9(4) COMP-5`	`short int`
AcuCOBOL	`PIC 9(9) COMP-5`	`long int`

C Floating-Point Data Types

The other numeric type is floating-point. Floating-point is a bit unusual, and COBOL programmers who are used to dealing with COBOL's fixed-point representation sometimes have a little trouble with it.

COBOL provides 18 digits of precision with a fixed-point decimal. The fixed point is created in the data division when the variable is declared:

```
01  GRAND-TOTAL           PIC 9(16)V99.
01  TO-THE-THOUSANDTH     PIC S9(14)V999.
```

In C, the `float` data type provides seven digits of precision while the `double` provides 15. The decimal point is not fixed, and the number will fit as long as it has the correct number of significant digits. A `float` could store `1,234,567.0`, `0.000009876543` and `55,666,770,000,000.0` all equally well, because none of the numbers exceeds seven digits of precision. The `double` type works in the same way.

`floats` and `doubles` use scientific notation to store a number. A `float` is stored as seven digits times a power of 10, as shown in Table 2.7.

Table 2.7. Examples of `float` storage.

Floating-Point Number	Stored As
1,234,567	1.234567×10^{6}
0.000009876543	9.876543×10^{-6}
55,666,770,000,000	5.566677×10^{13}

Some C compilers (notably Microsoft C/C++ 7.0) have implemented an additional floating-point type called a `long double` that provides additional precision and a larger range.

Table 2.8. Floating-point ranges and precision.

Type	*Range*	*Precision*
`float`	$\pm 3.4 \times 10^{38}$	7 digits
`double`	$\pm 1.7 \times 10^{308}$	15 digits
`long double`	$\pm 1.2 \times 10^{4932}$	17 digits

Listing 2.17 is a `float` version of the now-familiar Adder program. Please note that `printf()` uses a `"%f"` to format floating-point data when printing it to the screen. The `"%f"` format will work for both `float`s and `double`s.

Listing 2.17. adder.c—adding a range of doubles.

```
#include <stdio.h>

/*
This adds the range of float values between 1 and 2.16 in
increments of 0.2
*/

double var_a;
double var_b;

main()
{
     var_a = 0.0;
     var_b = 1.0;
     while(var_b <= 2.16)
          add_em_up;
     printf("%f",var_a);
}

add_em_up()
{
     var_a += var_b;
     var_b += 0.2;
}
```

You should notice a couple of things in Listing 2.17. First, the method of incrementing `var_b` is `var_b += 0.2` rather than `++var_b`, because the intention here is to increment by a value less than 1. Second, the variables `var_a` and `var_b` are initialized with `0.0` and `1.0` rather than `0` and `1`. This is strictly a formatting convention. The compiler should handle the initialization correctly either way, but using a number with an explicit decimal is a reminder that you are working with a floating-point type. It creates a handy reference when dealing with long listings.

C Floating-Point Arithmetic Operators

There are no special floating-point arithmetic operators, and all of those discussed so far also work with floating-point numbers, except the remainder operator. Because division in floating-point operations never produces a remainder, the compiler will return an error if you attempt to use a remainder operator on a floating-point type.

Mixing Integers and Floating-Point Types

COBOL has some useful warnings, one of which is high-order digit truncation. Several COBOL compilers would produce this error for Listing 2.18. The programmer is warned that moving `VAR-B` to `VAR-A` might result in a loss of higher-order digits. In Listing 2.18, `VAR-A` would actually end up containing the value `56789`.

Listing 2.18. TRUNCED.COB—high-order digit truncation.

```
IDENTIFICATION DIVISION.
PROGRAM-ID. TRUNCED.
ENVIRONMENT DIVISION.

DATA DIVISION.
WORKING-STORAGE SECTION.
01  VAR-A           PIC 9(5).
01  VAR-B           PIC 9(9).
```

continues

Listing 2.18. continued

```
PROCEDURE DIVISION.
MAIN-LOGIC SECTION.
PROGRAM-BEGIN.
    MOVE 123456789 TO VAR-B.
    MOVE VAR-B TO VAR-A.
    DISPLAY VAR-A.
EXIT-PROGRAM.
    EXIT PROGRAM.
STOP-RUN.
    STOP RUN.
```

C is not so friendly. Listing 2.19 provides an example of a similar problem in C. Moving `var_b` to `var_a` produces no warning by most compilers, and the results are unpredictable. Usually `var_a` ends up with some negative number, such as `-13825`. Results would be equally strange if `var_a` and `var_b` were declared as `unsigned short` and `unsigned long`, but the main point is that results are indeterminate. Both Borland and Microsoft C compilers will complain vigorously about this if you have your warning levels turned up. Borland will even produce an error sometimes.

Listing 2.19. trunced.c—truncation in C.

```
#include <stdio.h>

short var_a;
long var_b;

main()
{
     var_b = 999999999;
     var_a = var_b;
     printf("%hd",var_a);
}
```

In Listing 2.19, the `printf()` function uses `"%hd"` to format the output. This is a formatting flag indicating that the variable being printed has been explicitly declared as a `short int`. Similarly `"%ld"` is used for a `long int`.

This problem is compounded by `doubles` and `floats`. In general, you can assign the value

of any numeric type to any other numeric type. If the value will fit in the assigned range, the assignment will work. All of the following assignments will work without problems (assuming the data name correctly reflects the data type):

```
float_a = short_b;
double_c = long_d;
double_f = float_g;
long_h = short_i;
long_j = int_k;
float_a = unsigned_short_b;
double_b = unsigned_long_c;
unsigned_long_d = unsigned_short_e;
```

A `long` can hold the integer portion of a `float`. The result of the assignment in Listing 2.20 is that the value 12 is stored in `long_a` and the `.55` portion of the number is lost. The result of the addition in Listing 2.21 is that the value to be added is converted to 12 for each pass through the loop, ending with the value 48 in `long_a`.

Listing 2.20. Decimal truncation.

```
#include <stdio.h>

long long_a;
float float_b;

main()
{
     float_b = 12.55;
     long_a = float_b;
     printf("%ld",long_a);
}
```

Listing 2.21. Decimal truncation during addition.

```
#include <stdio.h>

long long_a;
float float_b;
```

continues

Listing 2.21. continued

```
main()
{
     float_b = 12.55;
     long_a = 0;
     while(long_a < 40)
          long_a += float_b;
     printf("%ld",long_a);
}
```

The result when a value won't fit is not a tidy truncation (as in COBOL), so be sure to start with a variable that will hold the values that you want and stick with that type throughout the calculations.

Notes on Rounding

A `float` is limited to seven digits of precision—not seven digits to the left of the decimal, but a total of seven digits. Using a `float` to represent dollars and cents limits you to $34,999.99 (not, because of the range limitation shown in Table 2.6, $99,999.99). This is not large enough for most business work, and causes truncation and rounding problems. I have given up using `floats` completely because of the inherent limit, and do all calculations with `doubles`, which are limited to $1,799,999,999,999.99—this should be enough for any standard business application. If you are working on the national debt, then by all means, get Microsoft C/C++ 7.0 and use `long doubles`.

Precedence of Operators

It seems you can't escape precedence of operators tables. Every book on programming languages I've ever read includes such a table. I have always operated on the basis that an equation should communicate to the next poor chap down the line who has to read my code, and he shouldn't have to memorize a table or dive into a book to figure out what I meant when I wrote:

```
var_a = 3 * 2 + 1 / -7;
```

so I always include parentheses—even when they are not needed:

```
var_a = (3 * 2) + (1 / -7);
```

Sometimes for compound operations, I go so far as to enclose the entire right-hand side of the equation in parentheses to ensure that what is happening is understood.

```
var_a -= (3 * (7/2));
```

However, to satisfy that longstanding tradition, Table 2.9 presents precendence for the operators covered so far.

Table 2.9. Precedence of operators.

Symbol	*Operation*	*Example*	
`++`	Pre- or post-increment	`++var_a;`	`var_b++;`
`--`	Pre- or post-decrement	`--var_c;`	`var_d--;`
`+`	Unary plus	`var_b = +2;`	
`-`	Unary minus	`var_a = -7;`	
`*`	Multiply	`var_a = 7 * 3;`	
`/`	Divide	`var_b = 6 / 3;`	
`%`	Remainder	`var_c = 21 % 4;`	
`+`	Addition	`var_a = 7 + 32;`	
`-`	Subtraction	`var_b = 7 - 32;`	
`=`	Simple assignment	`var_ a = 1;`	
`+=`	Compound addition	`var_b += 27;`	
`-=`	Compound subtraction	`var_c -= 15;`	
`*=`	Compound multiplication	`var_d *= 4;`	
`/=`	Compound division	`var_e /= 3;`	
`%=`	Compound remainder	`var_f %= 13;`	

In the preceding table, unary means relating to one operand. The single + or - used to denote the sign of a number are the primary unary operators.

I will not cover this precedence issue further. Once you are through this book, if you want a precedence table for all operators, you can find one in your compiler documentation.

Summary

C arithmetic operators are part of the enigma of C, and hopefully I have been able to take some of the mystery out of them.

C character data is similar to COBOL character data, but as you'll see in Chapter 3, the syntax for processing character data has some interesting twists to it.

3 C Characters and Strings

After numeric data types, the next most useful data type in C is the character data type. This is equivalent to COBOL's alphanumeric `PIC X` type. It is used extensively in C. In this chapter, I will first review the basics of character data types, and then introduce character handling in C. These basics will be more important to you in C than they were in COBOL.

This chapter covers the following topics:

- What a character is
- C's `char` data type
- Strings as arrays of characters
- Using double and single quotation marks
- The NUL string terminator
- Using `strlen()`
- Using `strcpy()` and `strcat()`

- Passing values to functions
- Pointers to strings
- Declarations versus definitions
- Local variables

What Is a Character?

Computer characters are stored in bytes. Each byte can hold eight bits of information. Since each bit can be set on or off, a byte can represent 256 (2^8) possible combinations of 8 bits. One of these combinations is all bits off, so the possible values in a byte are numbered 0 through 255.

The ASCII (American Standard Code for Information Interchange) character set employs the first 128 values (0 through 127) and defines what they represent.

Table 3.1 is a brief ASCII chart. Several of the ASCII codes represent nonprintable characters, and these are represented by their names. Some of these you may be familiar with because of their actions. For example, value 13 (CR) is a carriage return. This value sent to a printer causes the print head to return to column 1. The keyboard usually sends the CR code when you press the Enter key on a keyboard. Value 7 (BEL), when sent by the computer to the terminal, usually causes a beep or rings an alarm. The values from 32 through 126 are printable characters.

Table 3.1. ASCII Chart with decimal values.

Code	*Character*	*Code*	*Character*	*Code*	*Character*	*Code*	*Character*
0	NUL	32	SP	64	@	96	'
1	SOH	33	!	65	A	97	a
2	STX	34	"	66	B	98	b
3	ETX	35	#	67	C	99	c
4	EOT	36	$	68	D	100	d
5	ENQ	37	%	69	E	101	e
6	ACK	38	&	70	F	102	f

Code	Character	Code	Character	Code	Character	Code	Character
7	BEL	39	'	71	G	103	g
8	BS	40	(	72	H	104	h
9	HT	41	)	73	I	105	i
10	LF	42	*	74	J	106	j
11	VT	43	+	75	K	107	k
12	FF	44	,	76	L	108	l
13	CR	45	-	77	M	109	m
14	SO	46	.	78	N	110	n
15	SI	47	/	79	O	111	o
16	DLE	48	0	80	P	112	p
17	DC1	49	1	81	Q	113	q
18	DC2	50	2	82	R	114	r
19	DC3	51	3	83	S	115	s
20	DC4	52	4	84	T	116	t
21	NAK	53	5	85	U	117	u
22	SYN	54	6	86	V	118	v
23	ETB	55	7	87	W	119	w
24	CAN	56	8	88	X	120	x
25	EM	57	9	89	Y	121	y
26	SUB	58	:	90	Z	122	z
27	ESC	59	;	91	[	123	{
28	FS	60	<	92	\	124	¦
29	GS	61	=	93	]	125	}
30	RS	62	>	94	^	126	~
31	US	63	?	95	_	127	DEL

The nonprinting ASCII characters are given names because there are no characters that can display them. The nonprinting characters are used by keyboards, terminals, printers, and in telecommunications. In telecommunications particularly, there are no hard and fast rules about these characters, but Table 3.2 will give you a list of these characters, their full names, and some examples of how they are used. The examples are neither complete nor set in stone; they are just possible uses.

Table 3.2. Uses for nonprinting ASCII characters.

Code	*Name*	*Decimal Value*	*Sample Uses*
NUL	NUL	0	Communications: Sometimes transmitted by a sending device to kill time. This is common when transmitting to physical devices that cannot print or display data as fast as they can receive data. It allows the physical display or printer to "catch up" without sending a bunch of data that will be missed. Sometimes called a pacing character. Sometimes transmitted by a sending device to indicate a "break" condition. What the receiving device does depends on the application.
SOH	Start of Header	1	Communications: Introduces header information being sent.
STX	Start of Text	2	Communications: Introduces a block of text.
ETX	End of Text	3	Communications: Ends a block of text.
EOT	End of Transmission	4	Communications: Signals the end of a transmission. In some communications protocols that transmit multiple files, it is used to signal the end of a file.

Code	Name	Decimal Value	Sample Uses
ENQ	Enquiry	5	Communications: Used to ask the other end of the line for status. A status can be anything from "Yes I am here." to "I am here; I am station number 19; I received your last packet; I am ready to send if you are done."
ACK	Acknowledge	6	Communications: Used to acknowledge successful receipt of a packet of information.
BEL	Bell	7	Terminal: Sounds the terminal bell. Printer: Sounds the printer bell.
BS	Backspace	8	Terminal: Moves cursor back one position; may also delete the character at the new position. Printer: Moves the print head back one position. It cannot erase the character, but on early printers, underlining was done by printing the character, backspacing, and then printing an underline.
HT	Horizontal Tab	9	Commonly known as Tab. Terminal: Causes advance to the next display column on the screen. Printer: Advances to the next print column.
LF	Line Feed	10	Terminal: Moves the cursor down one line in the current column. Printer: Moves the print head down one line in the current column.

continues

Table 3.2. continued

Code	*Name*	*Decimal Value*	*Sample Uses*
VT	Vertical Tab	11	Printer: Some printers allow setting vertical tab positions as a number of lines to feed. A vertical tab can act as a multiline line feed.
FF	Form Feed	12	Printer: Ejects to the top of the next page. Terminal: On some terminals, causes the screen to clear.
CR	Carriage Return	13	Printer: Moves print head to the extreme left of the current row. Terminal: Moves the cursor to the extreme left of the screen in the current row.
SO	Shift Out	14	Printer: Returns the printer to the normal character set.
SI	Shift In	15	Printer: Some printers carry two font sets, the alternative set is enabled by sending SI to the printer, and then the default set is resumed by sending SO.
DLE	Data Link Escape	16	Communications: The next group of characters have a special meaning.
DC1–DC4	Device Control 1-4	17–20	The ASCII definition had no intention for these characters other than to make them usable (and definable) by hardware builders. DC1 and DC3 have become the de facto codes for pause and continue. Ctrl-S sends a DC3 and Ctrl-Q sends a DC1.

Code	Name	Decimal Value	Sample Uses
NAK	Negative Acknowledge	21	Communications: Sent to indicate "Not OK." This could be "No you can't transmit; I'm still busy sending," or "There was an error in the last packet of data."
SYN	Synchronous Idle	22	Communications: Transmitted on synchronous communications line as an idle signal.
ETB	End of Transmission Block	23	Communications: Sometimes sent instead of ETX to indicate that the block just ended was not of the usual length, short for whatever reason.
CAN	Cancel	24	Terminal: Some terminals allow a Cancel from the keyboard (Ctrl-X) to indicate that all characters typed since the last CR (carriage return) should be ignored.
EM	End of Medium	25	Communications: Last usable bytes have been sent.
SUB	Substitute	26	Communications: If a character is received garbled during a transmission, a SUB may be inserted in the stream of bytes to indicate an invalid character was received.
ESC	Escape	27	Terminal: First character in a special control sequence for the screen. Printer: First character in a special control sequence for the printer.
FS	File Separator	28	Communications: Used between files in a transmission.
GS	Group Separator	29	Communications: Used between groups of data in a transmission.

continues

Table 3.2. continued

Code	Name	Decimal Value	Sample Uses
RS	Record Separator	30	Communications: Used between records in a transmission.
US	Unit Separator	31	Communications: Used for units smaller than a record. FS, GS, RS, and US can be used arbitrarily as separators with the kind of general rule that the FS is used to divide up the largest chunks of data, and the US breaks up the smallest. A common file protocol might only use FS to separate files and RS to separate records.
SP	Space	32	The space character which doesn't display or print, so has been given the name SP.

Remember that all of the uses described above are pretty loose. Some terminals only receive an LF, but treat it as a CR-LF. Some printers only receive a CR but treat it as a CR-LF. Many telecommunications protocols don't use all of the COMMUNICATIONS characters, and some use them in ways that have nothing to do with the intentions of the ASCII standard.

For a detailed and excellent description of ASCII, I recommend *C Programmer's Guide to Serial Communications* by Joe Campbell, from Sams Publishing. Chapter 1 alone, on ASCII, makes this book worth the cover price.

The codes above 127 are undefined, and manufacturers of different equipment use them in different ways. Printer manufacturers frequently define the upper range of values as special or foreign language characters. If you send a value of, say, 214 to the printer, the result just might be Greek to you.

C *char* Data Type

The C `char` data type represents a single byte value that can hold any of the character values from 0 through 255. It is comparable to a COBOL `PIC X`. But it's not quite that simple.

A C char cannot be declared as an aggregate (as, for example, PIC X(20), which declares 20 bytes capable of holding alphanumeric information). To create space for more than one C char, you must declare an array of char data types. Luckily, the syntax is fairly simple. In addition, the printf() function uses another format character, %s, which is used for formatting output for a char array. Listings 3.1 and 3.2 display a now classic message in COBOL and C.

Listing 3.1. SHOWSTR.COB—displays a string.

```
IDENTIFICATION DIVISION.
 PROGRAM-ID. SHOWSTR.
* THIS PROGRAM DISPLAYS A STRING.
 ENVIRONMENT DIVISION.
 DATA DIVISION.
 WORKING-STORAGE SECTION.
 01  VAR-C                PIC X(20)
     VALUE "Hello World".

 PROCEDURE DIVISION.
 MAIN-LOGIC SECTION.
 PROGRAM-BEGIN.
     DISPLAY VAR-C.
 EXIT-PROGRAM.
     EXIT PROGRAM.
 STOP-RUN.
     STOP RUN.
```

Listing 3.2. showstr.c—displays a string.

```
#include <stdio.h>



char var_c[20] = "Hello World";



main()
{
     printf("%s\n",var_c);
}
```

While it is fortunate that the syntax for generating a `char` array is so simple, it's unfortunate that it happens to look so much like the COBOL syntax. It is too easy to lose sight of the fact that the `var_c` variable is not a string but an array of `char` data types.

Strings as Arrays of *char*

In fact, the `char var_c[20]` declaration would be better expressed in COBOL as

```
01  VAR-C PIC X OCCURS 20 TIMES.
```

Declared this way, COBOL would not be able to `DISPLAY VAR-C`, because the compiler would complain of a missing subscript. Listings 3.3 and 3.4 better represent the shape of the data.

Listing 3.3. SHOWSTR.COB—COBOL string as an array of characters.

```
 IDENTIFICATION DIVISION.
 PROGRAM-ID. SHOWSTR.
* THIS PROGRAM DISPLAYS A STRING.
 ENVIRONMENT DIVISION.
 DATA DIVISION.
 WORKING-STORAGE SECTION.
 01  THE-STRING PIC X(20)
     VALUE "Hello World".
 01  FILLER REDEFINES THE-STRING.
     05  THE-CHAR PIC X
         OCCURS 20 TIMES.

 PROCEDURE DIVISION.
 MAIN-LOGIC SECTION.
 PROGRAM-BEGIN.
     DISPLAY THE-STRING.
 EXIT-PROGRAM.
     EXIT PROGRAM.
 STOP-RUN.
     STOP RUN.
```

Listing 3.4. showstr.c—C string as an array of char data types.

```
#include <stdio.h>

char the_char[20] = "Hello World";

main()
{
     printf("%s\n",the_char);
}
```

Note the complex declaration required in COBOL to access a string as both a string and an array of characters, while at the same time initializing it in working storage. C, on the other hand, allows you to access the full string by its name, as well as to access the individual elements with a subscripted version of the name.

Listings 3.5 and 3.6 display the string and one element of the array. The `printf()` function uses yet another formatting character, `%c`, for a single character.

Listing 3.5. SHOWSTR.COB—displaying a string and a character.

```
 IDENTIFICATION DIVISION.
 PROGRAM-ID. SHOWSTR.
* THIS PROGRAM DISPLAYS A STRING.
 ENVIRONMENT DIVISION.
 DATA DIVISION.
 WORKING-STORAGE SECTION.
 01   THE-STRING PIC X(20)
      VALUE "Hello World".
 01   FILLER REDEFINES THE-STRING.
      05   THE-CHAR PIC X
           OCCURS 20 TIMES.

 PROCEDURE DIVISION.
 MAIN-LOGIC SECTION.
 PROGRAM-BEGIN.
      DISPLAY THE-STRING.
   DISPLAY THE-CHAR(1).
 EXIT-PROGRAM.
      EXIT PROGRAM.
 STOP-RUN.
      STOP RUN.
```

Listing 3.6. showstr.c—displaying a string and a character.

```
#include <stdio.h>

char the_char[20] = "Hello World";

main()
{
     printf("%s\n",the_char);
     printf("%c\n",the_char[0]);
}
```

The big difference (aside from COBOL's complex data declaration) is the subscript value of `[0]` on `the_char`. C uses zero-based subscripting, while COBOL, of course, uses one-based subscripting. It takes some getting used to, but it's clearer if you think of a C subscript as an offset from the base of the array rather than as a position. The *H* in *Hello World* is at offset 0 from the base of the array `the_char`. You'll get the hang of it after you work with it awhile.

Using Double and Single Quotation Marks

A single `char` in C is initialized, or assigned a value, by enclosing the character in single quotation marks. Listing 3.7 converts *Hello World* to the Elmer Fudd version, *Hewwo World,* before displaying it.

Listing 3.7. showstr.c—modifying characters in a string.

```
#include <stdio.h>

char the_char[20] = "Hello World";

main()
{
     the_char[2] = 'w';
     the_char[3] = 'w';
     printf("%s\n",the_char);
}
```

Note that the two *l*s of *Hello* are at offsets 2 and 3 rather than subscript 3 and 4. In fact, the technique of initializing or assigning a string to an array of `char` using double quotation marks is a shortcut in C. The actual syntax for initializing an array of any type is to enclose all the initializers in braces (`{}`) and separate them with commas. Listing 3.8 is a formal initialization of `the_char` using these rules.

Listing 3.8. showstr.c—formal string initialization.

```
#include <stdio.h>

char the_char[20] = {'H','e','l','l','o',' ','W','o','r','l','d'};


main()
{
      the_char[2] = 'w';
      the_char[3] = 'w';
      printf("%s\n",the_char);
}
```

This initialization assigns `'H'` to `the_char[0]`, `'e'` to `the_char[1]`, and so on until all initializers are exhausted. Since `the_char` is a global variable, the remainder of the array is set to zeroes.

Because arrays of `char` are such a common programming device, the double quotation mark method of initialization is included in the language to cut down on huge quantities of typing.

The NUL String Terminator

C strings are different from COBOL strings in another way. COBOL requires that values passed to another program be declared with their `PICTURE` in the called program as well as the calling program. If you

```
CALL "HEADLINE" USING THE-TITLE.
```

and `THE-TITLE` is a `PIC X(30)`, you would expect `HEADLINE` to include something like

```
LINKAGE SECTION.
01  PASSED-TITLE        PIC X(30).
PROCEDURE DIVISION USING PASSED-TITLE.
```

The linkage section is used so that if `HEADLINE` attempts to `DISPLAY PASSED-TITLE`, it knows to display 30 characters.

In contrast, look at Listing 3.9. This listing displays several lines of text by calling `printf()` repeatedly. In each case, `printf()` correctly identifies the length of the string and displays it appropriately on the screen.

In fact, `printf()` does not have some hotline to the compiler that allows it to extract the string length. Instead, a C string is little bit more than you see in the source code.

A C string is an array of printable characters that includes a NUL (ASCII 0—see Table 3.1) as the last character in the array.

Listing 3.9. paine.c—`printf()` using different string lengths.

```
#include <stdio.h>

char line1[50] = "These are the times that";
char line2[10] = "try";
char line3[20] = "men's souls.";

main()
{
     printf("%s\n",line1);
     printf("%s\n",line2);
     printf("%s\n",line3);
}
```

Putting double quotation marks around a string in C automatically adds the extra NUL to the end. The formal initialization of `line2` in Listing 3.9 would actually be

```
char line2[10] = {'t','r','y',0};
```

NUL-terminated strings are used throughout C, and `printf()` is just one of the many functions that use them.

The `printf()` function processes the passed string, putting one character at a time on the screen until a zero-valued character is encountered. Processing stops at that point. In fact, the `"%s"` format argument used by `printf("%s",str)` means that the next argument (`str` in this example) will be a NUL-terminated string.

Initializating a string using double quotation marks accomplishes one other task for you. If you leave the size of the array blank, the C compiler automatically calculates the size of

the array for you and creates the array with that size. This is very useful for string constants (as in Listing 3.9). Listing 3.10 is an example of letting the compiler sort out the size of the array for you.

In Listing 3.10, the compiler calculates that the array for `line1` requires space for 24 characters plus one extra space for the NUL terminator, and creates an array of 25 elements. Similary, `line2` will be created with space for three characters plus a NUL terminator, and `line3` will have space for 12 characters plus one for the NUL. Listing 3.11 shows how, in effect, the source code is viewed by the compiler.

Listing 3.10. paine.c—automatic array sizing.

```
#include <stdio.h>

char line1[] =
   "These are the times that";
char line2[] = "try";
char line3[] = "men's souls.";

main()
{
      printf("%s\n",line1);
      printf("%s\n",line2);
      printf("%s\n",line3);
}
```

Listing 3.11. paine.c—what the compiler saw.

```
#include <stdio.h>

char line1[25] =
   "These are the times that";
char line2[4] = "try";
char line3[13] = "men's souls.";

main()
{
      printf("%s\n",line1);
      printf("%s\n",line2);
      printf("%s\n",line3);
}
```

Note again in Listings 3.10 and 3.11 the free-form nature of the source code in the initialization of `line1`.

It's important that you understand NUL-terminated strings. They are used throughout C for processing alphanumeric data, so I will show you some of the C standard library functions for handling strings.

Using *strlen()*

The `strlen()` function is part of the standard C library (like `printf()`) and is used to find the length of a string. The syntax for `strlen()` is

```
length = strlen(str);
```

The `length` variable must be an `int` type and the `str` variable must be a character array. C functions can return a value, and the function can be used in an equation just as if it were a single numeric value. The `strlen()` function returns the count of all characters up to but not including the NUL terminator. The `strlen()` function returns an `int`. A function that returns an `int` can be used anywhere that an `int` can be used.

Listing 3.12 is a footnoted version of paine.c that displays the length of each string. The length of each line is extracted using `strlen()` and then displayed with a short preamble.

Listing 3.12. paine.c—with footnotes on string length.

```
#include <stdio.h>

char line1[] =
   "These are the times that";
char line2[] = "try";
char line3[] = "men's souls.";
int len1, len2, len3;

main()
{
     printf("%s\n",line1);
     printf("%s\n",line2);
     printf("%s\n",line3);

     printf("\n");          /* Insert an extra line feed */
     printf("Notes:\n");
```

```
    len1 = strlen(line1);
    printf("Character count for line 1 is ");
    printf("%d\n",len1);

    len2 = strlen(line2);
    printf("Character count for line 2 is ");
    printf("%d\n",len2);

    len3 = strlen(line3);
    printf("Character count for line 3 is ");
    printf("%d\n",len3);

}
```

There are a couple of additional points worth noting in this example. The `printf()` function calls are passed string constants as in `printf("The character count for line 1 is ")`. The `printf()` function can be used to print string constants in this manner. C, unlike COBOL, will allow you to pass a constant to a function or subroutine. Most COBOL compilers would insist that the string be assigned to a variable first, and then `printf()` could be called with the name of the variable.

The second point is that each string constant sent to `printf()` does not end with the `"\n"` line terminator. The result is that the length variables will be printed on the same line as the constant, providing a final display that looks something like this:

```
These are the times that
try
men's souls.

Notes:
Character count for line 1 is 24
Character count for line 2 is 3
Character count for line 3 is 12
```

Before leaving `strlen()`, remember that a function that returns an `int` can be used anywhere you might use an `int`. Listing 3.13 is a much shorter version of paine.c. The output is identical. The technique I used is to place `strlen()` inside the argument list to `printf()`. In English this might read, "Resolve the length of `line1` to an `int` using `strlen()`, and then use that `int` as the second argument to `printf()`." This is another one of those magic tricks that makes C so difficult to read. The technique is perfectly valid—since you have no other use for the variables `len1` through `len3`, why bother defining space for them in the program?

Listing 3.13. paine.c—passing the return value from a function to another function.

```
#include <stdio.h>

char line1[] =
   "These are the times that";
char line2[] = "try";
char line3[] = "men's souls.";

main()
{
     printf("%s\n",line1);
     printf("%s\n",line2);
     printf("%s\n",line3);

     printf("\n");       /* Insert an extra line feed */
     printf("Notes:\n");

     printf("Character count for line 1 is ");
     printf("%d\n",strlen(line1));

     printf("Character count for line 2 is ");
     printf("%d\n",strlen(line2));

     printf("Character count for line 3 is ");
     printf("%d\n",strlen(line3));

}
```

Using *strcpy()* and *strcat()*

Two more useful string functions are `strcpy()` and `strcat()`. The `strcpy()` function takes two string arguments and copies the second argument into the first. The `strcat()` function takes two string arguments and concatenates the two by appending the second string to the first.

The `strcpy()` function uses the NUL in the second string as the terminator for the copy. It will copy everything up to and including the final NUL. The `strcat()` function locates the position of the NUL in the first string, and begins copying the second string into that position.

Listing 3.14 tidies up paine.c by combining all the messages into one message. Note that spaces are inserted in the result by using `strcat()` to append spaces between each chunk of text. This is another example of passing a constant to a C function.

Listing 3.14. paine.c—combining strings.

```
#include <stdio.h>

char line1[] =
   "These are the times that";
char line2[] = "try";
char line3[] = "men's souls.";
char one_big_line[81];

main()
{
     strcpy(one_big_line, line1);
     strcat(one_big_line, " ");
     strcat(one_big_line, line2);
     strcat(one_big_line, " ");
     strcat(one_big_line, line3);
     printf("%s\n", one_big_line);
}
```

The output from this example will, of course, be

```
These are the times that try men's souls.
```

This brings me to one of the big differences between COBOL and C string handling. COBOL provides an exact string length by virtue of its `PICTURE` clause. When a `MOVE` takes place in COBOL between two alphanumeric variables, the compiler generates code to move the bytes for the length of the shorter variable, and fill the destination variable with spaces if it was not the shorter one.

C has no such tidy organization. C functions that use a string as a source process the string up to the first NUL character. C functions using a string as a destination assume that it is a large enough area of memory to hold the largest value that will be copied or concatenated into it.

Listing 3.15 provides an example of copying a string into too small a space. If you run the program, one of two things will happen. The computer may give you an error saying that you are attempting to write into invalid memory addresses, or the output will look something like the following:

```
These are the times that
These are the times that
e are the times that
```

In Listing 3.15, the compiler created `line2` with enough space for four characters: the three characters `try` plus one extra for the NUL. Copying `line1` to `line2` caused the first four characters to lay over the space for `line2`, but the remainder of the copy of `line1` went into memory either allocated for something else or not allocated at all. If your output looks like the example, it is because the rest of the memory that was modified by the copy of `line1` was the memory allocated to `line3`, which now holds part of the copy of `line1`. The `printf()` function processes its input string until a NUL is encountered; it has no knowledge of the size of the string space that was originally allocated by the compiler. So `printf()` just outputs characters merrily through memory until some NUL is encountered and then stops.

Listing 3.15. paine.c—running over memory.

```
#include <stdio.h>

char line1[] =
   "These are the times that";
char line2[] = "try";
char line3[] = "men's souls.";

main()
{
     strcpy(line2,line1);
     printf("%s\n",line1);
     printf("%s\n",line2);
     printf("%s\n",line3);
}
```

Destination strings for `strcpy()`, `strcat()`, and several other functions must be created with enough space to hold the largest string that will be built in them. If a string space is overwritten by something larger, results are unpredictable.

The `strcpy()` function is roughly analogous to the COBOL `MOVE` verb for alphanumeric data. The main difference is that the COBOL `MOVE` is bounded by the size of the source and destination fields as they are declared in `WORKING-STORAGE`. The C `strcpy()` is bounded by the terminating NUL character on the source string, and is unbounded in the destination string.

Passing Values to Functions

So far, you have placed actual values in memory and dealt with them directly. There is another method of accessing values that is characteristically used for strings, and in general used for arrays. COBOL has this mechanism; you've probably seen it without realizing what it meant. Listings 3.16 and 3.17 are a called and calling program that pass and return a string value.

Listing 3.16. SHOWSTR.COB—passing a string in COBOL.

```
 IDENTIFICATION DIVISION.
 PROGRAM-ID. SHOWSTR.
* THIS PROGRAM DISPLAYS A STRING
* BEFORE AND AFTER IT HAS BEEN
* MODIFIED BY MODSTR.COB
 ENVIRONMENT DIVISION.
 DATA DIVISION.
 WORKING-STORAGE SECTION.
 01  THE-STRING PIC X(20).

 PROCEDURE DIVISION.

 MAIN-LOGIC SECTION.
 PROGRAM-BEGIN.
   MOVE "HELLO" TO THE-STRING.
     DISPLAY THE-STRING.
     CALL "MODSTR"
          USING THE-STRING.
   DISPLAY THE-STRING.
 EXIT-PROGRAM.
     EXIT PROGRAM.
 STOP-RUN.
     STOP RUN.
```

Listing 3.17. MODSTR.COB—modifying a passed string in COBOL.

```
IDENTIFICATION DIVISION.
 PROGRAM-ID. MODSTR.
* THIS PROGRAM MODIFIES A PASSED
```

continues

Listing 3.17. continued

```
* STRING.
 ENVIRONMENT DIVISION.
 DATA DIVISION.
 WORKING-STORAGE SECTION.

 LINKAGE SECTION.
 01     PASSED-STRING PIC X(20).

 PROCEDURE DIVISION
    USING PASSED-STRING.

 MAIN-LOGIC SECTION.
 PROGRAM-BEGIN.
     MOVE "GOODBYE" TO PASSED-STRING.
 EXIT-PROGRAM.
     EXIT PROGRAM.
 STOP-RUN.
     STOP RUN.
```

You will recognize that these two programs linked together will display:

```
HELLO
GOODBYE
```

The variable `THE-STRING` is passed to modstr.cob and is modified. Upon return to showstr.cob, the new value is displayed. The interesting question in this pedestrian example is, *What exactly is passed to modstr.cob?*

One possible answer is that all 20 bytes of `THE-STRING` are copied somewhere, modstr.cob modifies these copies, and the 20 bytes are copied back to `THE-STRING` upon exit. Common sense dictates that this is unlikely, and that when modstr.cob is modifying `PASSED-STRING`, it is, in fact, modifying the area of memory occupied by `THE-STRING`. `THE-STRING` and `PASSED-STRING` both refer to the same 20 bytes of memory, but by different names.

The COBOL mechanism for passing a variable is to pass the address in memory of the variable. `CALL "MODSTR" USING THE-STRING` translates to "call the `MODSTR` program passing the address in memory of `THE-STRING`."

In modstr.cob, `PROCEDURE DIVISION USING PASSED-STRING.` is a signal that any reference to `PASSED-STRING` in modstr.cob is a reference to the address of a variable that has its actual working storage allocated in some higher-level calling program. The description of `PASSED-VALUE` in the `LINKAGE SECTION` is further information for the compiler, indicating

that the address or memory pointer named `PASSED-STRING` points to a variable (in some other module) with a `PIC X(20)` shape.

Within modstr.cob, `PASSED-STRING` could be called a pointer to a `PIC X(20)` field. C has a similar mechanism, but its rules are slightly different. COBOL always passes pointers, whether you are passing a numeric or alphanumeric variable. C passes a pointer when the value is an array, and a copy of the value when it is not. For now, this means that whenever you call a function with a numeric argument, a copy of the value is passed; when you call a function with a string argument, the address of the string is passed. Listing 3.18 shows the different passing logic using `printf()`.

Listing 3.18. prttypes.c—passing different data types.

```
#include <stdio.h>

int var_a = 1;
long var_b = 2;
float var_c = 2.2;
char var_d[] = "Hello World";

main()
{
     printf("%d\n",var_a);     /* passes a copy of var_a */
     printf("%ld\n",var_b);    /* passes a copy of var_b */
     printf("%f\n",var_c);     /* passes a copy of var_c */
     printf("%s\n",var_d);     /* passes the address of var_d */
}
```

Pointers to Strings

Pointers in C are declared by an asterisk in front of the variable name, for example:

```
char *passed_string;
```

The asterisk in the declaration tells the compiler that the variable, `passed_string`, contains the address of a `char` data type that should be defined somewhere else in the data. Listings 3.19, 3.20, and 3.21 compare a COBOL program and subroutine to a C program with a function call.

Listing 3.19. PAINE.COB—passing a string.

```
 IDENTIFICATION DIVISION.
 PROGRAM-ID. SHOWSTR.
* DISPLAYS PAINE'S QUOTE BY
* CALLING DISPIT
 ENVIRONMENT DIVISION.
 DATA DIVISION.
 WORKING-STORAGE SECTION.
 01  LINE1          PIC X(30) VALUE
         "These are the times that".
 01  LINE2          PIC X(30) VALUE
         "try".
 01     LINE3       PIC X(30) VALUE
         "men's souls.".
 PROCEDURE DIVISION.
 MAIN-LOGIC SECTION.
 PROGRAM-BEGIN.
     CALL "DISPIT" USING LINE1.
     CALL "DISPIT" USING LINE2.
     CALL "DISPIT" USING LINE3.
 EXIT-PROGRAM.
     EXIT PROGRAM.
 STOP-RUN.
     STOP RUN.
```

Listing 3.20. DISPIT.COB—displaying the string.

```
 IDENTIFICATION DIVISION.
 PROGRAM-ID. SHOWSTR.
* DISPLAYS A 30 BYTE STRING
 ENVIRONMENT DIVISION.
 DATA DIVISION.
 WORKING-STORAGE SECTION.
 LINKAGE SECTION.
 01  PASSED-STRING  PIC X(30).
 PROCEDURE DIVISION
     USING PASSED-STRING.
 MAIN-LOGIC SECTION.
 PROGRAM-BEGIN.
     DISPLAY PASSED-STRING.
 EXIT-PROGRAM.
     EXIT PROGRAM.
 STOP-RUN.
     STOP RUN.
```

Listing 3.21. paine.c—pointers to strings.

```
#include <stdio.h>

char line1[] =
   "These are the times that";
char line2[] = "try";
char line3[] = "men's souls.";

main()
{
     dispit(line1);
     dispit(line2);
     dispit(line3);
}

dispit(passed_string)
char *passed_string;
{

     printf("%s\n",passed_string);
}
```

The `dispit()` function in Listing 3.21 introduces the pointer-to-string syntax. The inclusion of the variable name in parentheses, `dispit(passed_string)`, indicates that the function `dispit()` will be receiving a passed value. The declaration just below the function name, `char *passed_string`, indicates that the value will be a pointer to a char type. Table 3.3 compares the differences between COBOL and C syntax and meaning when passing values.

Table 3.3. Passing values in COBOL and C.

Syntax	*Meaning*
	Passing values in C
`CALL "DISPIT" USING LINE1.`	Call the program `DISPIT` passing a pointer to the variable named `LINE1`.
`PROCEDURE DIVISION` ` USING PASSSED-VALUE.`	This program is passed a pointer to a variable which will locally be named `PASSED-VALUE`.
`LINKAGE SECTION.` `01   PASSED-VALUE     PIC X(20).`	The variable `PASSED-VALUE` will point to a `PIC X(20)`.
	Passing values in C
`dispit(line1);`	Call the function `dispit()` passing a variable named `line1`. The variable `line1` will be passed as a value or a pointer depending on how `line1` is declared in the program.

`dispit(passed_value)`
`{`
`}`
	This function, `dispit()`, will be passed a variable that will locally be named `passed_value`.

`dispit(passed_value)`
`char *passed_value;`
`{`
 	
`}`
	The variable, `passed_value`, will be a pointer to a `char` data type.

The two syntaxes share the tasks differently, but they both get the job done—indicating to the subroutine or function three key pieces of data:

- The function or subroutine that will receive one or more passed variables.
- The names that will be used locally by the variables.
- The shape that the variable takes inside the called function or subroutine.

You now know enough syntax to be able to take a closer look at some of the string library functions. The `strlen()` function counts all characters in a string up to but not including the the terminating NUL character, and returns the count of characters.

Listing 3.22 shows what `strlen()` might look like.

Listing 3.22. `strlen()`.

```
int str_idx = 0

strlen(str)                     /* Receives a variable we'll call str */
char *str;                      /* str is a pointer to char */
{
     str_idx = 0;               /* Init the index to 0 */
     while(str[str_idx] != 0)   /* If the character is not = NUL */
          ++str_idx;            /* increment the index */

     return(str_idx);           /* Return the count */
}
```

Just a couple of quick notes before I analyze this one. The `!=` is the C conditional comparison operator `NOT EQUAL`. The syntax for returning from a function is

```
return;                   /* vanilla return */
return value;             /* return with a specified value */
return(value);            /* same as return value; */
```

I prefer the `return(value)` version over `return value`, but you will see both in C listings.

The `strlen()` function is passed a pointer to a `char` (array), which is assumed to be NUL-terminated. An index is used to step through the string until the value in the array element is equal to zero. When that condition is met, the `while()` loop terminates, and the index is returned. The index is left pointing to the character that is equal to zero (NUL). Suppose, for example, that the passed string was `try` plus its closing NUL. The value at `str[0]` is `'t'`, at `str[1]` it is `'r'`, at `str[2]` it is `'y'`, and at `str[3]` the NUL is found. The non-NUL length of the string is 3, so there is no need to adjust the index; it correctly represents the length of the string.

Listing 3.23, an example of how `strcpy()` works, has an additional syntax convention that you need to know. If more than one command is to be executed within a `while` loop, all of the commands must be enclosed in opening and closing braces.

Listing 3.23. `strcpy()`.

```
int str_idx;

strcpy(dest,src)          /* Two variables we'll call dest and src */
char *dest, *src;         /* Both are pointers to char */
{
     str_idx = 0;                      /* Init the index to 0 */
     while(src[str_idx] != 0)          /* If the character is not = NUL */
          {
          dest[str_idx] = src[str_idx];  /* Copy src to dest */
          ++str_idx;                     /* Increment the index */
          }
/* The routine stopped copying at the final NUL */
/* so it is necessary to add a closing NUL to dest */
     dest[str_idx] = 0;
}
```

The `strcpy()` function copies up to and including the closing NUL character, so you need one extra action after the last byte is copied. Note also that individual elements of the `src` and `dest` variables are assigned by using the = operator.

Declarations versus Definitions

I'd like to clarify the difference between a C definition and a C declaration. A C declaration specifies the attributes of a variable, and the manner in which the compiler will treat the variable when it is used in expressions, function calls, and so on. A C definition is a declaration that actually reserves space in memory for the variable. COBOL has almost no equivalent; all variables are defined (and declared) in `WORKING-STORAGE`, and the compiler allocates space for them at compile time.

There is one exception: the declaration of a passed variable in the `LINKAGE SECTION` as described above. The `PICTURE` of a value in the `LINKAGE SECTION` does not reserve space in

memory; it merely tells the compiler the shape that the passed data is expected to have. The space for the data was reserved in some higher-level COBOL program.

The distinction between definition and declaration is more important in C, and it is necessary to have a fairly clear idea of what reserves space for data and what doesn't. For example, the declaration of data types under a function such as

```
strcpy(dest,src)
char *dest, *src;
{
}
```

in Listing 3.23 does not reserve any memory space. That space was already reserved by a higher-level function. The declaration simply tells the compiler how to treat references to `dest` and `src` within the body of the function.

Throughout this book, you will be exposed to more examples of declarations that do not define space in memory.

Local Variables

If `strlen()` and `strcpy()` as described in Listings 3.22 and 3.23 were both written in the same source code file, they could both use `str_idx` as the index to manipulate the strings, but C has a better mechanism for this. It is called a local variable. A variable defined inside a function can only be used by that function. If you consider a COBOL subroutine as a function, you will immediately see the similarity. The only `WORKING-STORAGE` that is available to both the called and calling program is the variable passed by the calling program. Any data declared in the `WORKING-STORAGE` of the called program is completely local to the called program. Listings 3.24 and 3.25 reprise `strlen()` and `strcpy()`, this time using a local variable for the index.

Listing 3.24. `strlen()` using local variables.

```
strlen(str)                     /* Receives a variable we'll call str */
char *str;                      /* str is a pointer to char */
{
     int idx;

     dx = 0;                    /* Init the index to 0 */
     while(str[idx] != 0)       /* If the character is not = NUL */
```

continues

Listing 3.24. continued

```
          ++idx;                    /* increment the index */

     return(idx);                   /* Return the count */
}
```

Listing 3.25. strcpy() using local variables

```
strcpy(dest,src)          /* Two variables we'll call dest and src */
char *dest, *src;         /* Both are pointers to char */
{
     int idx;

     idx = 0;                       /* Init the index to 0 */
     while(src[idx] != 0)           /* If the character is not = NUL */
          {
          dest[idx] = src[idx];     /* Copy src to dest */
          ++idx;                    /* increment the index */
          }
/* The routine stopped copying at the final NUL */
/* so it is necessary to add a closing NUL to dest */
     dest[idx] = 0;
}
```

Listing 3.26 combines them into one source code file. Note that both functions use `idx` as the variable name, but there is no naming conflict since each variable is used exclusively within its respective function. The compiler recognizes the variable inside the function and sets up a method of accessing a temporary variable that does not cause a name conflict.

Listing 3.26. strouts.c—strlen() and strcpy() in the same source code file.

```
strlen(str)
char *str;
{
     int idx;

     dx = 0;
```

```
    while(str[idx] != 0)
        ++idx;
    return(idx);
}


strcpy(dest,src)
char *dest, *src;
{
    int idx;        /* This name does not conflict with idx in strlen() */

    idx = 0;
    while(src[idx] != 0)
        {
        dest[idx] = src[idx];
        ++idx;
        }
    dest[idx] = 0;
}
```

There is one big difference in using local variables: they are not initialized by the compiler. You will recall that global numeric variables are initialized by the compiler to start with a value of zero. This is not the case with local variables (numeric or otherwise), and they must be explicitly initialized within the function.

Summary

This chapter covered a lot of material about strings and C functions, and it is worth taking a look at these again.

- A C string is an array of `char` type data.
- Most C string processing functions expect a string to end with a NUL.
- Initializing a string with a value in double quotation marks will cause the compiler to automatically generate the NUL terminator.
- An initialized C string does not have to have an explicit length, and the C compiler will calculate the length and use that for the size of the char array.
- The functions `strlen()`, `strcpy()` and `strcat()` all operate on NUL terminated strings.

When I introduced C functions, I compared them to COBOL paragraphs. They can be used to replace COBOL paragraphs when translating a COBOL program to C. But a C function also has additional powers. Because a C function can include its own local variables, a C function can also act like a complete COBOL subroutine, or a complete called COBOL program.

A value is passed to a function by including it within parentheses after the function name (instead of empty parentheses). A value is received by a function by placing a variable inside the parentheses at the top of the function and then declaring the data type of the variable. The declaration appears before the opening brace of the function.

This chapter covered a great deal more than strings, and in fact illustrated a lot about the C language. Chapter 4, "More on Strings and Pointers," continues with more about strings and yet another dose of C fundamentals.

4

More on Strings and Pointers

A good understanding of strings in C will lead to a solid understanding of concepts that appear throughout the C language. This chapter continues with strings, introducing such essential C ideas as

- Accessing parts of a string
- Working directly with pointers
- Centering a string
- Starting your C library
- Printing strings
- Escape sequences for strings and characters

Much of this chapter does not contain comparisons to COBOL, but with the background you received from previous chapters, you should have no trouble understanding what's happening.

Accessing Parts of a String

It is possible in C to access a portion of a string. As you recall, when a string (char array) is passed to a function, the name of the array causes the compiler to pass the address of the char array (rather than a copy of the array).

```
char a_string[] = "Hello world!";

     strlen(a_string);        /* Passes the address of the string */
```

C has an operator that can be used to force the compiler to pass the address of something rather than the value. This operator is the ampersand (&), and it precedes the variable in question.

```
char a_str = "yet another char array";

     do_something(a_str);        /* Passes the address of a_str */
     do_something(a_str[0]);     /* Passes the character at a_str[0] */
     do_something(&a_str[0]);    /* Passes the address of a_str[0] */
```

The first and third examples are equivalent. When C passes the address of a string (char array), it is, in fact, passing the address of the first element of the array, &a_str[0] in this example.

If the "address of" (&) operator can be used to address the 0th element of an array, it should be possible to address any element of an array. Listing 4.1 passes successively smaller chunks of a string by passing a pointer to different elements of the array.

Listing 4.1. shorter.c—passing part of a string.

```
#include <stdio.h>

char a_str[] = "Just a little bit shorter now!";

main()
{
     printf("%s\n",&a_str[0]);
     printf("%s\n",&a_str[7]);
     printf("%s\n",&a_str[18]);
}
```

The output from Listing 4.1 should look like this:

```
Just a little bit shorter now!
little bit shorter now!
shorter now!
```

Again notice that `printf()` doesn't care about the original length of the string; it prints only from the passed address up to the NUL at the end of the string.

With the "address of" operator, it is possible to try to work out the `strcat()` function. Recall that `strcat()` appends the second string to the first. Listing 4.2 is an example of how `strcat()` might create this effect.

Listing 4.2. strcat.c.

```
strcat(dest,src)
char *dest, *src;
{
     int len;

     len = strlen(dest);
     strcpy(&dest[len],src);
}
```

A desk check on this function can be worked out by assuming that `dest` contains the address of the string `Jose can `, and `src` contains the address of the string `you see?`. Table 4.1 lays out one possible arrangement for these values in memory.

Table 4.1. Memory layout for `dest` and `src`.

Address	1000	1001	1002	1003	1004	1005	1006	1007	1008	1009
Contents	'J'	'o'	's'	'e'	' '	'c'	'a'	'n'	' '	NUL
Address	1050	1051	1052	1053	1054	1055	1056	1057	1058	1059
Contents	'Y'	'o'	'U'	' '	'S'	'E'	'E'	'?'	NUL	

On entry to the function, `dest` contains the value 1000 and `src` contains the value 1050; both are values of addresses in memory. The first step of the function calculates the length of dest using strlen(). In this example, len will be set to 9, the length of Jose can , not including the NUL. The len variable is now used as an index into dest, and strcpy() will be passed the address of the ninth element of dest. Since the string is zero-based, this value will be 1009, the address of the NUL at the end of dest. The string you see? will be copied into memory starting at address 1009, thereby concatenating the two strings.

The strcat() function also illustrates the reusable nature of C code. Both strlen() and strcpy() are low-level functions. When it became necessary to create a strcat() function, it was quickly assembled by combining these two functions for a new type of result. C functions tend to be very small for just this reason. Small simpler functions can be combined into larger more complex actions while relying on already working (and presumably debugged) smaller functions.

Working Directly with Pointers

C has a more convenient mechanism for working with addresses of values. Unfortunately, the syntax can be confusing. You can use the asterisk (*) operator inside a function, but it has a different meaning inside a function than it has when you use it to declare the data passed to a function. Listing 4.3 is a revised example of the strlen() function using this syntax.

Listing 4.3. strlen()—using pointers.

```
strlen(str)
char *str;                 /* str is a pointer to char */
{
     int len;

     len = 0;
     while(*str != 0)      /* *str = the char pointed to by str */
          {
          ++len;
          ++str;           /* Increment the address */
          }
     return(len);
}
```

The variable str is used in several different ways. In the data declaration, just below the start of the function strlen(str), *str means "str is a variable that is an address of a char data type (or a pointer to a char)." Within the function, *str means "Retrieve the variable at the address in str." Since str is defined as a pointer to char, the compiler knows that the value to be retrieved will be the char at the address in str. In this context, *str and str[0] are equivalent. The first retrieves the character at the address in str, while the second retrieves the char at the address in str plus the offset [0].

Finally, you can combine str with the pre-increment operator, ++str. This is something that you cannot do in COBOL. COBOL passes an address into a subroutine, just as C passes an address into a function. Both COBOL and C allow you to modify the data pointed to by the address. But C will let you manipulate the variable as an address, as well as manipulate the contents of the variable.

I'll break this down with a concrete example. Listing 4.4 is a complete program that calls strlen() to extract the length of a string and then print it.

Listing 4.4. showsize.c—a sample program using strlen().

```
#include <stdio.h>

char sample_str[] = "The";

main()
{
     int len;

     len = strlen(sample_str);
     printf("The length of sample_str is ");
     printf("%d\n",len);
}

strlen(str)
char *str;              /* str is a pointer to char */
{
     int len;

     len = 0;
     while(*str != 0)    /* *str = the char pointed to by str */
          {
          ++len;
          ++str;        /* Increment the address */
          }
     return(len);
}
```

The first thing that happens is that the compiler compiles the program and the linker links it. The compiler and linker work jointly to allocate space for the program code and program data. When you run the program, `sample_str` resides at a specific address in memory. For this example, assume that `sample_str` has been created at the address 1040 in memory. When `strlen()` is first called, the value 1040 (the address of `sample_str`) is passed to `strlen()`. Table 4.2 describes the values in each variable after each pass through the `while()` loop within `strlen()`.

Table 4.2. Incrementing an address pointer.

After Pass	*Value of* `str`	*Value of* `*str`	*Value of* `len`
0 (entry)	1040	`'T'`	0
1	1041	`'h'`	1
2	1042	`'e'`	2
3	1043	0	3
Exit from loop	1043	0	3 (returned)

To recap: A variable preceded by an asterisk in the data declaration of a function indicates that the variable is an address pointing to some type of data. A variable preceded by an asterisk in the body of a function indicates the value pointed to by the address in the variable. You could think of these two different meanings for the asterisk as "passed address of" and "value at."

Listing 4.5 is a revised version of `strcpy()` using pointers instead of indexing. It also includes another one of those seemingly cryptic sets of C hieroglyphics.

Listing 4.5. `strcpy()` using pointers.

```
strcpy(dest,src)
char *dest, *src;
{
     while(*src)
          {
          *dest++ = *src++;
          }
     *dest = 0;
}
```

The line `*dest++ = *src++` can be deciphered if you apply rules that you have already learned. An English-language version of this might be, "Get the value at `src`, then increment `src`. Place the value at `dest`, then increment `dest`."

Listings 4.6 and 4.7 are two successive versions of `strcat()`. They show that not only can you increment an address, but you can perform arithmetic operations (addition and subtraction) on addresses and obtain the expected result. Listing 4.7 also substitutes a function that returns an `int` (in this case `strlen()`) for the `int` itself. This produces a very compact version of `strcat()`.

Listing 4.6. `strcat()` with pointers.

```
strcat(dest,src)
char *dest, *src;
{
     int len;

     len = strlen(dest);
     strcpy(dest + len,src);
}
```

Listing 4.7. `strcat()`—a shorter version.

```
strcat(dest,src)
char *dest, *src;
{

     strcpy(dest + strlen(dest),src);
}
```

Centering a String

So far I have referred only to string routines that exist in the standard C library. It's time to start building your own library of routines. These will be functions that you can call to perform tasks from any program. They rely on functions that already exist in the standard C library: `strcat()`, `strlen()`, `strcpy()`, and a few others. Each function is separately coded and explained, but to create a library, you will combine them all in one source code file before they are compiled.

Listing 4.8 is `strljust()`. It is intended to left-justify a passed string by eliminating all leading white space (tabs, spaces, and line feeds). It uses another header file, ctype.h, which is needed for calls to the `isspace()` function. The `isspace()` function is a standard library function. `isspace` is passed a single character; if the character is a space, tab, or line feed, the function returns a nonzero value.

Listing 4.8. `strljust()`—left justification.

```
#include <ctype.h>
#include <string.h>

strljust(str)
char *str;
{
     int len;

     len = strlen(str);
     while(isspace(*str) != 0)
          {
          strcpy(str,str + 1);      /* Copy &str[1] into &str[0] */
          str[len] = ' ';
          }
}
```

Different functions in the standard C library use different header files. So far you have only seen the <stdio.h> header file, which includes support information for `printf()` and some similar functions.

Most of the string functions use a header file named <string.h>, and the `isspace()` function used in Listing 4.8 uses the header file <ctype.h>. Your compiler documentation, particularly the library reference manual, provide information about what a function does, as well as any additional header files that need to be included to use that function. Listing 4.8 includes the appropriate header files for `isspace()` and `strlen()`.

Assuming that `strljust()` is passed a value of `"   three leading spaces"`, the initial `isspace(*str)` will return TRUE (nonzero). Everything one character to the right of the leading space will be copied one character to the left by `strcpy(str, str + 1)`. A space is then added to the end of the string.

The next `while()` iteration tests the new first character in the string. This continues until the `'t'` of `"three leading spaces"` is copied into the first position in the string. This use

of `strcpy()` is considered unacceptable by some because it copies a string over itself from left to right. Many people prefer a standard C function called `memmove()`. This function is passed a destination address, a source address, and the number of bytes to copy. It is guaranteed to correctly handle overlapping areas of memory no matter which direction the string is copied.

Normally, using `memmove()` to copy strings requires the use of `strlen()` to extract the length of the string. Then the length plus one (to include the NUL terminator at the end of the string) is moved. Since the memory that needs to be moved starts one position to the right of the string, use `strlen()` without adding the extra byte. Listing 4.9 revises `strljust()` accordingly, to extract the length of the string.

Listing 4.9. `strljust()`—using `memmove()`.

```
#include <ctype.h>

strljust(str)
char *str;
{
     int len;

     len = strlen(str);
     while(isspace(*str) != 0)
          {
          memmove(str,str + 1,len);
          str[len] = ' ';
          }
}
```

Listing 4.10 `strrev()` reverses a string. This may seem like a silly function, but you will soon see how it's used. The `strrev()` function works by setting up an additional `char` pointer to the end of the string (by adding the length of the string less 1 to `str`).

Listing 4.10. `strrev()`—reversing a string.

```
strrev(str)
char *str;
{
     char ch;
     char *end;
```

continues

Listing 4.10. continued

```
     end = str + strlen(str) - 1;

     while(str < end)
          {
          ch = *end;
          *end = *str;
          *str = ch;
          ++str;
          --end;
}
```

Bytes are swapped between the `end` pointer and the `str` pointer; `end` is then decremented and `str` is incremented. This continues until `end` and `str` cross each other. Note the use of local variables `*end` as a character pointer, and `ch` as a `char` to hold a single character for swapping between `*str` and `*end`.

The `strrev()` function could be tightened up a little by changing the logic inside the while loop to

```
ch = *end;
*end-- = *str;
*str++ = ch;
```

Listing 4.11 is `strrjust()` for right justification. It calls `strrev()` to reverse the string, then left-justifies it, and then reverses the string once more.

Listing 4.11. `strrjust()`—right justification.

```
strrjust(str)
char *str;
{
     strrev(str);
     strljust(str);
     strrev(str);
}
```

This is another good example of building from small blocks. The `strrev()` function can be used on its own if you ever need to reverse a string (perhaps encryption of some sort), and it becomes one of the building blocks for `strrjust()`.

For the next function, strtrunc(), you need to learn a new C operator. It is &&—the exact equivalent to COBOL's AND. It is used for combining two or more conditional tests and requires that they both be true. Listing 4.12 truncates a string by placing a NUL at the end of the last nonspace character in a string. It sets a pointer to the end of the string and then moves backward, replacing each space character with a NUL.

Listing 4.12. strtrunc()—truncating white space.

```
#include <ctype.h>

strtrunc(str)
char *str;
{
     char *end;

     end = str + strlen(str) - 1;

     while( (*str != 0) && ( isspace(*end) != 0 ) )
          {
          *end = 0;
          --end;
          }
}
```

The strtrunc() function can be tightened up by using the following logic:

```
*end-- = 0;
```

At first glance it would seem that strtrunc() could be more easily coded by writing

```
while( isspace(*end) != 0)
     *end-- = 0;
```

This version of strtrunc() contains two possible runaway conditions. First, an empty string could be passed, containing no characters at all. The logic at end = str + strlen() - 1 will cause end to point to an address one earlier than the beginning of str. As end is decremented and possibly filled with NULs, it writes over some other area of memory. The test (*str != 0) prevents the condition.

The second runaway occurs when a string is passed containing nothing but spaces. The end pointer starts out correctly pointing to somewhere within the string, but as it decrements, it always encounters spaces and writes past the beginning of the string. Instead, the test (*str != 0) picks up the point at which end reaches the beginning of the string and a NUL is shoved into that memory address. The additional test catches both possible runaways.

Listing 4.13, `struntrunc()`, does the opposite of `strtrunc()`. It pads a string at the end with spaces for a specified length. It is considerably simpler than `strtrunc()`: it works by concatenating a space to `str` until the length is correct.

Listing 4.13. `struntrunc()`—padding a string with spaces.

```
struntrunc(str,len)
char *str;
int len;
{
     while( strlen(str) < len)
          strcat(str," ");
}
```

You now have all the building blocks you need for string centering. Listing 4.14 centers a string within the length of the string as passed. It saves the original length of the string, and then truncates white space at the end of the string. The string is reversed and truncated again. This ensures that all leading and trailing white space is removed, and you are dealing only with the nonspace length of the string. The original width less the new width is divided by two to calculate the amount of padding needed, and the string is untruncated by this amount. The string is again reversed to restore the original order and untruncated by the original width. This results in a centered string.

Listing 4.14. `strcenter()`—centering a string.

```
strcenter(str)
char *str;
{
     int width,non_blank_len,padding;

     width = strlen(str);

     strtrunc(str);
     strrev(str);
     strtrunc(str);
     non_blank_len = strlen(str);

     padding = (width - non_blank_len ) / 2;

     struntrunc(str,padding);
     strrev(str);
     struntrunc(str,width);
}
```

To center a string within a 30-character space, you must initialize it with the full 30 characters—as shown in Listing 4.15.

Listing 4.15. titler.c—using `strcenter()`.

```
#include <stdio.h>

/* Title is initialized with 30 characters */
char title[] = "Year End Report              ";

main()
{
      strcenter(title);
      printf("%s\n",title);
}
```

Listing 4.16, `strncenter()`, is a more useful version. It is passed a string and a width for the centering, and assumes that memory is large enough to hold the centered result.

Listing 4.16. `strncenter()`—centering a string.

```
strncenter(str,width)
char *str;
int width;
{
      int non_blank_len,padding;

      strtrunc(str);
      strrev(str);
      strtrunc(str);
      non_blank_len = strlen(str);

      padding = (width - non_blank_len ) / 2;

      struntrunc(str,padding);
      strrev(str);
      struntrunc(str,width);
}
```

Listing 4.17 shows an example of using `strncenter()`. It ensures that the title is copied (or created in a space large enough for the work). Note that `work_buffer` is 51 characters long, but the centering is requested for 50 characters. Remember in working with strings that the memory areas to be used must be long enough to hold the entire string, plus one extra byte for the NUL.

Listing 4.17. title50.c—using `strncenter()`.

```
#include <stdio.h>

char title[] = Year End Report";

char work_buffer[51];

main()
{
     strcpy(work_buffer,title);
     strncenter(work_buffer,50);
     printf("%s\n",work_buffer);
}
```

A final comparison of Listings 4.14 and 4.16 reveals that the logic in the two functions is almost identical, except for the initial step of extracting the width of the passed string in `strcenter()`. From a debugging perspective, it makes more sense to deal with that code only once. Listing 4.18 is a revised version of `strcenter()` that extracts the width and then calls `strncenter()`, thereby preventing duplicate code.

Listing 4.18. `strcenter()`—improved version.

```
strcenter(str)
char *str;
{

     strncenter(str,strlen(str));
}
```

I have not included examples of `strnljust()` and `strnrjust()`, which would be versions that include passing widths for left and right justification, but as an exercise you might want to work out how to do them and add them to your library.

Starting Your C Library

Now you have a set of routines that can be used for string manipulation. How do you turn this into a library?

1. Create a Source Code File

The first step is to create a source code file containing one or more functions. Listing 4.19, stringer.c, includes all of the routine developed in the previous section including the improvements mentioned above. Note that ctype.h has to be included only once, at the top of the file. Create this file with your editor and name it stringer.c.

Listing 4.19. stringer.c—library string routines.

```
#include <ctype.h>

/* Left justify a string */
strljust(str)
char *str;
{
      int len;

      len = strlen(str);
      while(isspace(*str) != 0)
            {
            memmove(str,str + 1,len);
            str[len] = ' ';
            }
}

/* Reverse a string */
strrev(str)
char *str;
{
      char ch;
      char *end;

      end = str + strlen(str) - 1;

      while(str < end)
            {
            ch = *end;
```

continues

Listing 4.19. continued

```
          *end-- = *str;
          *str++ = ch;
}

/* Right justify a string */
strrjust(str)
char *str;
{
     strrev(str);
     strljust(str);
     strrev(str);
}

/* Truncate to last non-white character */
strtrunc(str)
char *str;
{
     char *end;

     end = str + strlen(str) - 1;

     while( (*str != 0) && ( isspace(*end) != 0 ) )
          {
          *end-- = 0;
          }
}

/* Pad a string for len with spaces */
struntrunc(str,len)
char *str;
int len;
{
     while( strlen(str) < len)
          strcat(str," ");
}

/* Center a string */
strcenter(str)
char *str;
{

     strncenter(str,strlen(str));
}

/* Center a string within width */
strncenter(str,width)
```

```
char *str;
int width;
{
     int non_blank_len,padding;

     strtrunc(str);
     strrev(str);
     strtrunc(str);
     non_blank_len = strlen(str);

     padding = (width - non_blank_len ) / 2;

     struntrunc(str,padding);
     strrev(str);
     struntrunc(str,width);
}
```

2. Compile the File

The next step is to compile the file into an unlinked object:

- Under DOS using the Microsoft C compiler, type

  ```
  cl /c stringer.c
  ```

  The `/c` switch indicates that the compile will stop before linking takes place.

- Under UNIX, type

  ```
  cc -c stringer.c
  ```

  The `-c` flag serves the same purpose as `/c` under DOS using Microsoft C.

- Under VAX VMS, type

  ```
  cc stringer.c
  ```

  The VAX C compiler does not automatically invoke the linker, so you do not need a switch to prevent linking.

3. Debug and Recompile

If there are errors in your code, correct them now. Common errors are misspelling a variable name in the body of the function or omitting the semicolon at the end of statements, omitting a brace, and other punctuation problems.

Once the corrections are complete, recompile until you have an error-free compilation.

- Under DOS, the output file will be named STRINGER.OBJ.
- Under UNIX, the output file will be named stringer.o.
- Under VAX VMS, the output file will be named STRINGER.OBJ.

4. Create a Library

The fourth step is to use the librarian to create a library and to add your object file to the library. In this example, the library will be called mylib.

- Under DOS, type

  ```
  lib mylib +stringer;
  ```

  This creates the library MYLIB.LIB and adds STRINGER.OBJ to the library.

- Under UNIX, type

  ```
  ar rv mylib.a stringer.o
  ```

  This creates the archive library mylib.a and adds stringer.o to it. Some versions of UNIX require that you further process the library (check your manuals) by running

  ```
  ranlib mylib.a
  ```

- Under VAX VMS, type

  ```
  LIBR/CREATE MYLIB.OLB
  LIBR/INSERT MYLIB.OLB STRINGER.OBJ
  ```

  This creates MYLIB.OLB and adds STRINGER.OBJ to it.

Listing 4.20 gives the library a little workout. Create titling.c with your editor, and compile and link as follows:

- Under MS-DOS Microsoft C, compile and link to create titling.exe by typing

  ```
  cl titling.c mylib.lib
  ```

- Under UNIX, you must specify the output filename with the `-o` switch, so compile and link to create titling by typing

  ```
  cc -o titling titling.c mylib.a
  ```

- Under VAX VMS, compiling and linking are two separate steps, so to compile, type

```
CC titling.c
```

and link by typing

```
LINK/EXE=TITLING TITLING.OBJ, MYLIB.OLB/LIB
```

Listing 4.20. Titling using `strncenter()`.

```
#include <stdio.h>

char title[] = Year End Report";

char work_buffer[51];

main()
{
     strcpy(work_buffer,title);
     strncenter(work_buffer,50);
     printf("%s\n",work_buffer);
     strljust(work_buffer);
     printf("%s\n",work_buffer);
     strrjust(work_buffer);
     printf("%s\n",work_buffer);
}
```

Routines in mylib that are needed by titling.c are extracted by the link step and included in the output file. You can create any other source code file that you wish that uses these routines, and it can be compiled and then linked with mylib.

Printing Strings

I have covered some of the simpler formatting strings used by `printf()`, but `printf()` is a very powerful library routine capable of a wide range of formatting options. This section explores this function in a bit more detail.

The simplest formatting string is one containing no format options. The passed string is printed as is:

```
printf("Hello World!");
```

or

```
char message[] = "Hello World!";

     printf(message);
```

A formatting string may also contain simple formatting characters. You have already seen several of these. They consist of a percent sign (%) followed by one or two characters to indicate the type of data to be printed, as shown in Listing 4.21.

Listing 4.21. prtopt.c—`printf()` options.

```
#include <stdio.h>

int an_int = 5;
long a_long = 6;
double a_double = 12.16;
char a_string[] = "Do not forsake me oh my darlin'";

main()
{
     printf("%d",an_int);
     printf("%ld",a_long);
     printf("%f",a_double);
     printf("%s",a_string);
}
```

A format string may contain formatting information for more than one value, and may also contain constants and newlines. The number of values passed to `printf()` must match the number of formatting characters, in the same order that they appear in the format string, as shown in Listing 4.22.

Listing 4.22. prtopt.c—`printf()` options.

```
#include <stdio.h>

int an_int = 5;
long a_long = 6;
double a_double = 12.16;
char a_string[] = "Do not forsake me oh my darlin'";

main()
{
     printf("%s on or before %d/%ld/93\n",a_string,an_int,a_long);
     printf("or I'll never pay you the %f that I owe you.\n",a_double);
}
```

The output from Listing 4.22 looks like this:

```
Do not forsake me oh my darlin' on or before 5/6/93
or I'll never pay you the 12.160000 that I owe you.
```

The first `printf()` is passed a format string containing formatting for three fields. Those three fields are passed in order as the next three arguments to `printf()`. The second `printf()` uses only one format field and one argument.

Table 4.3 lists the common formatting strings, the data type expected as an argument to `printf()`, and the output format that is printed.

Table 4.3. Common `printf()` formatting characters.

String	*Data Type*	*Output Format*
`"%d"` or `"%i"`	`int`	Signed decimal integer
`"%u"`	`unsigned int`	Unsigned decimal integer
`"%o"`	`int`	Unsigned octal integer
`"%x"` or `"%X"`	`int`	Unsigned hex integer using the digits 0123456789abcdef or 0123456789ABCDEF
`"%f"`	`double` (or `float`)	Signed value `[-]`*`dddd.dddd`*
`"%e"`	`double` (or `float`)	Scientific notation `[-]`*`d.dddd`* `e [+/-]`*`ddd`*
`"%g"`	`double` (or `float`)	Most compact version of `"%f"` and `"%e"` formats
`"%c"`	`int` (or `char`)	Single character
`"%s"`	String (array of `char`)	Printed up to first NUL

A format string can contain additional information that overrides or additionally formats the default output or input. You are already familiar with `"%ld"`, used in Listing 4.22 for a long integer. An `l` can be used with `d`, `i`, `u`, `o`, `X`, or `x` to indicate an expected long integer argument. Similarly an `h` can be used with `d`, `i`, `u`, `o`, `X`, or `x` to indicate an expected short integer argument. Microsoft C uses an `L` prefix with `f`, `e`, or `g` to indicate an expected long double argument.

A format string is made up of several parts, as shown in the following syntax:

`%[flags][width][.precision][prefix]type.`

Everything but the percent sign (`%`) and the type are optional, and the effect of these optional pieces varies depending on the basic types. The types are already listed in Table 4.3. The prefixes again are `h`, `l`, and `L`. The next most useful part is the width. This field indicates the number of spaces the field is to occupy. For numeric values this can be used to force columns of numbers to line up as in Listing 4.23.

Listing 4.23. column.c—using `printf()` to create columns.

```
#include <stdio.h>

int x = 1

main()
{
     while( x < 32000)
          {
          printf("%5d\n",x);
          x += 999;
          }
}
```

The output from column.c is

```
    1
 1000
 1999
.
.
.
10990
11989
.
.
.
```

and so on. The default action of a width specifier is to right-justify the requested output within the space requested by width. For strings, then, it is useful to use the flag with a format string. If the flag is a minus (-), it causes left justification within the width.

```
printf("%15s and all the ships at sea.\n","Hello world");
printf("%-15s and all the ships at sea.\n","Hello world");
```

outputs

```
                 Hello World and all the ships at sea.
Hello World                  and all the ships at sea.
```

The width part of a format string for numeric values can start with a `0`, causing the space to the left of the number to be filled with zeroes as in Listing 4.24. Compare this output to that produced by Listing 4.23.

Listing 4.24. column.c—using `printf()` with leading zeroes.

```
#include <stdio.h>

int x = 1

main()
{
     while( x < 32000)
          {
          printf("%05d\n",x);
          x += 999;
          }
}
```

The output from column.c will be;

```
00001
01000
01999
.
.
.
10990
11989
.
.
.
```

and so on. The flag value + can be used with numeric values to force signed output. The default value is to print a minus sign (-) only when the value is negative.

The precision specification is most useful with `doubles` and `floats`. This indicates the number of decimals to be printed and performs `ROUNDING`. When specifying the width of a `float` or `double`, the width is of the entire field as it will be printed, including the decimal and other formatting characters. If you want to print a signed number with six places before the decimal and two after, the natural inclination is to call this format `"%+6.2f"`. In fact, the correct format width must include the six digits, the sign, the decimal point, and two decimal places—or `"%10.2f"`. If you wanted this field to print with leading zeroes, you would use `"%+010.2f"`.

Your C library reference manual usually contains several examples of format fields, and you should look up the **`printf()`** function and look at them. Whenever you see a `printf()` function, take the time to understand how the formatting is being done. It is one of the most heavily used, and useful, C standard library routines.

One more note on `printf()`: If a percent sign precedes a character that has no special meaning to `printf()`, the second character is printed as is. This is the method to use for printing an actual percent sign. In the following example, the two percent signs in `"%d%%"` are printed as a single percent sign.

```
printf("Net profits were %d%%\n",profit_percentage);
```

Escape Sequences in Strings and Characters

You have already seen one of the C escape sequences that can be embedded in a C string—`"\n"`, which causes a newline to be output to the terminal. There are other "escaped" characters that can be placed in C strings, and you will come across them in listings. The escape character (\) is used to tell the compiler that the next character has a special meaning (the same way that `%` tells `printf()` that the next characters have a special meaning). The backslash is usually used when something can't be represented by typing it on the keyboard, or when the presence of the character in a string would be confusing. Table 4.4 lists the common escape sequences.

Table 4.4. Common escape sequences.

Escape Sequence	*Description*
`\a`	Rings terminal or printer bell
`\b`	Backspace
`\f`	Form feed on a printer; usually clears the screen

Escape Sequence	*Description*
	when printed to the screen
`\n`	Newline
`\r`	Carriage return
`\t`	Tab
`\"`	Double quotes
`\'`	Single quotes
`\\`	A backslash
`\nnn`	An ASCII character in octal, where *n* is an octal digit
`\xhh`	An ASCII character in hexadecimal, where *h* is a hexadecimal digit

Listing 4.25 illustrates the use of some escape sequences.

Listing 4.25. witchdoc.c—using escape sequences.

```
#include <stdio.h>

/*
 This program clears the screen, prints a silly message,
 and then rings the terminal bell
*/

char cls[]="\f";
char msg1[] = "He said \n\t\"Ooh eee ooh ah ah \n";
char msg2[] = "\tting tang walla walla wing bang.\"\n";
char msg3[]= "and it didn\'t make any sense.";
char bell[] = "\a";

main()
{
     printf("%s%s%s%s%s\n",cls,msg1,msg2,msg3,bell);
}
```

This bit of nonsense will probably clear the screen and then print as

```
He said
     "Ooh eee ooh ah ah
     ting tang walla walla wing bang."
and it didn't make any sense.
```

probably followed by the terminal bell sounding.

Escaped characters are also used within single quotes when referring to a single character.

```
str[5] = '\n';      /* Store a newline in str */
str[4] = '\f';      /* Store a form feed in str */
```

I have used the value 0 to represent NUL, but it is common practice in C code to represent a single NUL as `'\0'` (an escaped zero). This is perhaps a clearer indication of a NUL character than a 0 because it stands out more on the page:

```
if(*str != '\0')
```

Summary

You still haven't seen everything about strings and pointers, but you have seen a big piece of the subject. In Chapter 5, "Program Flow Control," you'll begin to deal with loops, conditional statements, and other aspects of program flow control. This is familiar territory, and immediate comparisons to COBOL are available.

5

PROGRAM FLOW CONTROL

Does C have a PERFORM UNTIL? Does C have an IF statement? Can I GO TO? Yes, yes, and yes (but it would be better if you didn't). Program flow control is at the heart of any programming, for without it, all programs would execute from the first instruction through to the last, with no repetitive processing. As a COBOL programmer, you are quite familiar with program flow control, and fortunately, C's program flow control is much like COBOL's. You should feel right at home with this chapter.

This chapter deals with a range of structures that you will recognize immediately:

- IF ELSE
- NEXT SENTENCE
- PERFORM WITH TEST BEFORE UNTIL
- PERFORM WITH TEST AFTER UNTIL
- PERFORM WITH TEST BEFORE VARYING UNTIL
- PERFORM *nn* TIMES
- C punctuation for flow control

- Multiple loop initialization
- Breaking and continuing flow control
- Calling functions within conditions
- The big IF—the C switch statement
- Using switch case logic in C
- The C conditional operator
- The dreaded GO TO
- Notes on COBOL SECTIONS and PERFORM THROUGH

IF ELSE

C's if-else syntax is very similar to COBOL's. In C, the condition that is being tested must be enclosed in parentheses:

```
if( var_a < var_b)
     do_something();
else
     do_something_else();
```

If more than one statement is to be performed as a result of an if or else testing true, all those statements must be enclosed in braces.

```
if( var_a < var_b)
     {
     do_step_one();
     do_step_two();
     }
```

As in the above example, an if() does not have to be matched with an else.

The C equivalent of IS EQUAL is a double equal sign (==), and C does not support IS NOT GREATER THAN and IS NOT LESS THAN. Instead, you must use "less than or equal to" and "greater than or equal to" respectively.

It is possible to combine tests using AND and OR. The C equivalent to AND is && and the C equivalent to OR is ¦¦ (two vertical bars). Table 5.1 summarizes COBOL and C comparison operators. The combined test operators have no space between the characters.

Table 5.1. COBOL and C comparison operators.

<table>
<tr><th>COBOL</th><th>C</th><th>Description</th></tr>
<tr><td><code>IS EQUAL</code></td><td><code>==</code></td><td>is equal to</td></tr>
<tr><td><code>IS NOT EQUAL</code></td><td><code>!=</code></td><td>is not equal to</td></tr>
<tr><td><code>IS LESS THAN</code></td><td><code><</code></td><td>is less than</td></tr>
<tr><td><code>IS GREATER THAN</code></td><td><code>></code></td><td>is greater than</td></tr>
<tr><td><code>IS NOT LESS THAN</code></td><td><code>>=</code></td><td>is greater than or equal</td></tr>
<tr><td><code>IS NOT GREATER THAN</code></td><td><code><=</code></td><td>is less than or equal</td></tr>
<tr><td><code>AND</code></td><td><code>&&</code></td><td>Boolean AND</td></tr>
<tr><td><code>OR</code></td><td><code>||</code></td><td>Boolean OR</td></tr>
</table>

Listing 5.1 demonstrates the `min()` and `max()` functions, which return the smaller and larger of two integers.

Listing 5.1. The `min()` and `max()` functions.

```
min(a,b)
int a, b;
{
     if(a < b)
          return(a);
     else
          return(b);
}

max(a,b)
int a,b;
{
     if(a > b)
          return(a);
     else
          return(b);
}
```

`if-else` can be be used in `if-else-if` constructions just as it is in COBOL. Listing 5.2 is a function from a menu program that dispatches to another function based on a passed menu selection.

Listing 5.2. Using `if-else-if` logic.

```
do_menu_pick(pick)
int pick;
{
     if(pick == 1)
          do_pick_1();
     else
     if(pick == 2)
          do_pick_2();
     else
     if(pick == 3)
          do_pick_3();
}
```

C includes one special `if` test for a nonzero condition. By placing a variable in parentheses and adding no comparison conditions, you are, in effect, testing for the condition in which the variable is not equal to zero, for example:

```
if(var_a)                        /* same as if(var_a != 0) */
     do_something();
```

Any test may be reversed by preceding it with the not operator (`!`); this is one way to pseudo-implement COBOL's `NOT LESS THAN` and `NOT GREATER THAN`.

```
     if(!(var_a < var_b))       /* if var_a not less than var_b */
          do_something();

/* or */
     if(!(var_a > var_b))       /* if var_a not greater than var_b */
```

This negation operation can be used on any test, so

```
if(!(var_a))          /* same as if(var_a == 0) */
```

is a valid test for a zero condition.

C also allows assignment operations within `if` tests. This presents some unusual looking constructions, such as

```
if((var_a = var_b) < var_c)
     do_something();
```

The effect of this assignment/comparison is to assign the value of var_b to var_a and then test whether var_a is less than var_c.

This feature of C has an unfortunate side effect. Both of the following if tests are valid:

```
if(var_a == var_b)
     do_something();
```

and

```
if(var_a = var_b)
     do_something();
```

The first tests whether var_a is equal to var_b. The second assigns the value of var_b to var_a and then tests whether var_a is nonzero. This is one of the biggest sources of bugs in programs by programmers coming from another language, and in fact causes plenty of headaches to experienced C programmers. There is no easy way around this. Just be aware of it and suspect it when your if logic seems to be misbehaving. Note, though, that some compilers (such as Borland) can be set so that a warning message is given when an assignment is made in a comparison statement.

When comparing against a constant, one partial fix is always to place the constant to the left of the comparison. For example, instead of

```
if( var_a == 5)
```

use

```
if( 5 == var_a)
```

The advantage of this is that if you mistype (5 = var_a), the compiler will return an error message, because a value cannot be assigned to a constant. For comparisons between variables, you just have to grit your teeth and remember which to use.

NEXT SENTENCE

C does not contain a NEXT SENTENCE statement, but it does contain a "do-nothing" that you can usually use to imitate NEXT SENTENCE logic. The "do-nothing" is a single semicolon with no statement, as shown in the following code:

```
if(var_a <= var_b)
     {
     if(var_a >= var_c)
          printf("var_a is in range\n");
     else
```

```
          ;       /*do nothing */
     }
else
     something_else();
```

However, in C you do not have to back yourself out of nested `if` corners. There is no need for the inside `else` in this example, so it would be better written as

```
if(var_a <= var_b)
     {
     if(var_a >= var_c)
          printf("var_a is in range\n");
     }
else
     something_else();
```

The braces make it clear to the compiler which `if` the `else` matches. The do-nothing statement is another problem area. C tends toward closing each statement with a semicolon. This can become an automatic habit and can get you into trouble, as in the following example:

```
if( (var_a <= hi) && (var_a >= lo) );
     printf("var_a is in range\n");
```

Because C doesn't care about indentation, the closing semicolon at the end of the `if` test actually transforms this piece of code into

```
if( (var_a <= hi) && (var_a >= lo) )
     ;          /* do nothing */
printf("var_a is in range\n");
```

So `var_a` will always be in range.

PERFORM WITH TEST BEFORE UNTIL

`PERFORM UNTIL` *`SOME CONDITION`* in COBOL contains an implied `TEST BEFORE`. The condition is tested before the first execution, and if the condition is true, the `PERFORM` is not executed. COBOL allows the inclusion of the test in the syntax, but it is implied even if not stated. Listings 5.3 and 5.4 are equivalent.

Listing 5.3. PERFORM UNTIL.

```
THE-LOOP.
   PERFORM ADD-UP
* IMPLIED TEST BEFORE
      UNTIL VAR-A IS GREATER THAN
         VAR-B.
```

Listing 5.4. PERFORM WITH TEST BEFORE UNTIL.

```
THE-LOOP.
   PERFORM ADD-UP
    WITH TEST BEFORE
    UNTIL VAR-A IS GREATER THAN
       VAR-B
```

You have already seen the C test-before syntax: the `while()` statement. The `while()` functions like an in-line `PERFORM` in COBOL. One statement may be placed immediately under the `while()`, or multiple statements may be grouped in braces under the `while()`. The big difference between the COBOL and C versions is that a `while()` operates as long as the condition is TRUE, but a `PERFORM UNTIL` operates as long as the condition is FALSE. Listings 5.5 and 5.6 illustrate this difference.

Listing 5.5. COBOL loops UNTIL the condition is TRUE.

```
THE-LOOP.
    MOVE 1 TO VAR-A.
    PERFORM
         UNTIL VAR-A > 10
         PERFORM ADD-UP
         ADD 1 TO VAR-A
    END PERFORM.
```

Listing 5.6. C loops `while` the condition is TRUE.

```
the_loop()
{
     var_a = 1;
     while(var_a <= 10)
          {
          add_up();
          ++var_a;
          }
}
```

Listing 5.7 illustrates an alternative method of testing that preserves a similarity to the COBOL test by using a negation.

Listing 5.7. C loops `while` a condition is not TRUE.

```
the_loop()
{
     var_a = 1;
     while(!(var_a > 10))
          {
          add_up();
          ++var_a;
          }
}
```

C `while()` tests are identical to `if()` tests including the nonzero condition. Any `while()` may use `&&` and `¦¦` to combine conditions. Note that like the `if()` test, a semicolon does not appear after a `while()` test.

PERFORM WITH TEST AFTER UNTIL

`PERFORM WITH TEST AFTER` is implemented with a completely different syntax in C, usually called `do while()` logic. The C `do while` is compared to `TEST AFTER` logic in Listings 5.8 and 5.9. The negation logic is used again because a `do while()` is just an upside-down `while()`; it continues executing as long as the condition is TRUE.

Listing 5.8. COBOL tests after one pass through the loop.

```
THE-LOOP.
    MOVE 1 TO VAR-A.
    PERFORM
    WITH TEST AFTER
         UNTIL VAR-A > 10
         PERFORM ADD-UP
         ADD 1 TO VAR-A
    END PERFORM.
```

Listing 5.9. C tests after one pass through the loop.

```
the_loop()
{
     var_a = 1;
     do{
          add_up();
          ++var_a;
          }while(!(var > 10));
}
```

For some perverse reason best known to compiler designers, the `do{}while()` requires a closing semicolon. If you do forget it, the compiler will warn you, so at least it isn't as bad as including a semicolon that shouldn't be there.

PERFORM WITH TEST BEFORE VARYING UNTIL

The `PERFORM VARYING` version of `PERFORM` is a powerful and often-used construction. C has an even more powerful control structure: `for()` logic. The syntax for a `for()` statement is

`for(`*`loop_initialization`*`;`*`loop_condition`*`;`*`loop_control`*`)`

The best way of explaining this is by comparing Listings 5.10 and 5.11, using `for()` logic in the C program.

Listing 5.10. Using PERFORM UNTIL.

```
THE-LOOP.
  PERFORM
  VARYING VA FROM 1 BY 1
         UNTIL VA > 10
         PERFORM ADD-UP
         ADD 1 TO VA
    END PERFORM.
```

Listing 5.11. Using for() logic.

```
the_loop()
{
     for(va = 1;!(va > 10);++va)
          {
          add_up();
          }
}
```

The `for` loop takes care of three basic functions that are performed over and over in programs:

1. Initialize for a loop.
2. Loop until some condition is met.
3. Do some sort of control at the bottom of each loop.

`PERFORM VARYING` embodies similar logic, but the `for()` statement takes this even further. The initialization statement may contain anything needed to initialize the loop, including a function call, multiple statements separated by commas, or nothing at all. The third statement for loop control is similar. It may contain one or more statements to perform at the bottom of the loop, or none at all.

Just to clarify this, I'll revisit a couple of the string functions from the previous chapter and redo them with `for()` logic. Listings 5.12 and 5.13 are the original and revised versions of `strrev()`. I've taken advantage of C's free-form structure to comment the three parts of the loop control.

Listing 5.12. `strrev()`—the original.

```
strrev(str)
char *str;
{
     char ch;
     char *end;

/*1*/end = str + strlen(str) - 1;

/*2*/while(str < end)
           {
           ch = *end;
           *end = *str;
           *str = ch;
/*3*/      ++str;
/*3*/      --end;
}
```

Listing 5.13. `strrev()`—with `for()` logic.

```
strrev(str)
char *str;
{
     char ch;
     char *end;

     for(end=str+strlen(str)-1;  /*1*/
         str < end ;             /*2*/
         ++str, --end)           /*3*/
          {
          ch = *end;
          *end = *str;
          *str = ch;
          }
}
```

Listings 5.14 and 5.15 compare the original and `for()` versions of `strtrunc()`.

Listing 5.14. `strtrunc()`—the original.

```
#include <ctype.h>

strtrunc(str)
char *str;
{
     char *end;

/*1*/ end=str+strlen(str)-1;

/*2*/ while((*str!=0) &&
                (isspace(*end)!=0))
          {
          *end = 0;
/*3*/     --end;
          }
}
```

Listing 5.15. `strtrunc()`—with `for()` logic.

```
#include <ctype.h>

strtrunc(str)
char *str;
{
     char *end;

     /*1, 2, and 3 combined */
     for(end=str+strlen(str)-1;(*str!=0)&&(isspace(*end)!=0);--end)
          {
          *end = 0;
          }
}
```

The `for()` construction is used extensively in C, and you will have to learn it well. The flexibility of being able to perform functions within the `for()` control statements is sometimes overused. To read C listings, you'll have to understand each of the three parts.

PERFORM nn TIMES

`PERFORM` *nn* `TIMES` is not supported in C, but the logic can obviously be imitated using a `for()` loop and a temporary variable. There is one thing worth taking a look at. Since C uses zero-based indexing, it is not uncommon for programmers to use zero initialization for counters. Thus, the code

```
PERFORM 10 TIMES
     PERFORM DO_SOMETHING
END PERFORM.
```

is very likely to be implemented by a C programmer as

```
for(counter = 0; counter < 10; ++counter)
     do_something();
```

This still performs `do_something()` 10 times, but until you get used to the tendency to count from zero, it is not immediately obvious what is happening.

This is a natural outgrowth of array initialization logic, such as that illustrated in Listing 5.16. The array `all_x` contains 10 elements. These will be indexed as elements 0 through 9. The initialization is easier to write with a condition of `idx < 10` rather than `idx <= 9`.

Listing 5.16. Array initialization.

```
char all_x[10];
int idx;

main()
{
     for(idx=0;idx < 10;++idx)
          all_x[idx] = 'X';
}
```

C Punctuation for Flow Control

Punctuation for flow control is a sticky subject. Fortunately, COBOL programmers are no strangers to punctuation hassles. There are three key rules to remember:

- When testing for equality, be sure to use == (equal equal), when assigning, use = (equal).
- `if()`, `while()` , and `for( ; ; )` are not concluded with semicolons.
- `do{} while()` is concluded with a semicolon.

The third rule is not such a big problem (because the compiler squawks about it), but the first two have probably caused more logic bugs in programs than any other problem in C.

Breaking and Continuing Flow Control

Unlike COBOL, C includes mechanisms that allow you to break out of controlled loops. The command naturally enough is `break`. A `break` is commonly used in syntax such as that illustrated in Listing 5.17. The `while(1)` control is, in fact, a sort of "do forever." The routine gets a value back from `get_menu_pick()`, and if the value is 99, the `while` loop is broken.

Listing 5.17. somemenu.c—using `break`.

```
#include <stdio.h>

main()
{
     int pick;

     while(1)
          {
          pick = get_menu_pick();
          if(pick == 99)
               break;
          if(pick == 1)
               do_pick_1();
          if(pick == 2)
               do_pick_2();
          }
}
```

Another version of "do forever" is

```
for( ; ; )
     {
     do_something();
     }
```

If you use a do-forever loop, you must make sure that some valid condition causes a break to terminate the loop.

Another use for the `break` command is simply to check a second condition somewhere in the body of the loop. Listing 5.18 is `strncpy()`. This routine copies all characters from `src` to `dest`, stopping either at the first NUL character or when `len` bytes have been copied—whichever comes first. You will find `strncpy()` in some C libraries. Listing 5.18 is not the most efficient coding, but it does illustrate the use of a `break`. Just for the sake of good form, Listing 5.19 shows a better version of `strncpy()`, but it doesn't use `break`.

Listing 5.18. `strncpy()` using `break`.

```
strncpy(dest,src,len)
char *dest, *src;
int len;
{
     int wlen;

     wlen = 0;
     while(len > wlen)
          {
          if(!(*src))                    /* (*src == 0 ) */
          if(wlen == len)
               break;
          *dest++ = *src++;
          ++wlen;
          }
     *dest = 0;
```

Listing 5.19. `strncpy()`—a better version.

```
strncpy(dest,src,len)
char *dest, *src;
int len;
{
     int wlen;
```

continues

Listing 5.19. continued

```
     wlen = 0;
     for(wlen = 0; (len > wlen) && (*src) ; ++wlen)
          {
          *dest++ = *src++;
          }
     *dest = 0;
```

C allows you to break out of the middle of a function by using a `return`. You have aleady seen this in the `min()` and `max()` functions shown in Listing 5.1.

A `continue` causes the code to skip to the end of the loop ready for the next iteration. In a `for()` loop, the loop-control logic is executed before looping, so a `continue` in a `for()` loop can be put to good use.

Listing 5.20 is a `vowelcpy()` function that copies only the vowels *a, e, i, o,* and *u* from a string. The function uses `continue` to skip consonants. The support function `is_a_vowel()` uses return logic to break out of the function.

Listing 5.20. `vowelcpy()`.

```
vowelcpy(dest,src)
char *dest,*src;
{
     for( ; *src != 0 ; ++src)
          {
          if(is_a_vowel(*src) == 0)
               continue;
          *dest++ = *src;
          }

is_a_vowel(ch)
int ch;
{
     if(ch == 'a')  return(1);
     if(ch == 'e')  return(1);
     if(ch == 'i')  return(1);
     if(ch == 'o')  return(1);
     if(ch == 'u')  return(1);
     return(0);
}
```

One thing in this listing that hasn't come up before is the passing of the character to `is_a_vowel()`. C promotes a single `char` to an `int` when extracting and passing it to functions. Even though it started as a `char`, it arrives inside the function as a an `int`. As an `int`, it can still be tested and treated as a character.

The logic in `vowelcpy()` is interesting. The `src` pointer is incremented in loop control, because the function should always increment the `src` pointer. The `dest` pointer is incremented only when a copy occurs. The `continue` statement skips the copy into `dest` and hits the bottom of the loop, where `++src` is executed as part of loop control.

The `continue` and `break` statements affect only the innermost loop. Listing 5.21 processes a string containing words and multiple spaces, and prints each word out on an individual line, one character at a time. It prints a newline when it contacts the first space, and then ignores remaining spaces until the next word begins.

Listing 5.21. wordbrk.c—using `break` and `continue`.

```
#include <stdio.h>

char some_words[]="These   are  some words     for testing";

main()
{
     wordy(some_words);
}

wordy(str)
char *str;
{
     while(1)
          {
          if(*str == 0)
               break;
          if(*str == ' ')
               {
               printf("\n");
               while(1)
                    {
                    if(*str != ' ')
                         break;
                    ++str;
                    }
               continue;
               }
```

continues

Listing 5.21. continued

```
          printf("%c",*str);
/*1*/     ++str;
          }
}
```

The inner loop breaks when it hits a nonspace character. The outer loop breaks when it hits a NUL. Each character in the string is printed using the `"%c"` format option. When a space is encountered, a newline is printed, and the inner loop takes control, stepping through `*str` until a nonspace character is hit. The continue logic is necessary because without it, the `++str` at point `/*1*/` would be executed after the blanks had been processed. The inner loop has already stepped up to the next nonblank character, so you do not want to execute another `++str`, or you will skip a character.

The Big *IF*

`GO TO DEPENDING` logic is little used in COBOL, but it is the closest analog to C's `switch-case` logic. Listings 5.22 and 5.23 compare the syntax of these two control structures.

Listing 5.22. ALPHANUM.COB.

```
 IDENTIFICATION DIVISION.
 PROGRAM-ID. ALPHANUM.
* THIS PROGRAM DISPLAYS A NUMBER
* AS A STRING.
 ENVIRONMENT DIVISION.
 DATA DIVISION.
 WORKING-STORAGE SECTION.
 01  VAR-A                PIC 99.

 PROCEDURE DIVISION.
 MAIN-LOGIC SECTION.
 PROGRAM-BEGIN.
     PERFORM NUM-TO-ALPHA THRU
          NUM-TO-ALPHA-EXIT
          VARYING VAR-A FROM 1 BY 1
               UNTIL VAR-A > 3.
 EXIT-PROGRAM.
```

```
     EXIT PROGRAM.
 STOP-RUN.
     STOP RUN.
 THE-OTHER SECTION.
 NUM-TO-ALPHA.
     GO TO
           1-TO-ALPHA
           2-TO-ALPHA
           3-TO-ALPHA
     DEPENDING ON VAR-A.
     GO TO NUM-TO-ALPHA-EXIT.
 1-TO-ALPHA.
     DISPLAY "ONE".
     GO TO NUM-TO-ALPHA-EXIT.
 2-TO-ALPHA.
     DISPLAY "TWO".
     GO TO NUM-TO-ALPHA-EXIT.
 3-TO-ALPHA.
     DISPLAY "THREE".
     GO TO NUM-TO-ALPHA-EXIT.

 NUM-TO-ALPHA-EXIT.
     EXIT.
```

Listing 5.23. alphanum.c.

```
#include <stdio.h>

main()
{
     int num;

     for(num = 1; num <= 3 ; ++num)
          num_to_alpha(num);
}

num_to_alpha(numbr)
int numbr;
{
     switch(numbr)
          {
          case 1:
               one_to_alpha();
               break;
```

continues

Listing 5.23. continued

```
          case 2:
               two_to_alpha();
               break;
          case 3:
               three_to_alpha();
               break;
          default:
               break;
          }
}

one_to_alpha()
{
     printf("one\n");
}

two_to_alpha()
{
     printf("two\n");
}

three_to_alpha()
{
     printf("three\n");
}
```

A C `switch-case` structure is more like an `if-else-if` statement than a `GO TO DEPENDING`. This is illustrated in Listings 5.24 and 5.25.

Listing 5.24. alphanum.c.

```
#include <stdio.h>

main()
{
     int num;

     for(num = 1; num <= 3 ; ++num)
          num_to_alpha(num);
}

num_to_alpha(numbr)
```

```
int numbr;
{
     switch(numbr)
          {
          case 1:
               one_to_alpha();
               break;
          case 2:
               two_to_alpha();
               break;
          case 3:
               three_to_alpha();
               break;
          default:
               break; /* do nothing */
          }
}


one_to_alpha()
{
     printf("one\n");
}

two_to_alpha()
{
     printf("two\n");
}

three_to_alpha()
{
     printf("three\n");
}
```

Listing 5.25. alphanum.c—using `if-else-if`.

```
#include <stdio.h>

main()
{
     int num;
```

continues

Listing 5.25. continued

```
     for(num = 1; num <= 3 ; ++num)
          num_to_alpha(num);
}

num_to_alpha(numbr)
int numbr;
{
     if(numbr == 1)
          {
          one_to_alpha();
          }
     else
     if(numbr == 2)
          {
          two_to_alpha();
          }
     else
     if(numbr == 3)
          {
          three_to_alpha();
          }
     else
          ;          /* do nothing */
}

one_to_alpha()
{
     printf("one\n");
}

two_to_alpha()
{
     printf("two\n");
}

three_to_alpha()
{
     printf("three\n");
}
```

A `switch-case` also differs from a `GO TO DEPENDING` in that the variable can be any value or expression. A `switch-case` is composed of three parts: the switch expression, the `case` constants (or a default), and the statements to be performed (which may include a break), as shown in the following syntax:

```
switch(expression)
     {
     case constant;
          statement;
          [statement;]
          [break;]
     case constant;
          statement;
          [break;]
     [default:]
          statement;
          [break;]
     }
```

The `break` statement causes a break to occur in the `switch` statement, and program control passes to the bottom of the entire `switch`. The `break` may be omitted. When it is missing, statements for the next `case` constant are executed as if they were logic for the preceding case (see Listing 5.28).

Using *switch-case* Logic in C

`switch-case` logic is used extensively in C. Listings 5.26 through 5.30 provide samples of different types of `switch-case` statements.

In Listing 5.26, each `menu_pick` option causes a single function to be called, and then the `switch` statement is exited by the `break` statement. The `break` statement after the default case causes nothing to happen if the `menu_pick` is any other value.

Listing 5.26. Usual `switch-case` logic.

```
switch(menu_pick)
     {
     case 1:
          do_pick_1();
          break;
     case 2:
          do_pick_2();
          break;
     default:
          break;
     }
```

In Listing 5.27, the `switch` tests if the value is a `'0'` and adds 1 to the `zero_count`. As no `break` appears, control falls through to the first statement under the default case. The character is tested to check whether it is a digit using the `isdigit()` function in the standard C library. If it is, the `digit_count` variable is incremented. The result is that the `zero_count` is incremented by 1 whenever `ch == '0'`, and `digit_count` is incremented by 1 whenever `ch ==` any digit.

Listing 5.27. `switch-case` fall-through by omitting `break` statements.

```
switch(ch)
     {
     case '0':
          ++zero_count;
     default:
          if(isdigit(ch))
               ++digit_count;
     }
```

In Listing 5.28, any vowel value for `ch` causes execution of `return_value = 1`; any other value sets `return_value` to 0.

Listing 5.28. `switch-case` using multiple cases.

```
int return_value;

switch(ch)
     {
     case 'a':
     case 'e':
     case 'i':
     case 'o':
     case 'u':
          return_value = 1;
          break;
     default:
          return_value = 0;
          break;
     }
return(return_value);
```

Listing 5.29 counts occurrences of the letter *a*, the other vowels, and any other character that is not a space.

Listing 5.29. Using fall-through and multiple cases.

```
switch(ch)
     {
     case 'a':
          ++letter_a;
     case 'e':
     case 'i':
     case 'o':
     case 'u':
          ++vowels;
     default:
          ++characters;
          break;
     case ' ':
          break;
     }
```

Listing 5.30 is a reprise of the `is_a_vowel()` function from Listing 5.20. The `switch case` is equivalent to the `switch case` in Listing 5.28. It uses return to force a return from the function, effectively "`breaking`" the switch. In Listing 5.30, the use of `break` statements is redundant, as the `return` will cause an exit from the function before the `break` is reached. Some compilers will notice this and provide the warning `statement not able to be reached`, because the `break` can never be executed.

Listing 5.30. `switch case` using `return` to `break`.

```
is_a_vowel(ch)
int ch;

     switch(ch)
          {
          case 'a':
          case 'e':
          case 'i':
          case 'o':
          case 'u':
               return(1);
```

continues

Listing 5.30. continued

```
                break ;          /* Redundant and can be omitted */
            default:
                return(0);
            }
}
```

The C Conditional Operator

`if-else` logic is so commonly used to perform a single `if-else` condition that C provides a special operator for this. The usual method of performing an `if-else` test for a `max()` function might be something like that shown in Listing 5.31.

Listing 5.31. `max()`.

```
max(a,b)
int a,b;
{
     int result;

     if(a > b)
          result = a;
     else
          result = b;
     return(result);
}
```

Listing 5.32 implements the same logic using the conditional operator (`?`). The C conditional operator consists of a conditional expression followed by a question mark. The next statement is a function or value to return if the condition tests TRUE, followed by a colon. The third part of the statement is what to do if the condition evaluates FALSE.

Listing 5.32. `max()` using the conditional operator.

```
max(a,b)
int a, b;
{
     result = (a>b) ? a : b ;
     return(result);
}
```

The conditional operator is tricky to get used to, and is very obscure to non-C programmers. If your code must be legible (as in the case of accounting software that must be audited), you might want to avoid it entirely, or at least comment it heavily. Even commented versions of this operator are a bit difficult to understand (as in Listing 5.33) unless you write out the whole `if` statement as a comment. Having written it out, you might as well have used it in the first place.

Listing 5.33. Attempting to comment the conditional operator.

```
max(a,b)
int a,b;
{
     result =
          /* if */          (a>b) ?
          /* then * /          a :
          /* else */           b ;
     return(result);
}
```

Having complained about how unreadable the conditional operator is, I must go on to say that it is extremely useful. Listing 5.34 uses the conditional operator to determine whether to print the singular or plural based on a `count`.

Listing 5.34. Using the conditional operator.

```
print_wrap_up(count)
int count;
```

continues

Listing 5.34. continued

```
    printf("There %s %d thing%s counted.\n",
                    (count == 1) ? "was" : "were",
                    count,
                    (count == 1) ? "" : "s");
}
```

Listing 5.34 will print any of several possible ways, depending on the value of `count`. The first conditional operation indicates that if `count` is 1, the value of the first string passed to `printf()` will be `was`, otherwise `were` is used. The second conditional operator passes an empty string for a value of 1 or an `s` for any other value as the third argument to `printf()`. The results could be

```
There was 1 thing counted.
There were 18 things counted.
There were 0 things counted.
```

The conditional operator may be nested, although it becomes even more unreadable. Listings 5.35 and 5.36 both compare two numbers, although the first is much easier to understand. They both return either `-1`, `0`, or `+1` based on the results of a comparison between two numbers.

Listing 5.35. Comparing two numbers.

```
comp_int(a,b)
int a,b;
{
      int result;
      if(a == b)
            result = 0;
      else
            {
            if( a< b)
                  result = -1;
            else
                  result = +1;
            }
      return(result);
}
```

Listing 5.36. Comparing two numbers using nested conditional operators.

```
comp_int(a,b)
int a,b;
{
     int result;
     result = (a==b) ? 0 : (a < b)?-1:+1 ;
     return(result);
}
```

You may also perform a function and return its value as the result of a conditional operator. Listing 5.37 is a `minmax()` function that is passed two values to compare, along with a compare code. If the code is `0`, the `min()` value is returned, otherwise the `max()` value is returned.

Listing 5.37. `minmax()`.

```
minmax(a,b,code)
int a,b,mode;
{
     return( (code == 0) ? min(a,b) : max(a,b) );
}
```

The Dreaded *goto*

C supports a `goto` statement. It is about as popular as boiled cabbage. The C `goto` is limited to going to a label inside a function. You may not `goto` anywhere outside the current function. The label is a C indentifier followed by a colon. Listing 5.38 illustrates a `goto`.

Listing 5.38. Using `goto`.

```
init_array(str,len)
char *str;
int len;
{
     int idx;
```

continues

Listing 5.38. continued

```
     idx = 0;
loop:
     str[idx] = 0;
     ++idx;
     if(idx < len)
          goto loop;
}
```

Of course, the above logic would be much better handled in a `while()` loop, and it is true that most problems that seem to require a `goto` to solve them can usually be better solved by organizing a proper set of conditions for loop control.

One possibly valid use of `goto` is in debugging logic. Consider Listing 5.39, which is a routine that takes multiple exits to get back to the caller. It evaluates a passed character and returns `1` for a digit, `2` for an uppercase character, `3` for a lowercase character, and `0` for all other character types.

Listing 5.39. Multiple exits.

```
what_is_it(ch)
int ch;
{
     if((ch <= '9') && (ch >= '0'))
          {
          return(1);
          }
     if((ch <= 'Z') && (ch >= 'A'))
          {
          return(2);
          }
     if((ch <= 'z') && (ch >= 'a'))
          {
          return(3);
          }
     return(0);
}
```

A common technique in debugging is to display the entry and exit to each function. In the above listing, the function has so many exits that a lot of extra coding would be needed for each condition. Instead, it might make sense to restructure the function as shown in Listing 5.40.

Listing 5.40. Capturing multiple exits.

```
what_is_it(ch)
int ch;
{
     int rc;

     printf("Entering what_is_it()\n");

     if((ch <= '9') && (ch >= '0'))
          {
          rc = 1;
          goto exit;
          }
     if((ch <= 'Z') && (ch >= 'A'))
          {
          rc = 2;
          goto exit;
          }
     if((ch <= 'z') && (ch >= 'a'))
          {
          rc = 3;;
          goto exit;
          }
     rc = 0;

exit:
     printf("Exiting what_is_it()\n");
     return(rc);
}
```

Notes on COBOL *SECTIONS* and *PERFORM THROUGH*

C does not support anything that resembles COBOL's `PERFORM` of a `SECTION` or `PERFORM THROUGH` logic. Since `goto` is limited in scope to the current function, there isn't even a good way to emulate COBOL's technique of allowing you to fall through paragraph after paragraph of code until an exit paragraph or new section is encountered. If you are accustomed to using that type of logic, you will have to start adjusting your thinking.

Summary

Aside from the absence of `PERFORM THROUGH` and `PERFORM` a `SECTION`, C control structures are very similar to COBOL. The conditional operator has an unusual syntax (`( ? : )`) but it is really just a fancy `if-else`.

The C `switch-case` has some analogs in COBOL, but it is more powerful than `GO TO DEPENDING`, and heavily used in C.

So far I have not covered user input, which is the subject of Chapter 6, "C Pointers, Input, and Output." That chapter starts with a review of pointers and offers some new information on pointers as they are needed for input. You will find C input functions much more flexible than COBOL's `ACCEPT` verb.

6

C Pointers, Input, and Output

How do you get data from the keyboard into your program? C has a good collection of input routines, but before you get into them, you need to learn a little bit more about pointers.

This chapter covers:

- Pointers to other data types
- Single character input
- Accepting user string input
- Formatted input
- Combining input and output

Pointers to Other Data Types

A pointer is the address of a variable. When a variable is passed in C, it is passed in one of two ways: either as an address (a pointer to the variable), called *pass by reference*; or as a copy of the variable, called *pass by value.*

C has the following default actions for passing values:

- If the variable is an array, it is passed by reference, and the address of the first element in the array is passed.
- If the variable is not an array, it is passed by value; a copy of the variable is made and passed.
- When a single character is passed, it is converted to an integer and passed as an `int`.

C also provides an address-of operator (`&`) that can be used to force the compiler to pass the address of a variable, even when the usual default action of the compiler would be to pass a copy of the value.

Listing 6.1 summarizes the syntax and what is happening in each case.

Listing 6.1. Passing by reference and by value.

```
#include <stdio.h>

int an_int = 5;
char a_str[]= "Hello world";

main()
{
     function1(a_str);     /* Passes the address of a_str */
     function2(an_int);    /* Passes a copy of an_int */
     function3(a_str[1]);  /* Copies a_str[1] ( 'e' ), converts */
                           /* it to an integer and passes it */
     function4(&a_str[3]); /* Calculates the address of a_str[3] */
                           /* and passes the address */
}
function1(str)
char *str;            /* passed value str is the address of a char */
{
}
function2(num)
int num;              /* passed value num is an integer */
```

```
{
}
function3(ch)
int ch;             /* passed value ch is an integer */
{
}
function4(addr)
char *addr;         /* passed value addr is the address of a char */
{
}
```

There is one function missing in Listing 6.1 that I have not mentioned before:

```
function5(&an_int); /* Passes the address of an_int */
```

```
function5(val)
int *val;        /* passed value val is the address of an integer */
{
}
```

It is possible to pass the address of any variable by preceding it with the ampersand (&). In the called function, the data type is specified as usual, but an asterisk is placed before the variable name to indicate that what was passed was an address.

Within the function, it is possible to access both the address of the variable and the variable itself. Accessing a variable through its address is necessary when you need to modify the variable itself, not just to pass a copy of the variable.

Listings 6.2 and 6.3 compare two ways of doubling a number. In Listing 6.2, a copy of an integer is passed to the function `double_it`. The copy of the variable is doubled and the value returned. The result is assigned to the original variable (the value returned by the `double_it` function).

Listing 6.2. Passing by value.

```
#include <stdio.h>

main()
{
     a_value;

     a_value = 22;
     a_value = double_it(a_value);
}
```

continues

Listing 6.2. continued

```
double_it(val)
int val;
{
     val *= 2;
     return(val);
}
```

In Listing 6.3, the address of an integer is passed to the function `double_it()`. The `double_it()` function acts directly on the variable by accessing it through the passed address. There is no need to return a value, because the variable is modified directly by `double_it()`. Note that the `*val` in the data declaration of the function means *passed address of* and the `*val` in the body of the function means the *value at* `val`.

Listing 6.3. Passing by value.

```
#include <stdio.h>

main()
{
     a_value;

     a_value = 22;
     double_it(&a_value);
}

double_it(val)
int *val;
{
     *val *= 2;     /* value at val is doubled */
}
```

Passing a value by reference is commonly used when a function must produce more than one value as part of its main action. Listing 6.4 is a routine that supposedly returns the current row and column of the cursor on the screen. A function that returns a single value could not do this. Listing 6.4 calls two functions: one to get the row and one to get the column (these functions are not included in the listing; just assume that each function returns an integer value representing the row and column respectively).

Listing 6.4. `get_row_and_col()`.

```
#include <stdio.h>

main()
{
     int row;
     int col;

     get_row_and_col(&row,&col);

     printf("Cursor was at row %d and column %d\n",row,col);
}

get_row_and_col(row, col)
int *row, *col;
{
     *row = get_row();
     *col = get_col();
}
```

Next, take at look a some simple C routines to get user input. Then consider some more complicated routines that use pointers to data to fill in variables from keyboard input.

Single Character Input

The simplest form of input is a single character. The C `getchar()` function returns a single key from the keyboard. The key is returned as an integer. Listing 6.5 is a shell for a menu routine that displays two prompts and an exit option, and accepts a single user keystroke followed by a carriage return.

Listing 6.5. simpmenu.c—using `getchar()`.

```
#include <stdio.h>

char pick1[]="1. First Selection";
char pick2[]="2. Second Selection";
char pick_exit[]="0. Exit Menu";
```

continues

Listing 6.5. continued

```
main()
{
    int ch;
    char *picked;

    while(1)
     {
     cls();         /*Clear screen */
     printf("\n\n\n");
     printf("\tPlease select:\n\n");
     printf("\t\t%s\n",pick1);
     printf("\t\t%s\n",pick2);
     printf("\n");
     printf("\t\t%s\n",pick_exit);
     printf("\n\n\n\n\n\n\n\n\n\n\n");
     printf("Enter a digit and press ENTER.\n");
     ch = getchar();
     getchar();          /* Extra getchar() picks up the \n */
     switch(ch)
          {
          case '1':
               picked = pick1;
               break;
          case '2':
               picked = pick2;
               break;
          case '0':
               picked = pick_exit;
               break;
          default:
               picked = "Not Valid";
               break;
          }
     printf("Your selection was <%s>\n",picked);
     printf("Please press enter\n");
     getchar();
     if(ch == '0')
          break;
     }
}

/*----
Clear screen by printing 25 new lines
------*/
cls()
{
```

```
     int idx;

     for(idx = 0; idx < 25; ++idx)
          printf("\n");
}
```

At first glance, it appears that the routine has an extra `getchar()` in it until you realize that `getchar()` returns every keystroke. The Enter keystroke is returned by `getchar` as a newline character. The extra `getchar()`, commented in the logic, clears away the newline character. The newline character isn't needed for any testing; so when it is returned by `getchar()`, it is not assigned to any variable.

This program also includes a lot of `"\n"` characters for formatting, and prints `"\n"` 25 times to clear the screen in the `cls()` function.

Accepting User String Input

The C function `gets()` is designed to accept user keyboard input. It is passed a buffer (a string array) into which the keyboard data is placed. The `gets()` function accepts all input until the user presses Enter. The value returned by the Enter key (usually a newline) is stripped from the buffer, and a trailing NUL is appended to the string. The buffer is expected to be large enough to hold all of the user input. Listing 6.6 illustrates `gets()` in action.

Listing 6.6. myecho.c—using `gets()`.

```
#include <stdio.h>

char work_area[512];

main()
{
     printf("Enter something that you want echoed.\n")
     printf("(no more than 510 characters)\n");
     gets(work_area);
     printf("You entered %s\n",work_area);
}
```

The `gets()` function is similar to `ACCEPT` in COBOL. It receives raw character data from the keyboard and drops it into memory at the address passed to it. The data in the `gets()` buffer is not formatted or converted to other data types. If you want to use the data in some other way, you process it with some other routine. Listing 6.7 collects keyboard input using `gets()` and then converts the input to an integer using the C library function `atoi()` (ASCII to integer). The `atoi()` function takes a string argument and returns an integer value representing the ASCII numerics found in the string.

This is probably a good time for you to start getting familiar with your library reference manual. This will be a separate manual or section of your main manual, usually called something like *Run Time Library Reference* or *C System Services*. It is a collection of all the available library functions, usually in alphabetical order, with the syntax and argument parameters for a call to the function. They frequently also include examples of using the function.

Appendix C, "The Standard C Library," contains generic manual entries for a large number of the standard C functions. They are provided for reference while studying this book. When using a function in a program, be sure to refer to the manual for that C compiler.

The summary or syntax portion of the manual describes any additional header files that need to be included for this function, as well as the argument types for the passed values. For now, take a look at the entry for `atoi()` in Appendix C. The entry indicates that you should include `<stdlib.h>` to use `atoi()`, and that the argument passed to `atoi()` is a pointer to a `char`. The function itself is also described as

```
int atoi(string)
```

indicating that it is a function that returns an integer value. You will learn about functions that return other than integer values in Chapter 8, "Scope, Storage, and Prototyping."

Listing 6.7 illustrates using `atoi()` with `gets()` to print factorials. The user enters an integer and its factorial is printed. The work variable that is used is a `long`, as factorials can get quite large. Note the use of combined operators and postdecrement in

```
lwork *= factorial--;
```

which causes `lwork` to be multiplied by `factorial`, and then decrements `factorial`.

Listing 6.7. factor.c—using `atoi()`.

```
#include <stdio.h>
#include <stdlib.h>
```

```
char work[10];
int factorial;
long lwork;

main()
{
     printf("Input a number to see its factorial.\n");
     printf("(no more than 3 digits)\n");
     gets(work);
     factorial = atoi(work);
     lwork = 1;
     while(factorial > 0)
          lwork *= factorial--;
     printf("%d factorial is %ld\n",factorial,lwork);
}
```

Formatted Input

C programmers have a love/hate relationship with `scanf()`, the C library routine for formatted input. It is awkward to use and clunky in some of the things that it does, but it also has some great features. The `scanf()` function is kind of a reverse `printf()` function. The `scanf()` function is passed a format string containing formatting characters that look very much like `printf()` formatting characters, plus a list of arguments that match in data type the formatting options in the format string.

The natural behavior of `scanf()` is to treat white space (spaces, tabs, and newlines) as the separators between fields. In Listing 6.8, if the user were to type `Hello world` and press Enter, the buffer would contain `Hello`, not `Hello world` as you might expect.

Listing 6.8. using `scanf()`.

```
#include <stdio.h>

char buffer[512];

main()
{
     printf("Please enter your message and press ENTER.\n");
     scanf("%s", buffer);
     printf("Your message was <%s>\n",buffer);
}
```

When `scanf()` encounters a formatting character such as `"%s"` (string format) in Listing 6.8, it looks for keyboard input. It starts by skipping all initial white space, and then begins saving characters until the next whitespace character is encountered. Because of this whitespace delimiter action, the `scanf()` function is awkward to use for string input. Most strings tend to have spaces in them (think of company names, street addresses, and so on). There are ways around this, which you will take a look at, but first consider `scanf()`'s general handling for input. Table 6.1 is a list of the common input format characters, the type of input expected, and the type of target variable.

Table 6.1. Common `scanf()` formatting characters.

Format	*Type of Input*	*Receiving Argument*
`"%d"`	Integer characters	Pointer to `int`
`"%ld"`	Integer characters	Pointer to `long`
`"%hd"`	Integer characters	Pointer to `short`
`"%o"`	Octal characters	Pointer to `int`
`"%lo"`	Octal characters	Pointer to `long`
`"%ho"`	Octal characters	Pointer to `short`
`"%x"`	Hexadecimal characters	Pointer to `int`
`"%lx"`	Hexadecimal characters	Pointer to `long`
`"%hx"`	Hexadecimal characters	Pointer to `short`
`"%u"`	Unsigned integer characters	Pointer to unsigned `int`
`"%lu"`	Unsigned integer characters	Pointer to unsigned `long`
`"%hu"`	Unsigned integer characters	Pointer to unsigned `short`
`"%U"`	Unsigned integer characters	Pointer to unsigned `long`
`"%f"`	Sign, digits, and decimal point	Pointer to `float`
`"%lf"`	Sign, digits, and decimal point	Pointer to `double`

Format	*Type of Input*	*Receiving Argument*
"%c"	A single character including any whitespace character	Pointer to char
"%s"	String of characters	Pointer to an array of characters large enough to hold the input field plus a terminating NUL.
"%n"	No input	Pointer to int. This int will receive the character count of the total number of characters processed to this point, since the call to scanf().

You will recognize most of these formatting characters from printf. There are others that allow input of numbers in scientific notation, and you should consult your library reference manual for details.

The arguments to scanf() are always pointers. Since you are asking scanf() to convert the input stream and store the result in a variable, it does scanf() no good to receive copies of the variables; it must have a pointer to know where the variable is.

One difference between scanf() and printf() formatting characters is scanf()'s use of "%lf" for a double. The call to the printf() function passes a copy of a float or double argument if there is one in the argument list. C promotes all floats to doubles before they are passed, so printf() always receives doubles. One formatting character is enough. The scanf() function, however, is always passed pointers as arguments. The value pointed to by a pointer cannot be promoted, so two separate format types are needed to indicate whether a pointer is pointing to a float ("%f") or a double ("%lf").

Some examples of scanf() in Listing 6.9 will illustrate the logic more clearly.

Listing 6.9. More examples of using scanf().

```
#include <stdio.h>

int an_int;
double a_double;
```

continues

Listing 6.9. continued

```
unsigned an_unsigned;
char a_string[22];

main()
{
     scanf("%d",&an_int);
     scanf("%lf",&a_double);
     scanf("%u",&an_unsigned);
     scanf("%s",a_string);
}
```

In Listing 6.9, `a_string` is automatically converted to a pointer by the compiler before being passed, so there is no need for the `&` operator.

A formatting string can be preceded by a width, which specifies the maximum number of characters that will be pulled for the conversion. The width may not be reached if a space appears in the input stream. In Listing 6.10, if the input stream contained `123456`, `x` becomes `123` and `y` would be `456`. If the input stream contained `12 3456`, the intervening space causes `x` to be set to `12`, and `y` becomes `345`, the first three characters of the second field.

Listing 6.10. Using width processing with `scanf()`.

```
#include <stdio.h>

main()
{
     int x,y;

     scanf("%3d %3d",&x,&y);
}
```

It is possible to use `scanf()` to accept and process an exact number of characters and terminate on an Enter key, but it takes some work. Let's look at various options.

The first logical choice is to try to process a 20-byte string, as shown in Listing 6.11.

Listing 6.11. `scanf()`—a 20-byte string.

```
#include <stdio.h>

char buff[21];

main()
{
      scanf("%20s",buff);
      printf("%s\n",buff);
}
```

If you try Listing 6.11 and enter a string containing spaces, you will find that only the characters up to the first space are saved in `buff`.

The `"%c"` format can be used to pull characters regardless of whether they are spaces or not. If you use a `"%c"`, it does not store the closing NUL needed for a string, so it is necessary to add the NUL. Listing 6.12 will take the next 20 characters, whatever they are, and place them in `buff`.

Listing 6.12. Using `scanf()` to accept a count of characters.

```
#include <stdio.h>

char buff[21];

main()
{
      scanf("%20c",buf);
      buff[20] = 0;
      printf("%s",buff);
}
```

Run Listing 6.12 and enter 20 or more characters followed by Enter. Only the first 20 characters are saved and printed. Run it again and enter five or six characters followed by Enter. Nothing happens yet. Enter another 20 or so characters and press Enter. Now the first 20 characters are saved and printed, including the newline in the middle of the data entry.

This still isn't what you're after. You need to let the user type whatever he or she wants and press Enter, and have the Enter signal the end of the input. You need the field to be able to receive anything (including spaces) except the actual newline generated when the user presses Enter.

There is one more format character available that I haven't yet mentioned. It is called the set character. This isn't really a character, but a list of characters that may be accepted in the input field. It replaces the s in a "%s" format string, and is enclosed in brackets ([ ]).

When a set is used, scanf() does add a NUL to the output buffer. The following scans a string containing only *a* and *c* and stops at the first occurrence of any other character.

```
scanf("%[ac]",buff);
```

The set may be expressed as a range by inserting a hyphen (-) between letters. The following example would accept all upper- and lowercase letters stopping at the first occurrence of any other character.

```
scanf("%[A-Za-z]",buff);
```

Of course, what you want is all characters except newline. This makes a long set to include in brackets—but scanf() also allows you to invert the set by including a caret (^) as the first character in the set. The following example will accept any characters except the upper- and lowercase alphabet characters.

```
scanf("%[^A-Za-z]",buff);
```

So what you want will logically be

```
scanf("%[^\n]",buff);
```

or every character except a newline. This can be improved by adding a maximum length:

```
scanf("%20[^\n]",buff);
```

Listing 6.13 can be used to test this. You should always get 20 or less characters, including spaces and input should terminate when the user presses Enter.

Listing 6.13. The final solution.

```
#include <stdio.h>

char buff[21];

main()
{
     printf("Enter anything you want\n");
     scanf("%20[^\n]",buff);
     printf("You entered <%s>\n",buff);
}
```

One more thing worth noting: `scanf()` puts nothing in the receiving argument if the first part of the input stream fails to convert. If the input were totally non-numeric in the following example, `x` would continue to have the value `1`. It is important when using `scanf()` to initialize all of the receiving variables.

```
x = 1;
scanf("%d",&x);
```

Combining Input and Output

Listing 6.14 is a simple program to accept input for a phone book. The `memset()` function initializes an address in memory with a value for the specified length. It is setting each memory area to zero for the length specified.

Listing 6.14. phone.c.

```
#include <stdio.h>

char name[31];
char address1[31],address2[31],address3[31];
char phone[16];

char prompt1[]="Name:";
char prompt2[]="Address 1:";
char prompt3[]="Address 2:";
char prompt4[]="Address 3:";
char prompt5[]="Phone:";

main()
{
     cls();
     get_name();
     get_address1();
     get_address2();
     get_address3();
     get_phone();

     printf("%s %s\n",prompt1,name);
     printf("%s %s\n",prompt2,address1);
     printf("%s %s\n",prompt3,address2);
     printf("%s %s\n",prompt4,address3);
     printf("%s %s\n",prompt5,phone);
```

continues

Listing 6.14. continued

```
}

get_name()
{
     printf("Enter %s\n",prompt1);
     memset(name,0,30);
     scanf("%30[^\n]",name);
     scanf("%*[^\n]");
     scanf("%*1[\n]);
}

get_address1()
{
     printf("Enter %s\n",prompt2);
     memset(address1,0,30);
     scanf("%30[^\n]",address1);
     scanf("%*[^\n]");
     scanf("%*1[\n]);
}

get_address2()
{
     printf("Enter %s\n",prompt3);
     memset(address2,0,30);
     scanf("%30[^\n]",address2);
     scanf("%*[^\n]");
     scanf("%*1[\n]);
}

get_address3()
{
     printf("Enter %s\n",prompt4);
     memset(address3,0,30);
     scanf("%30[^\n]",address3);
     scanf("%*[^\n]");
     scanf("%*1[\n]);
}

get_phone()
{
     printf("Enter %s\n",prompt5);
     memset(phone,0,15);
     scanf("%15[^\n]",phone);
     scanf("%*[^\n]");
     scanf("%*1[\n]);
}
```

```
cls()
{
     int idx;

     for(idx = 0; idx < 25; ++idx)
          printf("\n");
}
```

The other thing of interest in the listing is the use of

```
scanf("%*[^\n]");
scanf("%*1[\n]");
```

The `scanf()` function operates on the basis that all useful characters are scanned into the destination argument. If a character is not useful, scanning stops, and the character is saved and offered to the next `scanf()` or input function. There are two possibilities for unused characters in these routines. First, the user may enter more characters than the limit. If so, all characters over the limit are saved for the next `scanf()`. The

```
scanf("%*[^\n]");
```

picks up any extra characters the user types and disposes of them. The asterisk indicates that a field is read but not stored.

Second, because you use the `\n` as the point to stop scanning, the `\n` is left in the input stream for the next `scanf()`. You must clear the `\n` so that it does not interfere with the next `scanf()`. The line

```
scanf("%*1[\n]");
```

scans in one character that must be a newline, but the asterisk (*) indicates that the scanned data will not be saved anywhere.

Notice in Listing 6.14 (phone.c) the repetitive nature of the coding. For each of the fields, the last three steps are identical: clear the destination, `scanf()` in enough characters to satisfy the field, `scanf()` and dispose of any extra characters that were entered, and then `scanf()` in the closing `"\n"` character to clear it away.

You would think it would be possible to create a routine that is passed a receiver buffer and a length, and takes care of all these tasks. It is possible, but it takes some thought and a new library function. For this function to work, you need to be able to build a format string on the fly, because the length of the field will vary based on the passed length.

This should be possible because the format string is just another C NUL-terminated string. So far you have considered format strings as constants: You know the type and length, and you just code the format string directly as `"%20[^\n]"`.

The `printf()` function has a cousin function for formatting fields as if they were going to the screen, but in actual fact the formatted output is stored in another string. This function is called `sprintf()`, and it has the syntax

```
sprintf(dest,formatstr[[,arg]. . .]);
```

This is the same syntax as the `printf()` function, but an initial argument is inserted at the front of the list indicating the address in memory to place the data. Listing 6.15 stores `a one and a two` in `buffer`.

Listing 6.15. Using `sprintf()`.

```
#include <stdio.h>

char buffer[512];

main()
{
     sprintf(buffer,"%s %s","a one and","a two");
}
```

The `sprintf()` function is obviously the tool that you need to build the format string on the fly. Now let's work out how to do it. The format string will be

```
"%len[^\n]"
```

To `printf()` a percent sign, you need a double percent sign, and to insert an integer variable into a string you need `"%d"`, so the `sprintf()` call looks like this:

```
sprintf(format,"%%%d[^\n]",len);
```

The first two percent signs resolve into a single percent, and the `%d` resolves to the value of `len` (say, 20). The result in `format` would be

```
"%20[^\n]"
```

and that is exactly the type of format string that is needed for `scanf()`. Listing 6.16 is `getstr()`, a generic entry routine that is passed a receiving string and a length, and performs the functions described in Listing 6.14.

Listing 6.16. `getstr()`—a general-purpose entry routine.

```
/*----
Uses scanf() to get len characters into receiver and clears excess
```

```
characters and \n from the input stream.
------*/
getstr(receiver, len)
char *receiver;
int len;
{
     char format[20];

     sprintf(format,"%%%d[^\n]",len);        /* build format string */
     memset(receiver,0,len);                 /* clear receiver */
     scanf(format,receiver);                 /* get the data */
     scanf("%*[^\n]");                       /* clear excess input */
     scanf("%*1[\n]");                       /* clear final newline */
}
```

Listing 6.17 is a reprise of Listing 6.14, using `getstr()` for the input.

Listing 6.17. phone.c.

```
#include <stdio.h>

char name[31];
char address1[31],address2[31],address3[31];
char phone[16];

char prompt1[]="Name:";
char prompt2[]="Address 1:";
char prompt3[]="Address 2:";
char prompt4[]="Address 3:";
char prompt5[]="Phone:";

main()
{
     cls();
     get_name();
     get_address1();
     get_address2();
     get_address3();
     get_phone();

     printf("%s %s\n",prompt1,name);
     printf("%s %s\n",prompt2,address1);
     printf("%s %s\n",prompt3,address2);
     printf("%s %s\n",prompt4,address3);
     printf("%s %s\n",prompt5,phone);
```

continues

Listing 6.17. continued

```
}

get_name()
{
     printf("Enter %s\n",prompt1);
     getstr(name,30);
}

get_address1()
{
     printf("Enter %s\n",prompt2);
     getstr(address1,30);
}

get_address2()
{
     printf("Enter %s\n",prompt3);
     getstr(address2,30);
}

get_address3()
{
     printf("Enter %s\n",prompt4);
     getstr(address3,30);
}

get_phone()
{
     printf("Enter %s\n",prompt5);
     getstr(phone,15);
}

cls()
{
     int idx;

     for(idx = 0; idx < 25; ++idx)
          printf("\n");
}

/*----
Uses scanf() to get len characters into receiver and clears excess
characters and \n from the input stream.
------*/
getstr(receiver,len)
char *receiver;
```

```
int len;
{
     char format[20];

     sprintf(format,"%%%d[^\n]",len);          /* build format string */
     memset(receiver,0,len);                   /* clear receiver */
     scanf(format,receiver);                   /* get the data */
     scanf("%*[^\n]");                         /* clear excess input */
     scanf("%*1[\n]");                         /* clear final newline */
}
```

The getstr() function is useful enough that you might want to add it to your library for linking into other programs. To do this, create a source code file named getstr.c, and compile it and add it to your library after reviewing the steps in Appendix A, "Program Development."

The scanf() is certainly more useful than ACCEPT, but it has several limitations. Most professional C development is done with a commercial library or in-house set of routines that allow a much more flexible approach to screen I/O, usually allow something like block mode processing, and include the ability to format, display, accept, edit, and possibly validate groups of fields on a screen. Some of these are discussed in Appendix E, "Screen Handling and Indexed Files," and though this book walks you through the basics using scanf(), you'll soon find its limitations frustrating. Then you'll know it's time to investigate screen handlers.

Summary

This chapter includes a large part of what you need to know for C programming. You may want to review Listing 6.17; it incorporates almost everything covered in this chapter.

Something may be niggling at the back of your skull. It seems that phone.c is still full of repetitive actions. Each field is prompted for and then input separately. You'd think there should be some way to make this less repetitive. The next chapter covers arrays, and you will find that it is possible to use arrays to reduce phone.c to a much more compact piece of code.

7

Arrays in C

Aside from `char` arrays to hold strings, I haven't yet covered arrays in C. The use of an array for strings is a bit of a special case. Normally, C arrays are used very much like COBOL arrays.

This chapter covers the following topics:

- Arrays in C
- Multidimensional arrays
- Arrays of strings
- Arrays of pointers
- Phone book using arrays of pointers
- Pointers in memory
- Passing values to `main()`

Arrays in C

Any C data type can be stored singly or in an array. You have already experienced arrays of `char` data types, which are called *strings.* The string is a special type of array. C has provided special initialization capabilities for it, and a vast number of standard library routines are set up to copy, compare, print, convert, format, and otherwise fool around with strings. Once you start creating arrays of other data types, you step back into a field that is more like COBOL. An array declaration should already be familiar to you from your work with strings:

```
char a_string[11];              /* An array of 11 chars */
int value[15];                  /* An array of 15 integers */
double month_total[12];         /* An array of 12 doubles */
```

Array initialization is enclosed in braces and the individual elements are separated by commas. The example below creates and initializes five doubles.

```
double sum[5] = {12.7, 13.6, 12.0, 22.5, 11.17};
```

This example sets up the days in the months used for date processing.

```
int days_in_month[12] = {31,28,31,30,31,30,31,31,30,31,30,31};
```

Listing 7.1 is a routine to return the number of days in a passed month and year. The routine first adjusts the month from 1–12 to 0–11 so that it can be used as an index into the array. If the month is not 1 (January), the routine returns the value from the array. Otherwise it does some work to establish whether the year is a leap year: it uses the remainder operator to test if the year is evenly divisible by 4 but not evenly divisible by 100, in which case it is a leap year.

Listing 7.1. Days of the month routine.

```
/*-----------------------------------------------------------
This routine is passed a month and a year. It returns the days
in the month, adjusted for leap years. Year is passed as a full
year, and month is passed as 1-12.
-----------------------------------------------------------*/

int month_days[] = {31,28,31,30,31,30,31,31,30,31,30,31};

days_in_month(year, month)
int month, year;
{
     --month;
     if(month != 1)
```

```
            return(month_days[month]);
        else
        if( ( (year % 4) == 0) && ( (year % 100) != 0) ) )
            return(29);
        else
            return(month_days[month]);
}
```

Listing 7.2 is an example of using the `days_in_month()` routine to convert a Gregorian date (year, month, day) to a Julian date (yyddd). A Julian date is a five-digit number representing the year as the first two digits, and the day as the number of days from the beginning of the year. Since dates of this nature could be in the neighborhood of, for example, 93272, they are too large for a `short` integer. An integer could be used on a machine that used a four-byte integer as a default, but you would want a routine like this to be as portable as possible. The best way is to force the routine to return a `long` integer. So far, all the routines you have seen return either integers or nothing. How do you force a routine to return a value other than an integer? Listing 7.2 defines the type returned by the `Gregorian_to_Julian()` function by declaring it a `long` function, or a function returning a `long`.

Listing 7.2. Converting Gregorian to Julian dates.

```
long Gregorian_to_Julian(year, month, day)
int year, month, day;
{
     long result;
     int work;

     result = year % 100;
     result *= 1000;

     for(work = 1; work < month ; ++work)
          result += days_in_month(year, work);

     result += day;

     return(result);
}
```

Listing 7.2 is passed three integers: the year, the month, and the day. The year is immediately converted to the last two digits by using a remainder operator to lop off the century. The result is multiplied by 1000 to left-shift the value by three places.

The work index steps though all months up to but not including the passed month, and uses the `days_in_month()` function to add the days for each of those months to the result. Finally the days in the current month are added, and the result is returned.

Table 7.1 shows this one step at a time, assuming passed values of 1993, 4, 14 (April 14, 1993).

Table 7.1. Steps of `Gregorian_to_Julian()`.

Step	*Value of Result*	*Comments*
`result = year %100`	93	
`result *= 1000;`	93000	
`result += days_in_month(year, work)`	93031	`work = 1`
`result += days_in_month(year, work)`	93059	`work = 2`
`result += days_in_month(year, work)`	93090	`work = 3`
`result += day`	93104	

Multidimensional Arrays

C allows multidimensional arrays. Listing 7.3 is a two-dimensional array containing hourly pay rates based on an employees staff rating, and whether the work was done at regular rates, overtime rates, or holiday rates.

The array allows for four classes of employees, and the three different hourly rates.

Listing 7.3. Two-dimensional array.

```
double hourly_pay[4][3]=
{
     {5.00,7.50,10.00},
     {6.00,9.00,12.00},
     {7.00,10.50,14.00},
     {8.00,12.00,16.00}
};
```

Take particular note of the syntax of the initialization. The first array subscript declares the number of rows; the second declares the number of elements in each row. The entire initialization is enclosed in braces ({}); within those braces, the initialization for each row appears as a set of braces surrounding the three values for each row. Each row is terminated with a comma except for the last. This initialization is consistent for non-string arrays. Each level of the array is enclosed in its own set of braces. Listing 7.4 is an example of initializing a three-dimensional array of hourly pay rates which uses two tables, one for part-time employees, and one for full-time employees.

Listing 7.4. Initializing a three-dimensional array.

```
double hourly_pay[2][4][3]=
     {     {
/* Part Time     Regular   Overtime  Holiday */
                {5.00,     7.50,     10.00},
                {6.00,     9.00,     12.00},
                {7.00,     10.50,    14.00},
                {8.00,     12.00,    16.00}
           },
           {
/* Full Time */
                {6.00,     9.00,      12.00},
                {7.00,     10.50,     14.00},
                {8.00,     12.00,     16.00},
                {9.00,     13.50,     18.00}
           }
     };
```

Listing 7.5 uses the three-dimensional array to return a pay amount. The `get_pay()` function is called passing a type flag of `'P'`art time or `'F'`ull time, an employee class of `0-3`, a work time flag of `'R'`egular, `'O'`vertime, or `'H'`oliday, and the number of hours. The routine calculates the amount of pay and returns the amount as a double. The `get_pay()` function is explicitly declared as a function returning a double. Remember that single characters passed to a function are promoted to integers, so all the values passed to `get_pay()` are received as integers.

Listing 7.5. get_pay().

```
double hourly_pay[2][4][3]=
     {     {
/* Part Time   Regular   Overtime  Holiday */
               {5.00,    7.50,    10.00},
               {6.00,    9.00,     12.00},
               {7.00,    10.50,    14.00},
               {8.00,    12.00,    16.00}
          },
          {
/* Full Time */
               {6.00,    9.00,     12.00},
               {7.00,    10.50,    14.00},
               {8.00,    12.00,    16.00},
               {9.00,    13.50,    18.00}
          }
     };

double get_pay(type, class, rate, hours)
int type, class, rate, hours;
{

     double pay;

/* convert type to table 0 or 1 */
     if(type == 'P')
          type = 0;
     else
     if(type == 'F')
          type = 1;
     else
          return(0.00);
     if((class < 0) ¦¦ (class > 3) )
          return(0.00);

/* convert rate to entries 0 through 3 */
     switch(rate)
          {
          case 'R':
               rate = 0;
               break;
          case 'O':
               rate = 1;
               break;
          case 'H':
               rate = 2;
```

```
            break;
        default:
            return(0.00);
        }
    pay = hourly_pay[type][class][rate] * hours;
    return(pay);
}
```

The get_pay() function uses the fact that all integers passed to the function are copies of the originals, and modifies the values in them. This can be done safely with any variable that is passed by value, as modifying the local value (inside get_pay()) does not change the value in the calling function.

The limit on multidimensional arrays is determined by the compiler. There is theoretically no limit to the number of subscripts that can be used, but most compilers have some limit on the largest possible size that a data item may have. Microsoft C/C++ 7.0 is 64K, but that can be overridden with a switch allowing arrays of 4 gigabytes, or in less technical terms, an array so big that you would only be able to save it on an extremely expensive disk drive.

The 64K (or 4G) limit is the size of the array in bytes, not the number of elements in the array. An array of short integers would use two bytes for each element and so would allow half the number of elements as an array of char types.

Arrays of Strings

Obviously, it is possible to create an array of strings that is actually a two-dimensional array of characters. Listing 7.6 shows an array of four strings.

Listing 7.6. An array of strings.

```
char the_quote[4][50] = {
    {"Now is the time"},
    {"for every good man to"},
    {"come to the aid"},
    {"of the party."}
    };
```

Listing 7.7 shows an alternative method of initializing, based on C's special treatment of strings. Listing 7.6 is acceptable to some compilers, but the syntax shown in Listing 7.7 is preferred.

Listing 7.7. An array of strings.

```
char the_quote[4][50] = {
     "Now is the time",
     "for every good man to",
     "come to the aid",
     "of the party."
     };
```

I have seen one or two older C compilers have trouble with the first form of initialization (with the inside braces) so it is a good idea to get in the habit of using the initialization style in Listing 7.7 on a regular basis.

Listing 7.8 is an example of letting the compiler determine the size of the first subscript by leaving it blank. The second subscript informs the compiler that it will be reserving space for a number of 50-character data elements. The compiler uses the initialization (and braces) to calculate that this will be a 4X50 array.

Listing 7.8. Letting the compiler size the array.

```
char the_quote[][50] = {
     "Now is the time",
     "for every good man to",
     "come to the aid",
     "of the party."
     };
```

Listing 7.9 demonstrates printing an array of strings.

Listing 7.9. Printing an array of strings.

```
#include <stdio.h>

char the_quote[][50] = {
     "Now is the time",
     "for every good man to",
```

```
     "come to the aid",
     "of the party."
     };


main()
{
     text_out(the_quote);
}

text_out(text)
char text[4][50];
{
     int index;

     for(index = 0; index < 4; ++index)
          {
          printf("%s\n", text[index]);
          }

}
```

The `text_out()` function in Listing 7.9 has some flaws that make it unsuitable as a general array-printing routine. The first is that the number of strings in the array has to be known. It would be far better if `text_out()` could be passed an array of any length containing 50-byte strings and it would be able to know what to do with it. For this, borrow a leaf from `printf()` and other string handling routines that use a NUL terminator to stop processing strings. The `text_out()` function will process an array of strings until it encounters an empty string.

Listing 7.10 uses this method to control string printing, and `the_quote` array is initialized with one extra empty string to signal the end of processing.

Listing 7.10. Processing until an empty string is encountered.

```
#include <stdio.h>

char the_quote[][50] = {
     "Now is the time",
     "for every good man to",
     "come to the aid",
     "of the party.",
```

continues

Listing 7.10. continued

```
     ""            /* <-- printing stops here */
     };


main()
{
     text_out(the_quote);
}

text_out(text)
char text[][50];
{
     int index;

     for(index = 0; text[index][0] != 0; ++index)
          {
          printf("%s\n", text[index]);
          }

}
```

The difference in `text_out()` is the declaration of the passed text variable as `text[][50]` which identifies text as an array of unknown length containing elements of 50-byte strings. The `for()` logic tests to see if the first character of the string to be output is a NUL, and stops processing when a NUL is encountered.

Arrays of Pointers

The version of `text_out()` in Listing 7.10 is an improvement, but it still has the drawback that the array must contain 50-byte strings. The other disadvantage is that `the_quote` occupies 250 bytes of storage (five elements of 50 bytes each) even though the actual space required for the quote is quite small (69 bytes). Using pointers to strings instead of two-dimensional arrays of char can solve this problem.

You have already seen the use of a pointer to a string as an independent variable in functions such as `strrev` in Listing 7.11.

Listing 7.11. strrev()—the original.

```
strrev(string)
char *string;
{
     char character;
     char *end;

     end = string + strlen(string) - 1;

     while(string < end)
          {
          character = *end;
          *end = *string;
          *string = character;
     ++string;
     --end;
}
```

A pointer is itself a variable, and it is possible to create arrays of pointers.

```
char *char_ptr[10];        /* array of 10 pointers to chars */
int *numbers[5];           /* array of 5 pointers to ints */
```

Listing 7.12 is a version of `text_out()` that uses an array of pointers to strings.

Listing 7.12. Using an array of pointers.

```
#include <stdio.h>

char text_1[] = "Now is the time";
char text_2[] = "for every good man to";
char text_3[] = "come to the aid";
char text_4[] = "of the party.";
char text_5[] = "";

char *the_quote[] = {text_1, text_2, text_3, text_4, text_5};

main()
{
     text_out(the_quote);
}

text_out(text)
char *text[];
```

continues

Listing 7.12. continued

```
{
     int index;

     for(index = 0; text[index][0] != 0; ++index)
          {
          printf("%s\n", text[index]);
          }

}
```

Five strings are initialized to the values of the quote. An array of pointers to `char` is declared and initialized to point to each of the five values: `the_quote[0] = text_1`, `the_quote[1] = text_2`, and so on.

The `text_out()` function declares its passed data as an array of pointers to `chars`. Because a pointer can be treated as a array, the body of the `text_out()` function requires no modification.

The `text_out()` function now becomes a generic function that can be used to print an array of strings until an empty string is encountered.

So much for `text_out()`, but the initialization of `the_quote` seems cumbersome. The variables `text_1` through `text_5` are used only to initialize the pointer array `the_quote`. These are not again accessed.

C provides a mechanism for initializing pointers to strings. While processing pointers, the compiler checks to see if the pointer is initialized with a constant value. If a constant exists, the compiler creates storage for the constant, gives it no variable name, but initializes the pointer to point to the variable.

Listing 7.13 illustrates this effect. The compiler recognizes that `the_string_pointer` is a pointer, and sets aside data storage for `"world."` followed by a NUL. It then sets the address of `"world."` in `the_string_pointer`.

Listing 7.13. Initializing a pointer.

```
#include <stdio.h>

char the_string[] = "Hello";

char *the_string_pointer = "world.";
```

```
main()
{
     printf("%s %s\n", the_string, the_string_pointer);
}
```

If the_string_pointer is assigned a new value, the original string pointed to is lost. In Listing 7.14, the message is printed, and then the_string_pointer is reassigned to point to "Hello". The second printing of the message now displays

```
Hello Hello
```

At this point, the area of memory containing "world." is lost. There is no variable name associated with it, and there is no value that can be assigned to the_string_pointer that will get it to point back to "world.". This style of initialization can be used for constant values that will always be pointed to by the pointer in question.

Listing 7.14. Losing what's pointed to.

```
#include <stdio.h>

char the_string[] = "Hello";

char *the_string_pointer = "world.";

main()
{
     printf("%s %s\n", the_string, the_string_pointer);
     the_string_pointer = the_string;
     printf("%s %s\n", the_string, the_string_pointer);
}
```

Arrays of pointers may be initialized in the same way. Listing 7.15 is the final version of the program to initialize an array of strings and call text_out.

Listing 7.15. Initializing arrays of pointers.

```
#include <stdio.h>

char *the_quote[] = {
     "Now is the time",
     "for every good man to",
```

continues

Listing 7.15. continued

```
     "come to the aid",
     "of the party.",
     ""
     };


main()
{
     text_out(the_quote);
}

text_out(text)
char *text[];
{
     int index;

     for(index = 0; text[index][0] != 0; ++index)
          {
          printf("%s\n", text[index]);
          }

}
```

Phone Book Using Arrays of Pointers

By now you may have guessed that what I am leading up to is a repeat of the phone.c program from the Chapter 6, "C Pointers, Input, and Output," using arrays to eliminate the repetitive nature of the code. First review the version of phone.c in Chapter 6, and then take a look at Listing 7.16.

Listing 7.16. phone.c—using arrays of pointers.

```
#include <stdio.h>

char *prompt[]={
     "Name:",
     "Address 1:",
```

```
     "Address 2:",
     "Address 3:",
     "Phone:",
     ""
     };

char name[31];
char address_1[31],address_2[31],address_3[31];
char phone[16];

char *value[]={name, address_1, address_2, address_3, phone};

int length[]={30,30,30,30,15};

main()
{
     cls();
     get_entries(prompt, value, length);
     print_entries(prompt, value);
}


/*-----------------------------------------
Input values until the prompt string is empty
-----------------------------------------*/
get_entries(string, receiver, width)
char *string[], *receiver[];
int width[];
{
     int index;

     for(index = 0; string[index][0] != 0; ++index)
          {
          printf("%s ?\n", string[index]);
          getstr(receiver[index],width[index]);
          }
}


/*-----------------------------------------------
Print values until the input prompt string is empty
-----------------------------------------------*/
print_entries(string, receiver)
char *string[], *receiver[];
{
     int index;

     for(index = 0; string[index][0] != 0; ++index)
```

continues

Listing 7.15. continued

```
          {
          printf("%s %s\n", string[index],receiver[index]);
          }
}

cls()
{
     int index;

     for(index = 0; index < 25; ++index)
          printf("\n");
}

/*------------------------------------------------------
Uses scanf() to get length characters into receiver and
clears excess characters and \n from the input stream.
------------------------------------------------------*/
getstr(receiver, length)
char *receiver;
int length;
{
     char format[20];

     sprintf(format, "%%%d[^\n]",length);/* format string */
     memset(receiver, 0, length);  /* clear receiver */
     scanf(format, receiver);      /* get the data */
     scanf("%*[^\n]");             /* clear excess input */
     scanf("%*1[\n]");             /* clear final new line */
}
```

The first array is an array of pointers to prompts, terminated by an empty prompt.

Receivers are declared with data names as it is likely that these variables might need to be accessed by name. An array of pointers to `char` is declared and initialized to point to each receiver.

A third array of integers holds the length of each value to be entered by the user.

Pointers in Memory

When coding in C, it is useful to have a reasonable idea of what is going on in memory when you access an array, a variable, a pointer to a variable, and an array of pointers, so I

will try to address this without getting too technical. It will help your understanding of this and more complex data types.

Computers organize data in bytes. Each byte in a program has an address. Addresses in machines are usually either 16 bits (two bytes) or 32 bits (four bytes). For the sake of this discussion, I will assume a 16-bit address, but the principles are the same whether you are operating with 16 or 32 bits. All of this discussion is illustrated by a block of memory at addresses 1000 through 1099. The diagrams are arranged in blocks that are 10 bytes wide so that they will fit on the page, but the diagram is not intended to be an array. It is just not possible to string out a really long page with the addresses in consecutive order. The addresses are chosen at random as an example of how the compiler and linker might organize the data section of a program.

Listing 7.17 declares two string variables and passes them to `strcpy()`.

Listing 7.17. Two strings in memory.

```
#include <stdio.h>

char string_1[25] = "Hello ";
char string_2[] = "world.";

main()
{
     strcat(string_1, string_2);
}
```

Table 7.2 shows what the data might look like in memory. Assuming that the linker placed `string_1` at address 1002, 25 bytes would be reserved for storage. The `string_2` variable would probably be placed immediately after `string_1` at address 1027.

Table 7.2. A memory map for Listing 7.17.

Address	1000	1001	1002	1003	1004	1005	1006	1007	1008	1009
Contents			'H'	'e'	'l'	'l'	'o'	' '	NUL	NUL
Address	1010	1011	1012	1013	1014	1015	1016	1017	1018	1019
Contents	NUL	NUL	NUL	NUL	NUL	NUL	NUL	NUL	NUL	NUL

continues

Table 7.2. continued

Address	1020	1021	1022	1023	1024	1025	1026	1027	1028	1029
Contents	NUL	NUL	NUL	NUL	NUL	NUL	NUL	'w'	'o'	'r'
Address	1030	1031	1032	1033	1034	1035	1036	1037	1038	1039
Contents	'l'	'd'	'.'	NUL						

The call to `strcat()` actually passes the values 1002 and 1027 being the addresses of the two variables. After the call to `strcat()`, memory would look like Table 7.3. The value `"world."` has been concatenated to `"Hello "`, and the original value of `"world."` is unchanged. The variables `string_1` and `string_2` still refer to addresses 1002 and 1027.

Table 7.3. A memory map for Listing 7.17 after `strcat()`.

Address	1000	1001	1002	1003	1004	1005	1006	1007	1008	1009
Contents			'H'	'e'	'l'	'l'	'o'	' '	'w'	'o'
Address	1010	1011	1012	1013	1014	1015	1016	1017	1018	1019
Contents	'r'	'l'	'd'	'.'	NUL	NUL	NUL	NUL	NUL	NUL
Address	1020	1021	1022	1023	1024	1025	1026	1027	1028	1029
Contents	NUL	NUL	NUL	NUL	NUL	NUL	NUL	'w'	'o'	'r'
Address	1030	1031	1032	1033	1034	1035	1036	1037	1038	1039
Contents	'l'	'd'	'.'	NUL						

Listing 7.18 uses two strings and a pointer to a string.

Listing 7.18. Using two strings and a pointer to a string.

```
#include <stdio.h>

char string_1[25] = "Hello ";
char string_2[] = "world.";
char *string_pointer = string_1;

main()
{
     strcat(string_pointer, string_2);
     string_pointer = string_2;
}
```

In Listing 7.18, the new variable `string_pointer` will probably be created at the next address after `string_1`. It is located at address 1034, occupies two bytes, and contains the value 1002, the address of `string_1`, as shown in Table 7.4.

Table 7.4. A memory map for Listing 7.18.

Address	1000	1001	1002	1003	1004	1005	1006	1007	1008	1009
Contents			'H'	'e'	'l'	'l'	'o'	' '	NUL	NUL
Address	1010	1011	1012	1013	1014	1015	1016	1017	1018	1019
Contents	NUL	NUL	NUL	NUL	NUL	NUL	NUL	NUL	NUL	NUL
Address	1020	1021	1022	1023	1024	1025	1026	1027	1028	1029
Contents	NUL	NUL	NUL	NUL	NUL	NUL	NUL	'w'	'o'	'r'
Address	1030	1031	1032	1033	1034	1035	1036	1037	1038	1039
Contents	'l'	'd'	'.'	NUL	(addr	1002)				

The call to `strcpy()` again passes the values 1002 and 1027 but for different reasons. In Listing 7.17, the compiler knew that `string_1` was an array, and therefore passed a pointer to `string_1`, or a reference to `string_1`, effectively passing by reference. In Listing 7.18, the compiler does not see `string_pointer` as an array, and passes a copy of the value in `string_pointer`. The value in `string_pointer` happens to be a pointer to `string_1`, so the overall effect is the same, but the mechanisms are very different. An array is passed as a pointer to the array, a variable is passed as a copy of the value.

After the `strcat()` step, things are pretty much as they were in Table 7.3 (see Table 7.5).

Table 7.5. A memory map for Listing 7.18 after `strcat()`.

Address	1000	1001	1002	1003	1004	1005	1006	1007	1008	1009
Contents			'H'	'e'	'l'	'l'	'o'	' '	'w'	'o'
Address	1010	1011	1012	1013	1014	1015	1016	1017	1018	1019
Contents	'r'	'l'	'd'	'.'	NUL	NUL	NUL	NUL	NUL	NUL
Address	1020	1021	1022	1023	1024	1025	1026	1027	1028	1029
Contents	NUL	NUL	NUL	NUL	NUL	NUL	NUL	'w'	'o'	'r'
Address	1030	1031	1032	1033	1034	1035	1036	1037	1038	1039
Contents	'l'	'd'	'.'	NUL	(addr	1002)				

The second step in Listing 7.18 assigns the address of `string_2` to `string_pointer`. Table 7.6 shows the new values.

Table 7.6. A memory map for Listing 7.18 after `string_pointer = string_2`.

Address	1000	1001	1002	1003	1004	1005	1006	1007	1008	1009
Contents			'H'	'e'	'l'	'l'	'o'	' '	'w'	'o'
Address	1010	1011	1012	1013	1014	1015	1016	1017	1018	1019
Contents	'r'	'l'	'd'	'.'	NUL	NUL	NUL	NUL	NUL	NUL

Address	1020	1021	1022	1023	1024	1025	1026	1027	1028	1029
Contents	NUL	NUL	NUL	NUL	NUL	NUL	NUL	'w'	'o'	'r'

Address	1030	1031	1032	1033	1034	1035	1036	1037	1038	1039
Contents	'l'	'd'	'.'	NUL	(addr	1027)				

The value at 1034 is now 1027. A call to any function passing `string_pointer` will now pass the value 1027, which happens to be the address of `string_2`.

Listing 7.19 uses two strings and an array of pointers to the strings.

Listing 7.19. An array of pointers.

```
#include <stdio.h>

char string_1[25] = "Hello ";
char string_2[] = "world.";
char *string[] = {string_1, string_2};

main()
{
     strcat(string[0],string[1]);
}
```

In this example, `string_1` and `string_2` have been located as usual, and then the compiler created an array of two pointers at address 1034. The array contains the values 1002 and 1027, the addresses of `string_1` and `string_2`. The call to `strcat(string[0],string[1])` resolves `string[0]` as the value of `string[0]` (arrays are passed by reference, but individual elements of an array are passed by value). The `string[1]` variable is resolved in a similar manner, and the contents of `string[0]` and `string[1]` are passed the values 1002 and 1027. Because of the initialization, these are the addresses of `string_1` and `string_2`.

The effect of `strcat()` is identical to that in 7.18, but the address to be passed is resolved differently (see Table 7.7).

Table 7.7. A memory map for Listing 7.19.

Address	1000	1001	1002	1003	1004	1005	1006	1007	1008	1009
Contents			'H'	'e'	'l'	'l'	'o'	' '	NUL	NUL
Address	1010	1011	1012	1013	1014	1015	1016	1017	1018	1019
Contents	NUL	NUL	NUL	NUL	NUL	NUL	NUL	NUL	NUL	NUL
Address	1020	1021	1022	1023	1024	1025	1026	1027	1028	1029
Contents	NUL	NUL	NUL	NUL	NUL	NUL	NUL	'w'	'o'	'r'
Address	1030	1031	1032	1033	1034	1035	1036	1037	1038	1039
Contents	'l'	'd'	'.'	NUL	(addr	1002)	(addr	1027)		

Now take a look at what happens with an array of pointers to strings as passed to `text_out()` as in Listing 7.15. Listing 7.20 is a similar array of text strings, but it is shortened to prevent the memory map illustration from getting out of control.

Listing 7.20. Array initialization for `text_out`.

```
#include <stdio.h>

char *the_quote[]={
     "Daddy don't you",
     "walk so",
     "fast.",
     ""
     };

main()
{
     text_out(the_quote);
}

text_out(text)
char *text[];
```

```
{
     int index;

     for(index = 0; text[index][0] != 0; ++index)
          {
          printf("%s\n", text[index]);
          }

}
```

The compiler builds the strings into memory. The first string starts at address 1002, second at 1018, third at 1026, and the final empty string (a single NUL) at 1032. There are no elementary variables that refer to these addresses. Instead, at address 1033, the compiler builds an array of these four addresses.

The call to `text_out(the_quote)` passes the value 1033, the address of the array (see Table 7.8).

Table 7.8. A memory map for Listing 7.20.

Address	1000	1001	1002	1003	1004	1005	1006	1007	1008	1009
Contents			'D'	'a'	'd'	'd'	'y'	' '	'd'	'o'
Address	1010	1011	1012	1013	1014	1015	1016	1017	1018	1019
Contents	'n'	'''	't'	' '	'y'	'o'	'u'	NUL	'w'	'a'
Address	1020	1021	1022	1023	1024	1025	1026	1027	1028	1029
Contents	'l'	'k'	' '	's'	'o'	NUL	'f'	'a'	's'	't'
Address	1030	1031	1032	1033	1034	1035	1036	1037	1038	1039
Contents	'.'	NUL	NUL	(addr	1002)	(addr	1018)	(addr	1026)	(addr
Address	1040	1041	1042	1043	1044	1045	1046	1047	1048	1049
Contents	1032)									

Inside text_out, the data declaration char *text[] tells the compiler that the received value, 1033, is the address of an array, and the array elements are pointers to characters. The element type is important; it lets the compiler know the size of each element once you are inside text_out(). In the function, text[0] accesses the value at 1033 and 1034 which is 1002, text[1] accesses the value at 1035 and 1036 which is 1018, and so on. The result is that

```
printf("%s\n", text[0]);
```

passes the format string and the value 1002, which is the address of the string, "Daddy don't you", which is exactly what printf() expects.

There is another way to signal the end of an array of strings. The method just described sets the last element of the array to point to an empty string. It is also possible to set the last element of the array to point to nothing, as shown in Listing 7.21.

Listing 7.21. Terminating an array with no string.

```
#include <stdio.h>

char *the_quote[]={
     "Daddy don't you",
     "walk so",
     "fast.",
     0
     };

main()
{
     text_out(the_quote);
}

text_out(text)
char *text[];
{
     int index;

     for(index = 0; text[index] != 0; ++index)
          {
          printf("%s\n", text[index]);
          }

}
```

The compiler generates the same information except for the final string containing a single NUL. The array now at address 1032 contains four elements, but the last element contains an address of zero (see Table 7.9). In practice, this is not always a zero. Some computers translate this to another value, but whatever it is, it means "This doesn't point to anything." Compilers are set up to recognize that setting a pointer to zero or testing a pointer to see if it is zero is translated into a test for "points to nothing." This changes the way the testing is done in `text_out()`. The original test was "Stop when the first character of the string pointed to by the array element is NUL." The new test is "Stop when the array element points to nothing (is zero)."

Table 7.9. A memory map for Listing 7.21.

Address	1000	1001	1002	1003	1004	1005	1006	1007	1008	1009
Contents			'D'	'a'	'd'	'd'	'y'	' '	'd'	'o'
Address	1010	1011	1012	1013	1014	1015	1016	1017	1018	1019
Contents	'n'	'''	't'	' '	'y'	'o'	'u'	NUL	'w'	'a'
Address	1020	1021	1022	1023	1024	1025	1026	1027	1028	1029
Contents	'l'	'k'	' '	's'	'o'	NUL	'f'	'a'	's'	't'
Address	1030	1031	1032	1033	1034	1035	1036	1037	1038	1039
Contents	'.'	NUL	(addr	1002)	(addr	1018)	(addr	1026)	(addr	0000)
Address	1040	1041	1042	1043	1044	1045	1046	1047	1048	1049
Contents										

C provides a special syntax for setting a pointer to nothing. It is the word `NULL`, which is defined in the stdio.h file.

The initialization and testing in Listing 7.22 uses `NULL` instead of `0`. Don't confuse `NULL` (a C pointer to nothing) and NUL the ASCII 0 character. You can choose whether to use `0` or `NULL` for a pointer, but you need to know what `NULL` means when you are studying listings.

Listing 7.22. Terminating an array with no string.

```
#include <stdio.h>

char *the_quote[]={
     "Daddy don't you",
     "walk so",
     "fast.",
     NULL
     };

main()
{
     text_out(the_quote);
}

text_out(text)
char *text[];
{
     int index;

     for(index = 0; text[index] != NULL; ++index)
          {
          printf("%s\n", text[index]);
          }

}
```

The choice of whether to terminate arrays using a pointer to nothing or an empty string is yours, but the former is more common, as you will see shortly. Whichever you use, ensure that the target function tests correctly for the terminator, so it would be a good idea to choose one and stick to it.

Passing Values to *main()*

You have probably seen programs, such as editors, that can be started by typing the name of the program, followed by a space, followed by some additional argument, usually the name of a file.

```
edit myfile.txt
```

Obviously the operating system is smart enough to locate, load and run a program probably called EDIT.EXE (under MS-DOS), but how does the EDIT.EXE program know that it is supposed to open a file named myfile.txt?

The answer is that when I said that the function named `main()` was the starting point of a program, I lied. When a C program is loaded to be run, there are a series of steps taken before `main()` is executed that are mainly housekeeping. This section of a C program is sometimes referred to as the `STARTUP` logic. It is not accessible under most circumstances. There are exceptions to this, but they are beyond the scope of this book and are used only in very advanced programming. One of the things that `STARTUP` does is to collect all of the arguments on the command line that were used to start the program, and place them in an array of pointers to strings. Listing 7.23 is the program args.c. If you edit, compile and link this program, you can run it by typing anything on the command line, such as

```
args 1 2 3 Hello
```

Listing 7.23. args.c—passing command-line arguments.

```
#include <stdio.h>

main(argc, argv)
int argc;
char *argv[];
{

     int index;

     for(index = 0; argv[index]; ++index)
          {
          printf("%s\n", argv[index]);
          }
     printf("Total arguments = %d\n", argc);
}
```

The args.c program will print a list of all the arguments each on a separate line.

```
C:\TEST\ARGS.EXE
1
2
3
Hello
```

All previous entrances to `main()` have specified no arguments, and if you do not need or expect anything on the command line, `main()` is perfectly workable. The arguments are passed by `STARTUP` but just ignored in all the previous programs you have looked at.

Note that the construction for processing all the elements of the array in args.c is identical to that used in the final version of `text_out()`.

The two arguments "passed" to `main()` are traditionally called `argc` and `argv`. The `argc` (argument count) variable is an integer that contains the number of arguments on the command line including the name of the program itself. Under MS-DOS, the first argument is modified to represent the complete drive path and filename of the executable program. An argument is any group of characters up to a space, or any group of characters enclosed in quotation marks.

The second "passed" value, `argv` (argument values), is an array of pointers to strings, and these pointers point to each of the strings on the command line. The array is terminated with a `NULL` element. Some early C compilers did not include the final `NULL` array element, so it was necessary to use `argc` to control the number of elements to be printed as in Listing 7.24.

Listing 7.24. args.c—passing command-line arguments using `argc`.

```
#include <stdio.h>

main(argc, argv)
int argc;
char *argv[];
{

     int index;

     for(index = 0; index < argc; ++index)
          {
          printf("%s\n", argv[index]);
          }
     printf("Total arguments = %d\n", argc);
}
```

Modern C compilers also pass a third value, which can be ignored if not needed. It is also an array of pointers to strings, and points to things called environment variables. This third argument is rarely seen in C programs, but is usually called `envp` (environment pointers). Listing 7.25 is an expanded version of args.c that includes the environment pointers.

Listing 7.25. args.c—environment pointers.

```
#include <stdio.h>

main(argc, argv, envp)
int argc;
char *argv[],*envp[];
{

     int index;

     for(index = 0; argv[index]; ++index)
          {
          printf("%s\n", argv[index]);
          }
     for(index = 0; envp[index]; ++index)
          {
          printf("%s\n", envp[index]);
          }
}
```

Run Listing 7.25 on a DOS machine and you will see something like this:

```
C:\TEST\ARGS.EXE
COMMSPEC=C:\DOS\COMMAND.COM
PATH=C:\DOS;C:\BIN
TEMP=C:\WINDOWS\TEMP
```

The first line is the name of the program, `argv[0]`, and the remaining lines are the environment variables. If you need to extract environment variables, this is one way to do it.

Summary

You're almost there now. Pointers are used extensively in C. You should practice with them as often as you can, and make an effort to really understand how they are being used when you see one in a listing. Arrays of pointers to strings are used right at the beginning of all C programs if you extract and use either command-line arguments, or environment pointers.

Now you need to polish off one other area of data storage, and then start in on file I/O with examples of programs to read, store, and modify a file of data.

8

Scope, Storage, and Prototyping

C has some special types of storage that allow you to delimit which parts of the program have access to which data. Some of these are very similar to COBOL. These should round out your knowledge of C variables. This chapter also covers some of what you might call the "administration" of C—some of the extra typing that you have to do to get the job done. These topics include the following:

- Static functions
- Static and local variables
- The scope of variables and functions
- Life span versus visibility
- Storage classes
- Function types and prototypes
- The new style of passed variables
- Header files
- The `#define` macros

Static Functions

By default, all C functions are global. If you create two separate source code files containing functions and then compile and link them, any function in either file can call any function in the other file.

This is different from COBOL. If two COBOL programs are compiled and linked, one program cannot perform paragraphs in the other program. This is one of the key differences between C and COBOL. In COBOL, if you need to center strings for report titles, you would either have to write a COBOL program that could be called using the string and a length, or you would have to include the logic for centering in either a hand-coded paragraph or as a `COPY` file.

In C you can write a single function (not a complete program) to handle the centering, and link it into other programs.

As far as COBOL is concerned, all paragraphs within a source code file are invisible to any other program. In C the default is that all functions are visible.

Listing 8.1 is a program that calls a routine to center a string, and then prints it. Listing 8.2 is the support code containing `center()`, and two other functions used by the `center()` function. Listings 8.3 and 8.4 are COBOL equivalents. When set up as defaults, all of the functions in Listing 8.2 are available. Listing 8.1 calls only `center()`, but it could call `inschar()` or `right_shift()` by passing the correct values. In the COBOL equivalents, none of the paragraphs in center.cob (Listing 8.4) are available to displ.cob (Listing 8.3), and the entry to center.cob is only through the call to `"CENTER"`.

Listing 8.1. displ.c—displays a centered string.

```
#include <stdio.h>

char string[51] = "The Title";

main()
{
     center(string, 50);
     printf("<%s>\n",string);
}
```

Listing 8.2. center.c—centers a string.

```
center(string, len)
char *string;
int len;
{
     int tlen;

     tlen = strlen(string);
     tlen = (len - tlen) / 2;
     while(tlen)
          {
          inschar(string,' ',len);
          --tlen;
          }
}

inschar(string, ch, len)
char *string;
int ch, len;
{
     int temp_ch;

     shift_right(string, len);
     *string = ch;
}

shift_right(string, len)
char *string;
int len;
{
     int index1, index2;

     for(index2 = (len-1); index2 > 0; --index2)
          {
          index1 = index2 - 1;
          string[index2] = string[index1];
          }
}
```

Listing 8.3. DISPL.COB—displays a centered field.

```
IDENTIFICATION DIVISION.
PROGRAM-ID. DISPL.
```

continues

Listing 8.3. continued

```
* THIS PROGRAM CENTERS A STRING AND
* DISPLAYS IT.
 ENVIRONMENT DIVISION.
 DATA DIVISION.
 WORKING-STORAGE SECTION.

 01  A-STRING     PIC X(50) VALUE
     "The Title".
 01  THE-LENGTH   PIC 99 VALUE 50.

 PROCEDURE DIVISION.
 MAIN-LOGIC SECTION.
 PROGRAM-BEGIN.
     CALL "CENTER" USING A-STRING, THE-LENGTH.
     DISPLAY "<" A-STRING ">".
 EXIT-PROGRAM.
     EXIT PROGRAM.
 STOP-RUN.
     STOP RUN.
 THE-OTHER SECTION.
```

Listing 8.4. CENTER.COB.

```
 IDENTIFICATION DIVISION.
 PROGRAM-ID. CENTER.
* THIS PROGRAM CENTERS A STRING.
 ENVIRONMENT DIVISION.
 DATA DIVISION.
 WORKING-STORAGE SECTION.
 01  LENGTH-INDEX  PIC 99.
 01  INDEX1        PIC 99.
 01  INDEX2        PIC 99.
 01  CHAR-TO-INS   PIC X.
 01  THE-COUNT    PIC 99.

 LINKAGE SECTION.
 01  A-STRING.
     05  A-CHAR   PIC X OCCURS 50 TIMES.
 01  THE-LENGTH   PIC 99.

 PROCEDURE DIVISION USING A-STRING THE-LENGTH.
 MAIN-LOGIC SECTION.
 PROGRAM-BEGIN.
```

```
    PERFORM STRLEN.
    IF LENGTH-INDEX > 0
        COMPUTE LENGTH-INDEX =
           (THE-LENGTH - LENGTH-INDEX) / 2
        MOVE SPACE TO CHAR-TO-INS
        PERFORM INSCHAR
         VARYING THE-COUNT FROM 1 BY 1
           UNTIL THE-COUNT > LENGTH-INDEX.

EXIT-PROGRAM.
    EXIT PROGRAM.
STOP-RUN.
    STOP RUN.

THE-OTHER SECTION.
STRLEN.
    PERFORM DUMMY-ROUTINE
       VARYING LENGTH-INDEX FROM THE-LENGTH BY -1
          UNTIL    LENGTH-INDEX < 1
                OR A-CHAR(LENGTH-INDEX) NOT = SPACE.
DUMMY-ROUTINE.
    EXIT.

INSCHAR.
    MOVE THE-LENGTH TO INDEX2.
    PERFORM SHIFT-RIGHT.
    MOVE CHAR-TO-INS TO A-CHAR(1).

SHIFT-RIGHT.
    PERFORM UNTIL INDEX2 < 2
        COMPUTE INDEX1 = INDEX2 - 1
        MOVE A-CHAR(INDEX1) TO A-CHAR(INDEX2)
        SUBTRACT 1 FROM INDEX2
    END-PERFORM.
```

The is no way to change the fact that the paragraphs of center.cob are local to that source code file, but in C there is a way to override C's default activity and force a function to become local. Listing 8.5 is center.c with some changes. First, the routines have been rewritten in a more C-like manner, just to illustrate the different philosophy of C. The `right_shift()` function has been eliminated and the `inschar()` function has been made local to center.c by adding the keyword `static` before the function.

Listing 8.5. center.c—more C-like.

```
center(string, len)
char *string;
int len;
{
     int tlen;

     tlen = strlen(string);
     tlen = (len - tlen) / 2;
     while(tlen)
          {
          inschar(string,' ');
          --tlen;
          }
}


static inschar(string, ch)
char *string;
int ch;
{
     int temp_ch;

     do{
          temp_ch = *string;
          *string = ch;
          ch = temp_ch;
          ++string;
          }while(ch);
     *string = ch;
}
```

The `inschar()` function is created as a unique function within center.c. Only functions that appear within center.c may call the function. Listing 8.6 is a version of displ.c that attempts to insert an extra space at the beginning of the string by calling `inschar()` before calling `center`. If this file is compiled and linked with center.c (as shown in Listing 8.5) using the command

```
cl displ.c center.c
```

both files will compile correctly, but the linker will return the message

```
displ.obj(displ.c):error L2029: 'inschar' : unresolved external
```

Listing 8.6. displ.c—displays a centered string.

```
#include <stdio.h>

char string[51] = "The Title";

main()
{
     inschar(string, ' ');
     center(string, 50);
     printf("<%s>\n",string);
}
```

The `inschar()` function is "out of scope" inside displ.c. There are two main advantages to this. First, you can "hide" some of your code by creating a single entry point to a set of routines. If you have some complex processing that has to be done to calculate pay, you can create a file named getpay.c containing a single entry function named, for example, `get_pay()`. The only way to access the routine is to call the `get_pay()` function. Inside getpay.c there may be many routines that support `get_pay()` in order to resolve the salary, but none of them can be called from any other C module. This prevents routines from being misused.

Second, you can use function names multiple times. If you have a C program that maintains customers and customer tax codes, you might have two separate files: custmnt.c and codemnt.c. The entry points in each are `maintain_customers()` and `maintain_codes()` respectively, but both files could contain routines named `add_records()`, `change_records()`, and `delete_records()`, provided the functions were declared with the keyword `static`.

It is good practice to declare any function that is only relevant within a single source code file as a `static` function. When reading the source code file, `static` indicates that you will not have to search for the function being called from any other module, and as projects get bigger, you don't have to worry about name collisions.

Static and Local Variables

Functions have two scopes: global and local. Variables have three scopes: global, local, and block.

A global variable is one that is simply defined

```
char string[50] = "The title";
```

as in Listing 8.1 earlier in this chapter.

A block variable is one that is available only within a specific block of code, such as a function. In Listing 8.7, `index1` and `index2` are block variables. They are created temporarily by entry to the function and are destroyed when the function exits.

Listing 8.7. Block variables.

```
shift_right(string, len)
char *string;
int len;
{
     int index1, index2;

     for(index2 = (len-1); index2 > 0; --index2)
          {
          index1 = index2 - 1;
          string[index2] = string[index1];
          }
}
```

A block is one or more procedure statements enclosed in braces. Block variables must be defined immediately after the opening brace. Listing 8.8 is a variation on `right_shift()` that uses another block variable within the internal block. The variable `index2` is defined immediately after the opening brace of the main body of the function. The scope of `index2` is from its definition to the closing brace that ends block 1. Block 2 is the code within the `for()` loop. The variable `index1` is defined immediately after the opening brace of the `for()` loop. Its scope is from its definition to the end of block 2. Neither `index1` nor `index2` may be accessed outside the `shift_right()` function, and `index1` may not be accessed outside the `for()` loop.

Listing 8.8. Blocks within blocks.

```
shift_right(string, len)
char *string;
int len;
{                                        /* start block 1 */
     int index2;
```

```
     for(index2 = (len-1); index2 > 0; --index2)
          {                         /* start block 2 */
          int index1;
          index1 = index2 - 1;
          string[index2] = string[index1];
          }                         /* end block 2 */
}                                   /* end block 1 */
```

In practice very little C code is written with block variables other than those defined for the whole function, as shown in Listing 8.7.

The `index1` and `index2` variables are automatic. They are created at the beginning of the code block, and destroyed at the end. They are created with an unspecified value, and must be initialized in the procedure logic.

Local variables are defined outside of a function, but given a `static` storage class. Listing 8.9 is the `days_in_month()` function from Chapter 7. The array of `month_days[]` is used only by functions in the source code file containing the array, so it is a suitable candidate for local storage, and is given a `static` storage class.

Listing 8.9. Days of the month routine with local storage.

```
/*----
This routine is passed a month and a year. It returns the days
in the month, adjusted for leap years. Year is passed as a full
year, and month is passed as 1-12.
------*/

static int month_days[] = {31,28,31,30,31,30,31,31,30,31,30,31};

days_in_month(year, month)
int month, year;
{
     --month;
     if(month != 1)
          return(month_days[month]);
     else
     if( ( (year % 4) == 0) && ( (year % 100) != 0) ) )
          return(29);
     else
          return(month_days[month]);
}
```

Life Span versus Visibility

Functions and variables have two key attributes that are difficult to discuss because the C terminology and C keywords to describe them are ambiguous. These are *life span* and *visibility.*

The life span of a function or variable is the range of code over which a variable or function exists. All functions are permanent. They always exist in the program. They may not be visible when you are in some other part of the program, but they exist. All variables defined outside of functions are permanent. Again, they may not be visible, but the area of memory that contains that variable is still in existence. A variable or function that is permanent is sometimes called "static." This is not the same as the keyword `static`, but *static* in the English sense of *always there.* This is part of the confusion.

All variables that are defined inside functions or inside code blocks (except as noted below) are automatic. They are created on entry to the block of code, and are destroyed on exit.

A variable inside a function can be forced to become "static." In Listing 8.10, the string `emsg` is a permanent variable. It is defined inside `error_msg()`, and it is visible only inside the function.

Listing 8.10. A `static` variable within a function.

```
error_msg(msg)
{
     static char emsg[]= "error";

     printf("%s:%s\n", emsg, msg);
}
```

Visibility is controlled by the location of the variable or function and the keyword `static`. A variable defined inside a function or code block is visible only within that function or code block. A function given a storage class of `static` is only visible within that source code file. A variable defined outside a function with a storage class of `static` is visible only within that source code file. For both of these conditions it would be far better to have created a new keyword, such as *invisible* or *local* or *private,* because in these two instances, the keyword `static` affects the visibility of the variable, not its permanence.

On a variable defined inside a function, `static` actually means what it says: "Make this variable indestructible."

I have regularly used the clumsy phrase "variable outside a function"; you might think that there should be some term to describe this condition. In official C parlance, a variable defined outside a function is an external variable, and one defined inside a function is an internal variable. Unfortunately this clashes with another storage class, `extern`, that I haven't introduced yet (see "Storage Classes," later in this chapter), and I have been trying to avoid further confusion.

Table 8.1. summarizes these differences.

Table 8.1. The effect of `static` storage class used on functions and variables.

Used on	*Affects*	*Effect*
Function	Visibility	Makes the function invisible outside the current source code file.
Variable outside a function	Visibility	Makes the variable invisible outside the current source code file.
Variable inside a function	Permanence	Makes the variable permanent and allows it to be initialized in the definition.

None of this clarifies the position of variables passed to functions. These most closely approach automatic variables, but their life span is slightly different. True automatics are defined inside a function and created when the function is entered. Variables passed to functions are actually created by the calling function. They are used on a temporary basis by the called function, and then destroyed by the calling function after returning from the called function.

Listing 8.11 shows the relationship between created variables in a function calling `strlen()` and inside the function itself.

Listing 8.11. Relationship of variables.

```
#include <stdio.h>

char a_string[] = "Hello world";

main()
{
     int len;                  /*1*/

     len = strlen(a_string);   /*2*/
                               /*3*/
}

strlen(str)
char *str;
{
     int len;                  /*4*/

     len = 0;
     while(*str)
          {
          ++len;
          ++str;
          }
     return(len);
}
```

At point `/*1*/`, a temporary variable is created (`len`) for use inside `main()`. At point `/*2*/`, a temporary variable is created, and initialized to the address of `a_string`. This variable is immediately passed to `strlen`. At point `/*3*/`, this temporary variable is destroyed. At point `/*4*/`, a temporary variable (`len`) is created for use inside the function `strlen()`.

For all practical purposes, copies of variables passed to a function can be treated as automatics. Their life span is only slightly longer than a true automatic.

Storage Classes

A storage class is a modifier applied to a function or a variable that indicates to the compiler the scope, permanence, use, or access to a variable or function. In other words, a storage class is really a grab bag.

There are five storage classes, and you have seen two of them. The first is `static`. The second is `auto`, the default storage class of a variable defined within a function. Listing 8.12 is equivalent to `strlen()` in Listing 8.11: the compiler inserts an `auto` default storage class for `len`. The `auto` storage class is rarely seen in listings because it is implied in all internal variables, but you will see reference to automatic variables in discussions of C.

Listing 8.12. The `auto` storage class.

```
strlen(str)
char *str;
{
     auto int len;

     len = 0;
     while(*str)
          {
          ++len;
          ++str;
          }
     return(len);
}
```

The next type of storage is `register`. A `register` storage class can be applied to any automatic variable. It signals the compiler to use the fastest possible method to store and retrieve values from the variable. In the original C language, `register` actually meant, "Assign this variable to a machine register in the CPU and keep it there for the duration of the function." This produced very fast access to that register. Nowadays, it is up to compiler designers to decide what to do with the `register` storage class, but it usually creates a faster version of the function. Listing 8.13 is a faster version of `strlen()`. The `register` storage class may only be applied to variables within functions.

Listing 8.13. The `register` storage class.

```
strlen(str)
char *str;
{
     register int len;

     len = 0;
     while(*str)
```

continues

Listing 8.13. continued

```
          {
          ++len;
          ++str;
          }
     return(len);
}
```

The fourth storage class is extern. The extern storage class is used with declarations of variables rather than definitions of variables. It is used in one C source code file to indicate that a global variable is available in some other source code file, or somewhere else in the program. Listings 8.14 and 8.15 are assumed to be two separate source code files to be linked together after compilation. The variable the_title in Listing 8.14 is a global variable as it is not given a static storage class. Listing 8.15 accesses that variable by naming it again and giving it an extern storage class.

Listing 8.14. A global variable.

```
#include <stdio.h>

char the_title[] = "My title";

main()
{
     print_title();
}


Listing 8.15—Accessing a global variable

extern char the_title[];

print_title()
{
     printf("%s\n", the_title);
}
```

Some modern COBOL compilers provide a very similar mechanism. Listings 8.16 and 8.17 are the working storage of calling and called COBOL programs using globals.

Listing 8.16. COBOL calling working storage for globals.

```
WORKING-STORAGE SECTION.

01  THE-TITLE           GLOBAL
    PIC X(50)   VALUE "My Title".
```

Listing 8.17 COBOL called working storage for globals.

```
WORKING-STORAGE SECTION.

01  THE-TITLE           EXTERNAL
    PIC X(50).
```

The `extern` storage class must also be used to declare a variable that has not yet been defined, even though the variable appears in the current source code file. This sounds odd until you realize that C is completely free-form, meaning that data and functions can be placed in any order in a file, as in Listing 8.18. The `the_title` variable is declared at the top of the listing, but not defined until the end of the listing. Without the `extern` declaration at the start of the listing, the compiler would complain in `print_title()` of an undefined variable.

It is interesting to note (though not much used) that `the_title` at the end of Listing 8.18 could itself be given a storage class of `static`, making it local to this file. Most people think of `extern` as a reference to a global variable that is defined later or in another file, but `extern` actually is a reference to a variable that hasn't yet been defined. The variable itself could be a local variable if it appeared later in the same file. This again is an example of an instance where a better keyword could have been used, such as *declare.*

Listing 8.18. A global variable.

```
#include <stdio.h>

extern char the_title[];

main()
{
     print_title();
}
```

continues

Listing 8.18. continued

```
print_title()
{
     printf("%s\n", the_title);
}

char the_title[] = "My title";
```

The last storage class is `typedef`. I will cover `typedef` in more detail in Chapter 12, "C Structures," but for now you can think of a `typedef` as a way of creating an alias for a C data type. In Listing 8.19, `LONG_INT` becomes an alias for the C data type `long`.

Listing 8.19. Using `typedef`.

```
typedef long LONG_INT;

func()
{
    LONG_INT one, two;

    /* do something */
}
```

One frequent use for `typedef` is to create a specific data type to be used for a common type of function call. Suppose you create a set of date routines. In order to prevent confusion when calling these routines, you decide that all values will be passed and returned as long integers. You might use something like Listing 8.20. This style of coding helps to clarify what you are doing, and also makes it unnecessary to remember whether date routines use `long`s or `int`s; they just use `Date`s.

Listing 8.20. Using `typedef`.

```
typedef long Date


Date add_days(oldate, days_to_add)
Date oldate, days_to_add;
{
     Date result;
```

```
     /* do something to get result */

     return(result);
}

main()
{
     Date newdate, oldate, days_to_add;

     newdate = add_days(oldate, days_to_add);
}
```

Function Types and Prototypes

You have already glimpsed some functions that return types other than integers. Listing 8.21 returns the square of a `double` as a `double` type.

Listing 8.21. Function returning a `double`.

```
double dbl_square(value)
double value;
{
     value *= value;
     return(value);
}
```

There is a hitch: the return type of a function must be declared before the function is called. If it is not, the compiler assumes that the function returns an integer (the default return type). When the compiler finally gets to the function, it spits out an error message that the function has been redefined.

In Listing 8.22, the compiler first encounters the call to `dbl_square()` and assumes that the function returns an integer. It generates the logic to convert the returned integer into a `double` and store it in `the_square`. When the compiler reaches `dbl_square()`, it suddenly realizes that the function returns a double, but it has already generated logic to perform a conversion of an integer to a `double`. Compilers are not very good at backtracking, so it has no choice but to generate an error.

Listing 8.22. Automatic function declaration.

```
#include <stdio.h>

main()
{
     double the_square, the_value;

     the_value = 22.2;
     the_square = dbl_square(the_value);

     printf("Result is %f\n", the_square);
}

double dbl_square(value)
double value;
{
     value *= value;
     return(value);
}
```

There are two ways to handle this problem. The first is to code the program "upside down" so that the function is defined before it is called, as shown in Listing 8.23. The definition of the function acts as the declaration, and the compiler is very clear about what `dbl_square()` is before it gets to the call to the function.

Listing 8.23. Defining a function before it is called.

```
#include <stdio.h>

double dbl_square(value)
double value;
{
     value *= value;
     return(value);
}

main()
{
     double the_square, the_value;

     the_value = 22.2;
     the_square = dbl_square(the_value);

     printf("Result is %f\n", the_square);
}
```

The second (and probably more traditional) method is to declare the function before it is called. A function may be declared anywhere before it is called. Listings 8.24 and 8.25 are both valid declarations for `dbl_square()`.

Listing 8.24. Declaring a function.

```
#include <stdio.h>

double dbl_square();

main()
{
     double the_square, the_value;

     the_value = 22.2;
     the_square = dbl_square(the_value);

     printf("Result is %f\n", the_square);
}
```

Listing 8.25. Another method of declaring a function.

```
#include <stdio.h>

main()
{
     double the_square, the_value, dbl_square();

     the_value = 22.2;
     the_square = dbl_square(the_value);

     printf("Result is %f\n", the_square);
}
```

The minimum declaration of a function is the return type, the function name, and parentheses (`()`) followed by a semicolon.

Functions can return any type. For example, `strcat()` (see Chapter 3, "C Characters and Strings") with no return value actually returns a pointer to the destination string. Listing 8.26 is a corrected version of `strcat()` with the return type identified.

Listing 8.26. `strcat()` with a return value.

```
char *strcat(dest, src)
char *dest, *src;
{
     char *end;
     int len;

     len = strlen(dest);
     end = dest + len;
     strcpy(end, src);
     return(dest);
}
```

The `strcat()` function could be used as an argument to any function that itself requires a pointer to a `char`, as shown in Listing 8.27. Note that `strcat()` is declared before it is used.

Listing 8.27. Using a returned pointer.

```
#include <stdio.h>

char one[50] = "One for the money ";
char two[] = "two for the show";

main()
{
     char *strcat();

     printf("%s\n", strcat(one, two));
}
```

A function declaration can be used to do more than just identify the return type. A function declaration can also list the types of values expected by a function. If a function declaration includes this information, the compiler does additional syntax checking, and will warn you if the types passed to the function do not match the types expected by the function. This type of function declaration, which includes the types of values to pass, is called a *function prototype.* Listing 8.28 includes a function prototype for `strcat()` and an error that the compiler will catch. In the listing, `strcat()` is called, passing only one pointer. The prototype states that two pointers to `char` are expected. Without the prototype, this would have caused a logic error that would have to be picked up in debugging. With the prototype, the compiler returns an error that can be picked up immediately.

Listing 8.28. Using a prototype.

```
#include <stdio.h>

char one[50] = "One for the money ";
char two[] = "two for the show";

char *strcat(char *, char *);

main()
{

     printf("%s\n", strcat(one));
}
```

The New Style of Passed Variables

As C became popular, people recognized that the original definition of the language had some cracks in it. A committee was set up to standardize and, in many cases, improve C syntax and that of its sister language, C++. This new C is now known as ANSI C. One of the changes concerned the method of typing variables received by a function. In the new style, the variables are named and typed inside the parentheses of the function definition. Listing 8.29 is `strcat()` with the new style of variable types. You should compare this to Listing 8.26 to get a feel for differences.

Listing 8.29. `strcat()` with new style passed values.

```
char *strcat(char *dest, char *src)
{
     char *end;
     int len;

     len = strlen(dest);
     end = dest + len;
     strcpy(end, src);
     return(dest);
}
```

The Microsoft C manual refers to the style in Listing 8.26 in a manner that indicates that it is antiquated. There are still millions of lines of code out there using this "old" style, and there are still compilers around that will not accept the "new" style, whereas most new compilers will accept the "old" style. It is a good idea to get used to the new style, as it will eventually be the standard, but for now recognize both types as they appear in listings.

Header Files

You have been using stdio.h in all your programs so far. The `typedef` descriptions, function declarations, and function prototypes are the type of "administration" that are placed in a header file. For example, string.h is a standard library header file for the string handling library routines. string.h will contain function prototypes for all the string library routines. A sample of what you might find in string.h is shown in Listing 8.30.

Listing 8.30. Sample string.h file.

```
int strlen(char*);
char *strcpy(char*, char*);
char *strcat(char*, char*);
char *strupr(char*), *strlwr(char*);
```

These would be prototypes for functions which specify that `strlen()` returns an integer while all the other functions return pointers to `char`, and each function requires either one or two `char` pointers as arguments.

With this information in string.h, it is possible simply to copy string.h into any file that calls a string handling routine, as shown in Listing 8.31. Compare this to Listing 8.28, and notice that now that string.h is included, it is no longer necessary to declare `strcat()`.

Listing 8.31. Using a prototype.

```
#include <stdio.h>
#include <string.h>

char one[50] = "One for the money ";
char two[] = "two for the show";
```

```
main()
{

     printf("%s\n", strcat(one));
}
```

You will be creating your header files starting with Chapter 10, "Basic Maintenance Modules," and there is one thing to note in the syntax. When an `#include` file is enclosed in angle brackets, it refers to an `#include` file in a special library (directory) of `#include` files that contains header files for standard C routines.

A header file enclosed in quotation marks, for example,

```
#include "myheader.h"
```

is a user-created header file and should be searched for in the current library (directory).

#define Macros

C also provides a substitution directive that can be used to create values and assign them to text strings. I have already mentioned the use of `NULL` to mean the value of a pointer to nothing. Using the define macro, this would be written:

```
#define NULL    0
```

This line or something similar will appear in stdio.h, but such `defines` can appear in the source code file as well. Whenever the compiler encounters the string `NULL`, it substitutes the remainder of the string in the text of the source code file.

So a line reading

```
if(ptr == NULL)
```

would first be translated to

```
if(ptr == 0)
```

and then compiled.

You could in fact use the `define` macro to change the appearance of the C language. Listing 8.32 is a header file that translates some of C's unusual operators into more COBOL-like syntax.

Listing 8.32. cobop.h—using `#define` to change the language.

```
#define    NOT_EQUAL           !=
#define    IS_EQUAL            ==
#define    NOT_LESS_THAN       >=
#define    NOT_GREATER_THAN    <=
```

In Listing 8.33, this file has been included, and the program has been written using the defined operators. Note the use of double quotation marks around cobop.h to indicate that it is a user-created header file.

Listing 8.33. Using the changes.

```
#include <stdio.h>
#include "cobop.h"
main()
{
     int index;

     for(index = 0; index NOT_GREATER_THAN 17; ++index)
          {
          if(index NOT_EQUAL 2)
               process(index);
          }
}
```

The `#include` directive and the `#define` directive are called *preprocessor* (before the processing) directives. They are acted on before the actual compilation takes place. An `#include` file is included and then compiled, and a substitution (`#define`) directive is processed first to perform the indicated text substitution.

The `#define` directive can be used to create macros that behave like Level 88 COBOL data items. Listing 8.34 uses `#define` to create tests for entry errors during screen processing.

Listing 8.34. Testing for entry errors.

```
#include <stdio.h>

int screen_error_flag = 0;
#define   no_screen_error          screen_error_flag == 0

main()
{
     screen_error_flag = 0;

     display_screen();
     validate_entries();
     if(no_screen_error)
          write_data();
}
```

Assuming that `validate_entries()` sets `screen_error_flag` when an error occurs, the test after the call to `validate_entries()` is converted to

```
if(screen_error_flag == 0)
```

The C `#define` preprocessor is a text substitution mechanism only, and does no other processing. In the example

```
#define   TOTAL          1 + 2

     value = TOTAL;
```

the second line is translated to

```
value = 1 + 2;
```

and not

```
value = 3;
```

The `#define` directive is also useful for creating named constants that can be used to shortcut code and make values easier to remember. In Chapter 7, "Arrays in C," Listing 7.5 included a routine to `get_pay()` that was passed a full-time/part-time flag (`P`/`F`) and a regular/overtime/holiday flag (`R`/`O`/`H`), as well as a numeric employee class. Refer to Listing 7.5 and note that inside the function the `P`/`F` and `R`/`O`/`H` flags had to be converted to indexes into the array. It would be easier to create a pay.h file containing `#define` clauses for each of the types as in Listing 8.35.

Listing 8.35. pay.h.

```
#define   PART_TIME          0
#define   FULL_TIME          1

#define   CLASS_A            0
#define   CLASS_B            1
#define   CLASS_C            2
#define   CLASS_D            3

#define   REGULAR_RATE       0
#define   OVERTIME_RATE      1
#define   HOLIDAY_RATE       2
```

Using this header file, the `get_pay()` routine could be called (as shown in Listing 8.36), and `get_pay()` itself could be simplified, as shown in Listing 8.37. Compare Listing 8.37 to Listing 7.5, and you will see how much more compact the new version is.

Listing 8.36. Calling the new `get_pay()`.

```
#include <stdio.h>
#include "pay.h"

double pay;

double get_pay(int, int, int, int);

main()
{
     pay = get_pay(PART_TIME, CLASS_A, HOLIDAY_RATE, 8);
}
```

Listing 8.37. New `get_pay()`.

```
static double hourly_pay[2][4][3]=
     {    {
/* Part Time   Regular   Overtime  Holiday */
               {5.00,    7.50,     10.00},
               {6.00,    9.00,     12.00},
               {7.00,    10.50,    14.00},
               {8.00,    12.00,    16.00}
```

```
          },
          {
/* Full Time */
               {6.00,    9.00,     12.00},
               {7.00,    10.50,    14.00},
               {8.00,    12.00,    16.00},
               {9.00,    13.50,    18.00}
          }
     };

double get_pay(type, class, rate, hours)
int type, class, rate, hours;
{

     double pay;

     if( (type < 0) || (type > 1) )
          return(0.00);
     if( (class < 0) || (class > 3) )
          return(0.00);
     if( (rate < 0) || (rate > 2) )
          return(0.00);

     pay = hourly_pay[type][class][rate] * hours;
     return(pay);

}
```

There is more to learn about #define directives, and there are other preprocessors besides #include and #define. These are covered in detail in Chapter 15, "Tips, Tricks, and Advanced Techniques."

Summary

C has some powerful features in the #define and #include preprocessor directives, and some annoying overhead in the need to declare certain functions before they are called. Even so, C is more "relaxed" than COBOL, and offers a lot of leeway in how you want to code things.

The next chapter covers file I/O, another critical piece of the C puzzle.

9

STREAM FILE I/O

You now are ready to tackle the first type of C file I/O, called stream files. I will conclude this discussion with a file-based version of the phone book program in the next two chapters.

In this chapter, you will learn about:

- C stream files
- Opening, closing, reading, and writing files
- Using `stdin` and `stdout`
- Character- versus record-based I/O
- Field-based I/O
- Moving around in a stream file

Stream Files

Stream files are files containing ASCII characters organized into separate lines by line terminators: usually a carriage return, a line feed, or a combination of both. Editor text files are stream files to a C program. They are called stream files because they are rather like tape files. They can be read from beginning to end, rewound, and subjected to other actions that are similar to tape processing. The files arrive as a stream of bytes. They are equivalent to COBOL's line sequential file type.

Compared to COBOL's `SELECT` and `FD` statements, the C syntax for file processing is very simple. Listing 9.1 is a program to open a file named on the command line and display it on the screen, rather like the MS-DOS TYPE command.

Listing 9.1. show.c—types out a file.

```
#include <stdio.h>
#include <process.h>

FILE *showfile;

main(int argc, char *argv[])
{
     int ch;

     showfile = fopen(argv[1],"r");

     if(showfile == NULL)
          {
          printf("File %s not found.\n", argv[1]);
          exit(0);
          }

     while( (ch = fgetc(showfile)) != EOF)
          putchar(ch);

     fclose(showfile);
}
```

A variable that is a pointer to a `FILE` data type is declared. This is a data type described in stdio.h.

The `fopen()` function is used to open the file named in the second argument on the command line. Remember that the first argument is the name of the program. The `fopen()` function expects to receive two pointers to `char`: the first contains the name of the file and the second contains the open mode. The open mode for `fopen()` is `"r"` which causes the file to be opened in input (read) mode. The file must exist before the open.

The `fopen()` function returns a pointer to a file which is assigned to `showfile`. If the open fails, `fopen()` returns `0` (or NULL). The routine checks for this condition and exits before any further processing is done. The `exit()` function is similar to a return, but causes an exit from the entire program and returns the value in parentheses as an integer, to the operating system. The prototype for `exit()` is in <process.h>

Once the open is successful, the `fgetc()` function is used to pull characters one at a time from the file. Look at the `while` statement for a moment. Inside the parentheses, `fgetc()` is called passing the pointer to the open file `showfile`. The return value is assigned to `ch`. This result is then compared to `EOF`.

`EOF` is a defined macro in stdio.h which is usually:

```
#define     EOF          -1
```

and represents an end-of-file condition. There is no ASCII character that has the value `-1`: they are in the range of 0 through 127 (or 0 through 255 if you include all the possible values of a character in a file). So `-1` or `EOF` is returned by the `fgetc()` function to indicate that an end of file has been reached.

Each character that is received is printed on the screen using the `putchar()` function, which takes a single character as the argument and displays it on the screen.

Opening, Closing, Reading, and Writing Files

The `fopen()` function allows several open modes, and these affect what happens to the file if it already exists. Table 9.1 summarizes the open modes and the effect on preexisting and nonexistent files.

Table 9.1. Summary of `fopen()` modes.

Open Mode	*Open Type*	*Effect on File*
`"r"`	read	The file must exist before the open.
`"w"`	write	Creates a new file destroying any copy of the file that existed before the open.
`"a"`	append (write)	The file is created if it does not exist. The file is added to at the end if it existed before the open.
`"r+"`	read /write	The file must exist before the open.
`"w+"`	read /write	Creates a new file destroying any copy of the file that existed before the open.
`"a+"`	read /append	Creates a file if it doesn't exist and appends it to an existing file.

Listing 9.2 uses two files, opened input (read) and output (write) to imitate a `COPY` command. Listing 9.2 includes some additional error checking to ensure that the program is invoked with two filenames, that both files can be opened, and that both files do not have the same name. The `strcmp()` function used for this argument is passed two strings and returns zero if they are equal and nonzero if they are not equal.

Listing 9.2. dupl.c—file copying.

```
#include <stdio.h>
#include <process.h>

FILE *infile, *outfile;

main(int argc, char *argv[])
{
     int ch;

/* Must be three arguments: program name, infile, outfile */
     if(argc < 3)
          usage();

     printf("Copying %s to %s\n", argv[1], argv[2]);

/* infile and outfile cannot have the same name */
```

```
     if(strcmp(argv[1], argv[2]) == 0)
          {
          printf("Cannot copy file into itself. \n\n");
          usage();
          }
     infile = fopen(argv[1], "r");

     if(infile == NULL)
          {
          printf("Cannot open %s. \n\n", argv[1]);
          usage();
          }

     outfile = fopen(argv[2], "w");

     if(outfile == NULL)
          {
          printf("Cannot create %s. \n\n", argv[2]);
          usage();
          }

     while( (ch = fgetc(infile)) != EOF)
          fputc(ch, outfile);

     fclose(infile);
     fclose(outfile);
     exit(0);
}


/*---------------------------------
Display syntax information and abort
---------------------------------*/
usage()
{
     printf("syntax:\n");
     printf(" dupl infile outfile \n\n");
     printf("Copies infile to outfile. \n");
     exit(0);
}
```

Errors on the command line are handled by calling a `usage()` routine that displays the syntax for the command. The `usage()` routine uses `exit()` to abort the program. The `exit()` routine is a standard library function that does some cleanup on a program, including closing all open files. The `fputc()` function prints a character to a file and is passed arguments of the character and the `FILE` pointer.

Listing 9.3 opens a file and reads in characters counting words and prints the total. This program has a slight twist. The program can be started with just a filename, or it can be started with a -w switch plus a filename. If the -w switch exists, each word is printed on the screen as it is counted.

Listing 9.3. wcount.c—word counting.

```
#include <stdio.h>
#include <ctype.h>
#include <process.h>

FILE *infile;

int show_words = 0;

long count = 0;

main(int argc, char *argv[])
{
     int ch, argi;
     char *fname;
     static char warning[] = "warning: unknown switch";

     fname = NULL;

/* 2 or 3 arguments program name, optional switch infile */
     if( (argc < 2) || (argc > 3) )
          usage();

/*
 * Step through the arguments. If the argument doesn't start
 * with '-' then use this argument as the file name.
 * If the argument starts with '-' then check if the next
 * character is 'w'. If it is then set the show_word flag.
 * If any other switches show up then print a warning message.
 */

     for(argi = 1; argi < argc; ++argi)
          {
          if( argv[argi][0] != '-')
               fname = argv[argi];
          else
          if(argv[argi][1] == 'w')
               show_words = 1;
          else
               printf("%s %c\n", warning, argv[argi][1]);
```

```
          }

/*
 * The file name should have been an argument that
 * does not start with -
 */

     if(fname == NULL)
          {
          printf("No file named. \n");
          usage();
          }

     printf("Counting words in %s.\n", fname);

     infile = fopen(fname, "r");

     if(infile == NULL)
          {
          printf("Cannot open %s.\n\n", fname);
          usage();
          }

/* Pull each character and send it to the handler */
     while( (ch = fgetc(infile)) != EOF)
          {
          handle_char(ch);
          }

     fclose(infile);

     printf("Total words = %ld\n", count);
}

/*-----------------------------------------------------------
Handle each character based on whether we are entering or
leaving white space. This function handles two activities:
counting words, and deciding what to send to the display
routine.
Word counting.
1. If entering non-space, increment the word counter. The word
   counter is only incremented for the first letter of each word
   which is good enough to get the count right.

Displaying
1. If a character is not a space, then it is automatically
   sent to the display routine.
```

continues

Listing 9.3. continued

```
2. If the character is a space, and we have just exited from a
   non-space (end of a word), then a new line is sent to
   the display routine.
---------------------------------------------------------------*/
handle_char(int ch)
{
     static inspace = 1;

     if( isspace(ch) )
          {
          if( ! inspace )
               {
               display_char('\n');
               }
          inspace = 1;
          }
     else
          {
          if( inspace )
               {
               ++count;
               }
          display_char(ch);
          inspace = 0;
          }
}

/*-------------------------------------------------------
Is passed a character, but only prints it if the show_word
switch is on.
-------------------------------------------------------*/

display_char(int ch)
{
     if(show_words)
          putchar(ch);
}

/*-----------------------------------
Display syntax information and abort
-----------------------------------*/
usage()
{
     printf("syntax:\n");
     printf(" wcount [-w] infile \n\n");
```

```
        printf("Counts words in infile.\n");
        printf("-w causes each word to be printed \n");
        exit(0);
}
```

For the purposes of this program, a word is any string of nonspace characters.

Using *stdin* and *stdout*

C provides a mechanism unlike anything in COBOL, called *redirection.* It allows a file to be opened, input, and used as if it were characters being typed at the keyboard. Another file can be opened, output, and can be used to capture all output that would normally go to the screen.

In order to understand this, it is necessary to tackle it a piece at a time. First, C considers the keyboard and screen to be stream files. When a C program is started, these two devices are opened as files (another bit of work done in the `STARTUP` code). The C program also provides `FILE` pointers through which these files can be accessed. The keyboard is called `stdin` and the CRT is called `stdout`. When a C program calls a function to print a character on a screen such as `putchar('h')`, the `putchar()` function actually just converts this into a write to the `stdout` file. Listing 9.4 is an example of what the `putchar()` and `getchar()` functions might look like in the standard library.

Listing 9.4. `putchar()` and `getchar()` become file I/O.

```
putchar(int ch)
{
        fputc(ch, stdout);
}

int getchar()
{
        int ch;

        ch = fgetc(stdin);
        return(ch);
}
```

The `stdin` and `stdout` `FILE` pointers are defined in stdio.h and are available in any program that includes stdio.h. All stream-based I/O to the screen and from the keyboard works in the same way: it is translated into a file I/O request using `stdin` or `stdout` as the `FILE` pointers.

Because all keyboard and screen I/O is already treated as file I/O, C has little trouble replacing the screen device with an output file and the keyboard device with an input file.

Listing 9.5 seems to be a rather simple program. It takes input from the keyboard and writes it to the screen until an end-of-file is encountered.

Listing 9.5. pass.c—input and output characters.

```
#include <stdio.h>

main()
{
     int ch;

     while( ( ch = getchar()) != EOF)
          putchar(ch);
}
```

If you compile and run this program under MS-DOS or UNIX, characters typed at the keyboard are echoed to the screen after each return is pressed.

Under MS-DOS, Ctrl-Z is used as an end-of-file character; UNIX uses Ctrl-D. Accordingly, you hold down the Ctrl key and press D or Z to end the program.

Using the *pass* Program

The program doesn't seem to do much until you add redirection. Redirection is signaled on the command line by an angle bracket. In the following code, the left angle bracket (<) indicates that input is to be taken from the named file rather than the keyboard.

```
pass <file.txt
```

The right angle bracket (>) indicates that output is to be sent to the named file rather than the screen. The following code takes its input from file.txt and puts the output on the screen. This is effectively a display program such as show.c using redirection instead of an explicitly named file.

```
pass <file.txt
```

The following code takes its input from file.txt and writes its output to newfile.txt instead of the screen. Thus, pass, used in this way, becomes a copy program.

```
pass <file.txt >newfile.txt
```

For a complete discussion of redirection under MS-DOS, see Appendix D, "Filters, Pipes, and Redirection."

Using redirection is common in C programs, and you will frequently read a program that seems to be taking input from the keyboard using `getchar()` and putting it on the screen using `putchar()`. It won't seem to make much sense. Usually, the comments for such a program will refer to the program as a filter that does something with `stdin` before passing it to `stdout`. It is the intention in such a program that it be used with redirected input and output.

Character versus Record I/O

The `fgetc()` and `fputc()` functions are character-based I/O. C also supports record-based I/O for stream files. Listing 9.6 reads records from a file and displays them 21 lines at a time on the screen. At the end of 21 lines the user is asked if more is wanted. Press Enter to cause another 21 lines to be displayed. Press N or Q followed by Enter to end the display.

Listing 9.6. Record-based I/O.

```
/*-----------------------------
Displays a file 21 lines at time
-----------------------------*/
#include <stdio.h>

FILE *infile;

main(argc, argv)
int argc;
char **argv;
{
     if(argc != 2)
          usage();
```

continues

Listing 9.6. continued

```
     infile = fopen(argv[1], "r");

     if(infile == NULL)
          {
          printf("File %s not found.\n", argv[1]);
          usage();
          }
     mor(infile, argv[1]);
     fclose(infile);
}

mor(inf, name)
FILE *inf;
char *name;
{
     char fbuf[81];
     int len;

     memset(fbuf, 0, 81);
     printf("== %s ==\n", name);
     while(fgets(fbuf, 79, inf))
          {
          len = strlen(fbuf);
          if(len)

               {
               --len;
               if(fbuf[len] == '\n')
                    fbuf[len] = 0;
               }
     if(!(more_filt(fbuf)))
          exit(0);
     }
     printf("End-of-file press ENTER\n");
     getchar();

}

static more_lines = 0;
#define MAX_MORE      21

more_filt(str)
char *str;
{
```

```
    int ch;

     puts(str);
     ++more_lines;
     if(more_lines < MAX_MORE)
          return(1);
     more_lines = 0;
     puts("more? ");
     ch = getchar();
     ch = toupper(ch);
     switch(ch)
          {
          case 'Q':
          case 'N':
          return(0);
          }
     return(1);
}

usage()
{
     printf("syntax: mor file.ext\n\n");
     printf("Prints a file %d lines at a time.\n",MAX_MORE);
     exit(0);
}
```

Field-Based I/O

C also supports field-based I/O. Once you realize that `printf()` and `scanf()` write to `stdout` and read from `stdin`, it does not require a long bow to reach the conclusion that there must be file versions of these functions.

The `fprintf()` function uses the exact same syntax as `printf()`, except that the first argument is a `FILE` pointer. The `fscanf()` function is identical. The first argument is also a `FILE` pointer.

The `printf()` and `scanf()` functions are actually two families of related functions, as shown in Table 9.2.

Table 9.2. The `printf()` and `scanf()` families.

Function	*To/From*
`printf(format, [arguments,...]);`	To `stdout`
`sprintf(char*, format, [arguments,...]);`	To `char` address
`fprintf(FILE*, format, [arguments,...]);`	To `FILE`
`scanf(format, arg pointer,...);`	From `stdin`
`sscanf(char*, format, arg pointer,...);`	From `char` address
`fscanf(FILE*, format, arg pointer,...);`	From `FILE`

Building a Phone Book Program with File I/O

Rather than beat the syntax of `fprintf()` and `fscanf()` to death, let's just cut to the chase and write a phone book maintenance program. But before I wrap up this chapter and start the design, we should take a look at four additional functions that operate on stream files.

Moving Around in a Stream File with *ftell()* and *fseek()*

The `ftell()` function is passed a `FILE` pointer argument and returns a long value that represents the current position in the file.

The `fseek()` function is passed a `FILE` pointer, a long offset, and a code. The code is defined in <stdio.h> and is either `SEEK_SET`, `SEEK_CUR`, or `SEEK_END`.

- `SEEK_SET` positions the `FILE` pointer to an offset from the beginning of the file such that the next I/O request will be performed at that position.
- `SEEK_CUR` seeks to an offset from the current position.

- `SEEK_END` seeks to a position from the end of the file working backwards. For `SEEK_END` to work correctly, it should be passed a negative value.

For the moment, on MS-DOS machines, `fseek()` works correctly on text files only when doing an `fseek()` from the start of the file (`SEEK_SET`), and only on a long value that was previously obtained by a call to `ftell()`. C was originally designed on a computer that stored text files with a newline as the record terminator. It became standard to program as if text records ended with only the newline terminator. The MS-DOS machine used a carriage return and a newline. When C was ported to MS-DOS, text files were read in such a way that the CR-LF (carriage-return, line-feed, or newline) was translated as a newline only. When writing to a file, a single newline in a program is translated to a CR-LF pair in the file. This keeps C programs consistent in the use of newline as a text record terminator, and still stores files on the disk with the correct CR-LF combination expected by MS-DOS. This works fairly well, but does cause problems for functions such as `fseek()` and `ftell()`.

One way around this is an extension to `fopen()` for MS-DOS files in Microsoft C compilers (and probably others). You can add an additional byte to the open mode to indicate that the open is to be in translated or untranslated mode. A `"t"` is used for translated or text mode; a `"b"` is used for untranslated mode, usually referred to as binary mode.

```
fopen("file.txt", "rt");      /* Open for reading in text mode */
fopen("file.txt", "wb");      /* Open for writing in binary mode */
```

In text mode, carriage-return-line-feed (CR-LF) combinations are translated into single line feeds (LF) on input and line-feed characters are translated to CR-LF combinations on output. MS-DOS in many cases uses Ctrl-Z as an end-of-file and in text mode, Ctrl-Z is interpreted as an end-of-file on input. When opening for reading or reading/writing, `fopen()` checks for and removes a Ctrl-Z at the end of the file if possible. This is done for the `fseek()` function, which may behave unpredictably near the end of a file if the file contains Ctrl-Z. In binary mode (untranslated), these translations are not done.

Binary mode causes complications when combined with text mode. A record read in binary mode will contain a CR-LF combination `"\r\n"` as the end of record as these are not translated. If this is written to a file that is opened for writing in text mode, the CR is passed to the file, but the LF is translated into a CR-LF pair, causing an extra CR to appear in the file. Unless you specifically need to deal with carriage returns, Ctrl-Z characters, or have some special problems with `fseek()` and `ftell()`, use text mode. This is the default for most MS-DOS C compilers, and you do not need to add the `"t"` to the open mode. Review your compiler documentation on this. You will usually find a manual section that specifically discusses text files, text processing, or stream files, and covers the CR-LF translation problem and how to deal with it. Except for exceptional problems, just don't deal with it.

The other two functions are `rewind()` and `feof()`. The `rewind()` function is passed a `FILE` pointer of an open file, and "rewinds" the file to the beginning.

The `feof()` function is passed a `FILE` pointer to an open file, and returns a nonzero value if the file is at the end, and a zero if not. It can be used for testing end of file as in

```
if(feof(file))
    printf("File is at end.\n");
```

Listing 9.7 is an example of using `fseek()`, `ftell()`, `rewind()`, and `feof()`. The program onerec.c is started by naming a text file on the command line as in

```
onerec file.txt.
```

The first 300 records are read in, but the position in the file is saved before each read, in an array of long `fpos[]`. After the file is loaded, the user is asked for a record number to display and the record number is used as an index into the array. The file is moved to that position using `rewind()` and `fseek()`, and the record is read and displayed.

As I am leading you toward a formal maintenance module, I have formalized the C code in numerous ways.

The header files string.h and stdlib.h are included. The `memset()` function used in `getstr()` is declared in string.h and the `atoi()` function used in `show_records()` is declared in stdlib.h. The remaining standard library functions are declared in stdio.h (`fopen()`, `fseek()`, `scanf()`, and so on).

The maximum number of records in this program and the maximum length of a record are defined as constants, and the defined constants are used throughout the program instead of hard coded constants. This has the advantage of allowing these to be changed by changing the `#define` statements.

Formal declarations with prototypes are made for all of the functions in this program. Each function including `main()` is given a return value, and all functions other than `main()` are made `static`. The use of the `void` data type needs some explanation.

A `void` function definition or declaration as in Listing 9.7 indicates that the function does not return any useful value. Modern C compilers such as Microsoft C/C++ 7.0 or Visual C++ check that the return type of a function is actually returned by the function and provide errors or warnings if the return value is of the wrong type. This error checking will include warnings such as "function returns no value." Using void to declare a function makes it "okay" for the function to have no return value.

A `void` inside the parentheses of a function declaration or definition indicates that the function receives no passed values.

Prototyping is an excellent way to cross-check various areas of code that commonly produce bugs. Prototyping checks the following conditions:

- Is a function being passed all the arguments it needs?
- Are the arguments of the correct type for the function?
- Is the function supposed to return a value but somehow exiting without returning a value?
- Is a higher-level function expecting a return value from a program but not actually receiving one?
- Is the function returning the correct type of value?

You will notice our old friend `getstr()` dolled up with its formal declaration and data typing.

The array of `fpos[]` file positions is initialized to `-1` as `0` is a valid return from `ftell()` for the first record.

In Listing 9.7, it is not necessary to use `rewind()` to restart the file before each `fseek()`, but is included to illustrate `rewind()`.

Listing 9.7. Using `fseek()`, `ftell()`, and `rewind()`.

```
#include <stdio.h>
#include <string.h>
#include <stdlib.h>


#define   MAX_RECS             300
#define   MAX_LEN              257

long fpos[MAX_RECS];

char buf[MAX_LEN];


/*-------------------------------------
Declarations for functions in this module
-------------------------------------*/
static void show_records(FILE*);
static void getstr(char*, int);
static void init_fpos(void);
```

continues

Listing 9.7. continued

```
int main(int argc, char *argv[])
{

     FILE *f1;
     long ftell();
     int fidx;

     init_fpos();

     f1 = fopen(argv[1],"r");
     if(f1 == 0)
          {
          printf("File %s not found.\n",argv[1]);
          return(0);
          }
     fidx = 0;

     do{
          if(feof(f1))
               break;
          fpos[fidx] = ftell(f1);
          ++fidx;
          if(fidx >= 300)
               break;
          }while(fgets(buf, MAX_LEN, f1));

     show_records(f1);
     fclose(f1);
     return(0);
}

/*-----------------------------------------------------
Ask for the record to display. If it is zero, then exit.
If the number is in range, than check if a record of
that number was actually found. If not, display a message;
otherwise, display the record.
-----------------------------------------------------*/

static void show_records(FILE *fil)
{
     char rec[4];
     int nrec;

     while(1)
          {
```

```
        printf("Record to display (1-%d)?\n", MAX_RECS);
        getstr(rec, 3);
        nrec = atoi(rec);
        if(nrec == 0)
             break;
        if((nrec < 1) || (nrec > MAX_RECS) )
             {
             printf("Record out of range.\n");
             continue;
             }
        --nrec;
        if(fpos[nrec] == -1)
             {
             printf("File not that big.");
             continue;
             }
        rewind(fil);
        fseek(fil, fpos[nrec], SEEK_SET);
        fgets(buf, MAX_LEN, fil);
        fputs(buf,stdout);
        }

}


/*------------------------------------------------------------
Uses scanf() to get len characters into receiver and clears
excess characters and \n from the input stream.
------------------------------------------------------------*/
static void getstr(char *receiver, int len)
{
     char format[20];

     sprintf(format,"%%%d[^\n]",len);  /* build format string */
     memset(receiver, 0, len);         /* clear receiver */
     scanf(format, receiver);          /* get the data */
     scanf("%*[^\n]");                 /* clear excess input */
     scanf("%*1[\n]");                 /* clear final new line */
}

void init_fpos(void)
{
     int index;

     for(index = 0; index < MAX_RECS; ++index)
          fpos[index] = -1;
}
```

Summary

Stream files are an efficient way of processing text files. C supports a wide range of routines for accessing stream files that makes it possible to use stream files as data files.

These are enough basic functions to put together a complete phone book program with file I/O. The next chapter uses these functions to design and code a complete maintenance module.

10

Basic Maintenance Modules

You now have enough material to engage in basic maintenance modules. Before I drift too far from the mother tongue (COBOL), this chapter presents a COBOL model on which maintenance modules can be based. Basic maintenance design leads to the idea of encapsulation, which should come naturally to a C programmer.

In this chapter, you will learn about:

- Basic maintenance
- Encapsulation
- Starting the C design
- Low-level screen I/O
- Testing for `#defined` values
- Menuing
- Utility routines

A review of the COBOL model will make dealing with a long C program much less painful.

Basic Maintenance

Listing 10.1 is phonemnt.cob, a complete maintenance module for a phone book with add, change, delete, look up, and display modes.

Listing 10.1. PHONEMNT.COB.

```
 IDENTIFICATION DIVISION.
 PROGRAM-ID. PHONEMNT.
* THIS PROGRAM MAINTAINS A PHONE FILE.
 ENVIRONMENT DIVISION.
 INPUT-OUTPUT SECTION.
 FILE-CONTROL.
     SELECT OPTIONAL PHONE-FILE
         ASSIGN TO "phone.bok"
         ORGANIZATION IS RELATIVE
         ACCESS MODE IS DYNAMIC
         RELATIVE KEY IS PHONE-KEY
         FILE STATUS IS DATA-FILE-STATUS.

     SELECT OPTIONAL PHONE-SEQ-FILE
         ASSIGN TO "phone.bok"
         ORGANIZATION IS RELATIVE
         ACCESS MODE IS SEQUENTIAL
         RELATIVE KEY IS PHONE-KEY
         FILE STATUS IS DATA-FILE-STATUS.


 DATA DIVISION.
 FILE SECTION.
 FD  PHONE-FILE
     LABEL RECORDS ARE STANDARD.
 01  PHONE-RECORD.
     05  PHONE-LAST-NAME       PIC X(20).
     05  PHONE-FIRST-NAME      PIC X(20).
     05  PHONE-NUMBER          PIC X(15).

 FD  PHONE-SEQ-FILE
     LABEL RECORDS ARE STANDARD.
 01  PHONE-SEQ-RECORD          PIC X(55).
```

```
 WORKING-STORAGE SECTION.

* Variables Associated with Main maintenance.
 01   SCREEN-ERROR-STATUS       PIC 9 VALUE 0.
      88 SCREEN-ENTRY-ERROR     VALUE 1.
 01   FORMATTED-QUESTION.
      05   FORMATTED-MODE       PIC X(10).
      05   FILLER               PIC X(20) VALUE
           "this record? ".

* Variables associated with FILE-IO.
 01   DATA-FILE-STATUS          PIC XX VALUE "00".
 01   PHONE-KEY                 PIC 9(6) VALUE ZEROES.
 01   WHICH-FILE                PIC X(3) VALUE SPACE.
 01   SAVE-SEARCH-KEY           PIC X(20) VALUE SPACE.

* Variables for MENU-ENTRY SECTION.
 01   MENU-TABLE.
      05   MENU-ENTRIES.
           10   MENU-1  PIC X(30) VALUE "Add Records".
           10   MENU-2  PIC X(30) VALUE "Change Records".
           10   MENU-3  PIC X(30) VALUE "Delete Records".
           10   MENU-4  PIC X(30) VALUE "Look Up a Record".
           10   MENU-5  PIC X(30) VALUE "Display Records".
           10   MENU-6  PIC X(30) VALUE SPACE.
           10   MENU-7  PIC X(30) VALUE SPACE.
           10   MENU-8  PIC X(30) VALUE SPACE.
           10   MENU-9  PIC X(30) VALUE SPACE.
      05   FILLER REDEFINES MENU-ENTRIES.
           10   MENU-ENTRY PIC X(30) OCCURS 9 TIMES.

 01   MENU-INDEX       PIC 99.
 01   MENU-PICK        PIC S9.
 01   MENU-MESSAGE     PIC X(79) VALUE SPACE.
 01   FORMATTED-MENU-PICK.
      05   FILLER          PIC X(20) VALUE SPACE.
      05   PICK-NUMBER     PIC 9.
      05   FILLER          PIC XX VALUE ". ".
      05   PICK-LITERAL    PIC X(30).

* Variables for MID-LEVEL-SCREEN SECTION.
 01   LAST-NAME-FIELD          PIC X(20) VALUE SPACE.
 01   FIRST-NAME-FIELD         PIC X(20) VALUE SPACE.
 01   NUMBER-FIELD             PIC X(15) VALUE SPACE.

 01   PROMPT-1                 PIC X(10) VALUE "Last Name".
 01   PROMPT-2                 PIC X(10) VALUE "First Name".
```

continues

Listing 10.1. continued

```
 01  PROMPT-3                PIC X(10) VALUE "Number".

* Variables for LOW-LEVEL-SCREEN SECTION.
 01  SCROLLING-MESSAGE       PIC X(79) VALUE SPACE.
 01  SCROLL-WORK             PIC X(79) VALUE SPACE.
 01  SCREEN-ROWS             PIC 99 VALUE 25.
 01  SCROLL-COUNT            PIC 99 VALUE ZEROES.
 01  AT-ROW                  PIC 99.
 01  ONE-CHAR                PIC X.

 PROCEDURE DIVISION.
 MAIN-LOGIC SECTION.
 PROGRAM-BEGIN.
     PERFORM MAINTAIN-FILE.

 EXIT-PROGRAM.
     EXIT PROGRAM.
 STOP-RUN.
     STOP RUN.

*-----------------------------------------------------------
 BASIC-MAINTENANCE SECTION.
*-----------------------------------------------------------
 MAINTAIN-FILE.
     PERFORM MENU-9.
     PERFORM MAINTAIN-RECORDS
         UNTIL MENU-PICK = 0.

 MAINTAIN-RECORDS.
     IF MENU-PICK = 1
         PERFORM ADD-RECORD
     ELSE
     IF MENU-PICK = 2
         PERFORM CHANGE-RECORD
     ELSE
     IF MENU-PICK = 3
         PERFORM DELETE-RECORD
     ELSE
     IF MENU-PICK = 4
         PERFORM LOOK-UP-RECORD
     ELSE
     IF MENU-PICK = 5
         PERFORM DISPLAY-RECORDS.

     PERFORM MENU-9.
```

```
ADD-RECORD.
    PERFORM OPEN-APPEND-DATA-FILE.
    PERFORM ADD-RECORD-INIT.
    PERFORM ADD-RECORD-ENTRY.
    PERFORM CLOSE-DATA-FILE.

ADD-RECORD-INIT.
    PERFORM CLEAR-SCREEN-FIELDS.

ADD-RECORD-ENTRY.
    MOVE 0 TO SCREEN-ERROR-STATUS.
    PERFORM ENTER-FIELDS.
    PERFORM VALIDATE-FIELDS.
    IF SCREEN-ENTRY-ERROR
        PERFORM ERROR-MESSAGE
        GO TO ADD-RECORD-ENTRY
    ELSE
        PERFORM LOAD-RECORD
        PERFORM WRITE-DATA-RECORD.

CHANGE-RECORD.
    PERFORM OPEN-IO-DATA-FILE.
    MOVE "Change" TO FORMATTED-MODE.
    PERFORM ENTER-KEY.
    IF DATA-FILE-STATUS NOT = "10"
        PERFORM CHANGE-RECORD-INIT
        PERFORM CHANGE-RECORD-ENTRY
    ELSE
        PERFORM RECORD-NOT-FOUND.
    PERFORM CLOSE-DATA-FILE.

CHANGE-RECORD-INIT.
    PERFORM LOAD-SCREEN.

CHANGE-RECORD-ENTRY.
    MOVE 0 TO SCREEN-ERROR-STATUS.
    PERFORM ENTER-FIELDS.
    IF SCREEN-ENTRY-ERROR
        PERFORM ERROR-MESSAGE
        GO TO CHANGE-RECORD-ENTRY
    ELSE
        PERFORM RELOAD-RECORD
        PERFORM REWRITE-DATA-RECORD.

ENTER-KEY.
    PERFORM ENTER-KEY-ENTRY.
    PERFORM CHECK-IF-CORRECT-KEY.
```

continues

Listing 10.1. continued

```
CHECK-IF-CORRECT-KEY.
    PERFORM CLEAR-SCREEN.
    PERFORM LOAD-SCREEN.
    PERFORM DISPLAY-FIELDS.
    PERFORM THIS-ONE.
    IF ONE-CHAR NOT = "y" AND "Y"
        PERFORM FIND-NEXT-DATA-RECORD
        IF DATA-FILE-STATUS NOT = "10"
             GO TO CHECK-IF-CORRECT-KEY.

ENTER-KEY-ENTRY.
    PERFORM CLEAR-SCREEN.
    MOVE 0 TO SCREEN-ERROR-STATUS.
    PERFORM GET-KEY-ENTRY.
    PERFORM VALIDATE-KEY.
    IF SCREEN-ENTRY-ERROR
        PERFORM ERROR-MESSAGE
        GO TO ENTER-KEY-ENTRY
    ELSE
        PERFORM FIND-DATA-RECORD.

THIS-ONE.
    MOVE 1 TO SCROLL-COUNT.
    PERFORM SCROLL-UP.
    MOVE FORMATTED-QUESTION TO SCROLLING-MESSAGE.
    PERFORM SCROLL-MESSAGE.
    PERFORM GET-ONE-CHAR.

DELETE-RECORD.
    PERFORM OPEN-IO-DATA-FILE.
    MOVE "Delete" TO FORMATTED-MODE.
    PERFORM ENTER-KEY.
    IF DATA-FILE-STATUS NOT = "10"
        PERFORM DELETE-DATA-RECORD
    ELSE
        PERFORM RECORD-NOT-FOUND.
    PERFORM CLOSE-DATA-FILE.

LOOK-UP-RECORD.
    PERFORM OPEN-INPUT-DATA-FILE.
    MOVE "Stop at" TO FORMATTED-MODE.
    PERFORM ENTER-KEY.
    IF DATA-FILE-STATUS NOT = "10"
        NEXT SENTENCE
    ELSE
        PERFORM RECORD-NOT-FOUND.
```

```
    PERFORM CLOSE-DATA-FILE.


DISPLAY-RECORDS.
    PERFORM OPEN-INPUT-DATA-FILE.
    PERFORM READ-NEXT-DATA-RECORD.
    PERFORM DISPLAY-EACH-RECORD
        UNTIL DATA-FILE-STATUS = "10".
    PERFORM CLOSE-DATA-FILE.

DISPLAY-EACH-RECORD.
    PERFORM CLEAR-SCREEN.
    PERFORM LOAD-SCREEN.
    PERFORM DISPLAY-FIELDS.
    PERFORM PRESS-ENTER.
    PERFORM READ-NEXT-DATA-RECORD.

DISPLAY-STUB.
    PERFORM CLEAR-SCREEN.
    PERFORM MESSAGE-AT-CENTER.
    PERFORM PRESS-ENTER.

PRESS-ENTER.
    MOVE "Press ENTER to continue. . ." TO SCROLLING-MESSAGE
    PERFORM SCROLL-MESSAGE.
    PERFORM GET-ONE-CHAR.

*--------------------------------------------------------------
PHONE-MAINTENANCE SECTION.
*--------------------------------------------------------------

ENTER-FIELDS.
    PERFORM GET-ENTRIES.

DISPLAY-FIELDS.
    PERFORM DISPLAY-ENTRIES.

VALIDATE-FIELDS.
    PERFORM VALIDATE-KEY.

VALIDATE-KEY.
    IF LAST-NAME-FIELD = SPACE
        MOVE 1 TO SCREEN-ERROR-STATUS.

CLEAR-SCREEN-FIELDS.
    MOVE SPACE TO
        LAST-NAME-FIELD
```

continues

Listing 10.1. continued

```
          FIRST-NAME-FIELD
          NUMBER-FIELD.

 RELOAD-RECORD.
      IF LAST-NAME-FIELD NOT = SPACE
          MOVE LAST-NAME-FIELD TO PHONE-LAST-NAME.
      IF FIRST-NAME-FIELD NOT = SPACE
          MOVE FIRST-NAME-FIELD TO PHONE-FIRST-NAME.
      IF NUMBER-FIELD NOT = SPACE
          MOVE NUMBER-FIELD TO PHONE-NUMBER.

 LOAD-RECORD.
      MOVE LAST-NAME-FIELD TO PHONE-LAST-NAME.
      MOVE FIRST-NAME-FIELD TO PHONE-FIRST-NAME.
      MOVE NUMBER-FIELD TO PHONE-NUMBER.

 LOAD-SCREEN.
      MOVE PHONE-LAST-NAME TO LAST-NAME-FIELD.
      MOVE PHONE-FIRST-NAME TO FIRST-NAME-FIELD.
      MOVE PHONE-NUMBER TO NUMBER-FIELD.

 GET-ENTRIES.
     PERFORM GET-KEY-ENTRY.
     DISPLAY PROMPT-2 " ? ".
     ACCEPT FIRST-NAME-FIELD.
     DISPLAY PROMPT-3 " ? ".
     ACCEPT NUMBER-FIELD.

 GET-KEY-ENTRY.
     DISPLAY PROMPT-1 " ? ".
     ACCEPT LAST-NAME-FIELD.

 DISPLAY-ENTRIES.
     DISPLAY PROMPT-1 " : " LAST-NAME-FIELD.
     DISPLAY PROMPT-2 " : " FIRST-NAME-FIELD.
     DISPLAY PROMPT-3 " : " NUMBER-FIELD.

*--------------------------------------------------------------
 FILE-IO SECTION.
*--------------------------------------------------------------
 OPEN-APPEND-DATA-FILE.
      OPEN EXTEND PHONE-SEQ-FILE.
      MOVE "SEQ" TO WHICH-FILE.

 OPEN-IO-DATA-FILE.
      PERFORM OPEN-APPEND-DATA-FILE.
      PERFORM CLOSE-DATA-FILE.
```

```
    OPEN I-O PHONE-FILE.
    MOVE "DYN" TO WHICH-FILE.

OPEN-INPUT-DATA-FILE.
    PERFORM OPEN-APPEND-DATA-FILE.
    PERFORM CLOSE-DATA-FILE.
    OPEN INPUT PHONE-FILE.
    MOVE "DYN" TO WHICH-FILE.

CLOSE-DATA-FILE.
    IF WHICH-FILE = "DYN"
        CLOSE PHONE-FILE
    ELSE
        CLOSE PHONE-SEQ-FILE.
    MOVE SPACE TO WHICH-FILE.

READ-NEXT-DATA-RECORD.
    READ PHONE-FILE NEXT RECORD
        AT END MOVE "10" TO DATA-FILE-STATUS.

READ-DATA-RECORD.
    READ PHONE-FILE
        INVALID KEY MOVE "23" TO DATA-FILE-STATUS.

WRITE-DATA-RECORD.
    WRITE PHONE-SEQ-RECORD FROM PHONE-RECORD.

REWRITE-DATA-RECORD.
    REWRITE PHONE-RECORD.

DELETE-DATA-RECORD.
    DELETE PHONE-FILE RECORD.

FIND-DATA-RECORD.
    MOVE LAST-NAME-FIELD TO SAVE-SEARCH-KEY.
    MOVE 1  TO PHONE-KEY.
    PERFORM START-NLT-PHONE-KEY.
    IF DATA-FILE-STATUS NOT = "10"
        PERFORM FIND-NEXT-DATA-RECORD.

FIND-NEXT-DATA-RECORD.
    PERFORM READ-NEXT-DATA-RECORD.
    IF DATA-FILE-STATUS NOT = "10"
        IF PHONE-LAST-NAME NOT = SAVE-SEARCH-KEY
            GO TO FIND-NEXT-DATA-RECORD.

START-NLT-PHONE-KEY.
```

continues

Listing 10.1. continued

```
    START PHONE-FILE KEY NOT LESS THAN PHONE-KEY
        INVALID KEY MOVE "10" TO DATA-FILE-STATUS.

*------------------------------------------------------------
 MENU-ENTRY SECTION.
*------------------------------------------------------------
 MENU-9.
     MOVE SPACE TO MENU-MESSAGE.
     PERFORM MENU-ROUTINE.

 MENU-ROUTINE.
     PERFORM DISPLAY-MENU.
     PERFORM GET-PICK.
     IF MENU-PICK = ZERO
         NEXT SENTENCE
     ELSE
     IF MENU-PICK < 0
         MOVE "Invalid Entry" TO MENU-MESSAGE
         GO TO MENU-ROUTINE
     ELSE
         MOVE MENU-PICK TO MENU-INDEX
         IF MENU-ENTRY(MENU-INDEX) = SPACE
             MOVE "Invalid Entry" TO MENU-MESSAGE
             GO TO MENU-ROUTINE.

 DISPLAY-MENU.
     PERFORM CLEAR-SCREEN.

     MOVE MENU-MESSAGE TO SCROLLING-MESSAGE.
     PERFORM SCROLL-MESSAGE.
     MOVE 3 TO SCROLL-COUNT.
     PERFORM SCROLL-UP.

     MOVE "Please Select:" TO SCROLLING-MESSAGE.
     PERFORM SCROLL-MESSAGE.
     MOVE 1 TO SCROLL-COUNT.
     PERFORM SCROLL-UP.

     PERFORM DISPLAY-ONE-MENU-PICK
         VARYING MENU-INDEX FROM 1 BY 1
           UNTIL MENU-INDEX > 9.

     MOVE 3 TO SCROLL-COUNT.
     PERFORM SCROLL-UP.
```

```
    MOVE 0 TO PICK-NUMBER.
    MOVE "Exit" TO PICK-LITERAL.
    MOVE FORMATTED-MENU-PICK TO SCROLLING-MESSAGE.
    MOVE 20 TO AT-ROW.
    PERFORM MESSAGE-AT-ROW.


DISPLAY-ONE-MENU-PICK.
    IF MENU-ENTRY(MENU-INDEX) NOT = SPACE
        MOVE MENU-ENTRY(MENU-INDEX) TO
            PICK-LITERAL
        MOVE MENU-INDEX TO PICK-NUMBER
        MOVE FORMATTED-MENU-PICK TO SCROLLING-MESSAGE
        PERFORM SCROLL-MESSAGE.

GET-PICK.
    PERFORM GET-ONE-CHAR.

    MOVE ONE-CHAR TO MENU-PICK WITH CONVERSION
        ON EXCEPTION MOVE -1 TO MENU-PICK.

*------------------------------------------------------------
MID-LEVEL-SCREEN SECTION.
*------------------------------------------------------------

ERROR-MESSAGE.
   PERFORM CLEAR-SCREEN.
   MOVE "An error occurred during entry"
       TO SCROLLING-MESSAGE.
   PERFORM MESSAGE-AT-CENTER.
   PERFORM PRESS-ENTER.

PLEASE-WAIT.
   PERFORM CLEAR-SCREEN.
   MOVE "Please Wait" TO SCROLLING-MESSAGE.
   PERFORM MESSAGE-AT-CENTER.

RECORD-NOT-FOUND.
   PERFORM CLEAR-SCREEN.
   MOVE "Record not Found" TO SCROLLING-MESSAGE.
   PERFORM MESSAGE-AT-CENTER.
   PERFORM PRESS-ENTER.

PRESS-ENTER.
   MOVE "Press ENTER to continue. . ." TO SCROLLING-MESSAGE
   PERFORM SCROLL-MESSAGE.
   PERFORM GET-ONE-CHAR.
```

continues

Listing 10.1. continued

```
*--------------------------------------------------------------
 LOW-LEVEL-SCREEN SECTION.
*--------------------------------------------------------------

 CLEAR-SCREEN.
     MOVE SPACE TO SCROLL-WORK.
     PERFORM DISPLAY-SCROLL-WORK SCREEN-ROWS TIMES.

 SCROLL-UP.
     MOVE SPACE TO SCROLL-WORK.
     PERFORM DISPLAY-SCROLL-WORK SCROLL-COUNT TIMES.

 SCROLL-MESSAGE.
     MOVE SCROLLING-MESSAGE TO SCROLL-WORK.
     PERFORM DISPLAY-SCROLL-WORK.

 DISPLAY-SCROLL-WORK.
     DISPLAY SCROLL-WORK.

 MESSAGE-AT-ROW.
     IF AT-ROW > SCREEN-ROWS
         SUBTRACT SCREEN-ROWS FROM AT-ROW
         GO TO MESSAGE-AT-ROW.
     COMPUTE SCROLL-COUNT = SCREEN-ROWS - AT-ROW - 1.
     PERFORM SCROLL-MESSAGE.
     PERFORM SCROLL-UP.

 MESSAGE-AT-CENTER.
     COMPUTE AT-ROW = SCREEN-ROWS / 2.
     PERFORM MESSAGE-AT-ROW.

 GET-ONE-CHAR.
     MOVE SPACE TO ONE-CHAR.
     ACCEPT ONE-CHAR.
```

The phonemnt.cob program uses the irreducible minimum for screen I/O, doing all the work through `DISPLAY` and `ACCEPT` verbs. Most COBOL languages come with a vendor-specific screen-handling routine. I have avoided these "screen handlers," to keep the COBOL as vanilla as possible.

The program maintains a relative file containing last name, first name, and phone number. In change, delete, and lookup mode, the last name is treated as a key value, and the user is asked for a last name in order to locate the record to process.

Encapsulation

Listing 10.1 is broken into sections that represent discrete sets of activities within the program. The sections communicate with each other through variables and there is an effort to isolate the sections from one another. This is a sensible practice in COBOL. It allows you to use phonemnt.cob as a boilerplate for other maintenance modules by changing those sections that are file and screen input-specific.

In order to create a new maintenance module, the `BASIC-MAINTENANCE`, `LOW-LEVEL-SCREEN`, `MID-LEVEL-SCREEN` and `MENU-ENTRY` sections do not need to change at all. A few changes in the `PHONE-MAINTENANCE` sections plus a few global search and replaces in the `FILE-IO` section will convert this to a maintenance module for any other file.

- The `LOW-LEVEL-SCREEN` section takes care of row positioning, displaying messages, scrolling the screen, and getting a single character input.
- The `MENU-ENTRY` section displays and accepts values for a generic nine pick menu.
- The `MID-LEVEL-SCREEN` section carries generic warnings and other messages to be displayed on the screen.
- The `BASIC-MAINTENANCE` section is a skeleton for maintenance that relies heavily on the `PHONE-MAINTENANCE` and `FILE-IO` sections for services.

Aside from a few tricks, this is a pretty standard maintenance module. When a file is opened, it is first opened in append (extend) mode to ensure that the file exists. This avoids logic to do with creating the file if it does not exist. Because of COBOL restrictions on file `OPENS`, it is necessary to have two `SELECT` and `FD` entries to allow for opening in `EXTEND` mode. The two-file problem means that the `CLOSE-DATA-FILE` paragraph needs a flag to tell it which file to close.

The program does all adds in append mode, all lookup and display in input mode, and all delete and change in I/O mode.

In change mode, it allows you to press Enter on an empty field without changing the field in the file, as it uses `RELOAD-RECORD` to verify that the entry fields are not blank before moving the data to the record.

Starting the C Design

It is possible to encapsulate a C version of this program in a similar way. The design here and in Chapter 11, "Phone Book Maintenance," breaks the sections into separate C modules.

In COBOL, the parts of phonemnt.cob that are common to all maintenance are left untouched, while the main program is edited to change the maintenance to some other file.

In C, the generic routines would be separated into individual C source code files, compiled, and linked with other modules containing the file specific parts. This modular design concept is inherent in C work, and you should start to think of projects in this way rather than think of each program as a separate and complete entity on its own.

There is an old saw that the best time to design a program is after it is written. I have had the luxury of writing these programs and modules to test them, and then tidying them up so that everything fits neatly together. In the real world, this doesn't happen, but it is helpful to see something broken into pigeon holes and nicely categorized. Several of the routines used for this maintenance module are generic enough that they can become a library of routines, and are not specific to the phone maintenance program.

Low-Level Screen I/O

Low-level screen I/O is a relative term, and an arbitrary point at which I decided to create a module. Listing 10.2 includes two types of routines: routines to print data on the screen, and routines to get input from the keyboard.

Listing 10.2. Screenlo.c—low-level screen I/O.

```
/*------------------
screenlo.c

Low level screen IO
------------------*/

#include "screenlo.h"


/*----------------------------------------------
          Positioning and printing routines
----------------------------------------------*/

/*----------------------------------------------
Scroll up a number of lines by printing a newline
to the screen.
----------------------------------------------*/
```

```
void scroll_up(int count)
{
     while(count--)
          printf("\n");
}

/*--------------------------------
Clear screen with SCREEN_ROW scrolls
--------------------------------*/
void cls(void)
{
     scroll_up(SCREEN_ROWS);
}

/*----------------------------------
Print a message and scroll up one line
----------------------------------*/
void scroll_message(char *message)
{
     printf("%s\n", message);
}


/*------------------------------------------------------------
Print a message and scroll up to position the message
at a specific row.

1.   Use the remainder operator to force row into 0 - 24 range.
2.   Rows to Scroll is SCREEN_ROWS - row - 1
3.   Print the message
4.   Scroll up
------------------------------------------------------------*/
void message_at_row(int row, char *message)
{
     row %= SCREEN_ROWS;
     row = (SCREEN_ROWS - row) - 1;
     scroll_message(message);
     scroll_up(row);
}

void message_at_center(char *message)
{
     message_at_row(SCREEN_ROWS / 2, message);
}
```

continues

Listing 10.2. continued

```
/*------------------------------------------------------------
          Character and String Entry routines
--------------------------------------------------*/

/*--------------------------------------------------------
Pick up a single character from the keyboard and return it,
or -1 if only ENTER was pressed.
--------------------------------------------------------*/
int get_one_char(void)
{
     int pick, ch;

     pick = -1;
     while( (ch = getchar()) != '\n')
          pick = ch;
     return(pick);
}

/*-------------------------------------------------
Uses scanf() to get len characters into receiver and
clears excess characters and the final \n from the
input stream.
-------------------------------------------------*/
char *getstr(char *receiver, int len)
{
     char format[20];

     /* build format string */
     sprintf(format, "%%%d[^\n]",len);

     scanf(format, receiver); /* get the data */
     scanf("%*[^\n]");      /* clear excess input */
     scanf("%*1[\n]");      /* clear final new line */
     return(receiver);
}
```

Routines to print to the screen include the following:

- Scroll up a number of lines.
- Clear the screen by scrolling a screenful of lines.
- Print a single line followed by a newline.

- Print a string and scroll it up a number of lines to position it at a specific row.
- Print a message and scroll it to the center of the screen.

Routines to get keyboard input include getting a single character followed by the Enter key. This routine returns the last key struck before the Enter key is pressed, or `-1` if only Enter is pressed. A second routine is another incarnation of `getstr()`.

Nothing comparable to `getstr()` appeared in phonemnt.cob because COBOL requires that an `ACCEPT` verb use a named variable. C allows a generic string input routine, so I have created one in screenlo.c

Throughout Listing 10.2, you will see reference to `SCREEN_ROWS`. This is a constant defined in screenlo.h.

Testing for *#defined* Values

Before you take a look at the header file for screenlo.c you need to learn a few new C preprocessor commands.

C includes a preprocessor command that allows you to define text substitution macros. The `#define` directive was discussed in Chapter 8, "Scope, Storage, and Prototyping." An example would be

```
#define SCREEN_ROWS 25
```

These defined values are sometimes called manifest constants. C also includes directives that allow you to test whether such a `#define` exists, and to conditionally compile a portion of code or not.

In Listing 10.3, the program is set up so that as the compiler is processing the source code, it checks to see if a #define `SCREEN_ROWS` exists. If it does, the compiler compiles the line

```
row = SCREEN_ROWS;
```

otherwise it compiles the line

```
row = 24;
```

This is called conditional compilation and is used extensively in C.

Listing 10.3. Using `#ifdef-#else-#endif`.

```
void last_row_message(char *msg)
{
     int row, col;

#ifdef     SCREEN_ROWS
     row = SCREEN_ROWS;
#else
     row = 24;
#endif

     col = 1;
     move_to(row, col);
     printf(msg);
}
```

The `#ifndef` (if not defined) is the complement of `#ifdef` as shown in Listing 10.4 which `#defines` `SCREEN_ROWS` if it has not already been defined.

Listing 10.4. Using `#ifndef`.

```
#ifndef   SCREEN_ROWS

#define   SCREEN_ROWS    24

#endif


void last_row_message(char *msg)
{
     int row, col;

     row = SCREEN_ROWS;
     col = 1;
     move_to(row, col);
     printf(msg);
}
```

The important thing to remember about `#ifdef` and family is that they control what code is compiled. This is not code that is executed while the program is running. Conditional compilation is somewhat similar to COBOL debugging lines. COBOL allows you

to place a `'D'` in column 7 to create a debugging line. This line is compiled depending on compiler options. Some COBOL compilers use `"WITH DEBUGGING MODE"` as a clause in the `SOURCE-COMPUTER` paragraph; others have a debugging switch at compile time. In either case, lines that contain a `'D'` in column 7 disappear when debugging is turned off.

Conditional compilation in C is much more powerful and is used to control the compilation of large areas of source code. Listing 10.5 is an example of debugging style logic. The entry and exit from each routine is passed to a function that displays this information if `DEBUGGING` is defined. Commenting of the #define of `DEBUGGING` eliminates the code that calls the functions, and eliminates the `entering()` and `exiting()` functions which are presumably only used for debugging.

Notice that `DEBUGGING` does not have to be defined with a value.

```
#define    DEBUGGING
```

is enough. Now `#ifdef DEBUGGING` will return TRUE and the appropriate pieces of code will be compiled.

Listing 10.5. Using `#ifdef` for debugging.

```
#define    DEBUGGING /* Comment out when not debugging */

some_func()
{
#ifdef    DEBUGGING
     entering("some_func");
#endif

/*
     Some real logic here
*/

#ifdef    DEBUGGING
     exiting("some_func");
#endif
}

#ifdef    DEBUGGING
entering(char *func_name)
{
     printf("Entering %s()\n", func_name);
}

exiting(char *func_name)
```

continues

Listing 10.5. continued

```
{
     printf("Exiting %s()\n", func_name);
}

#endif
```

Newer compilers use a preferred syntax for this test, as shown in Listing 10.6.

Listing 10.6. Testing for a defined constant.

```
some_func()
{
#if  defined(DEBUGGING)
     entering("some_func");
#endif

/*
     Some real logic here
*/

#if  defined(DEBUGGING)
     exiting("some_func");
#endif
}
```

The `#ifndef` command may be coded

```
#if  !defined(DEBUGGING)
```

This command is commonly used to prevent a file from being included twice during a compile.

The technique is illustrated in Listings 10.7 and 10.8, which show two alternative methods.

Listing 10.7. Preventing a double `#include`.

```
#ifndef   SOME_VALUE
#define   SOME_VALUE
```

```
(text of the file)

#endif     /* SOME_VALUE */
```

Listing 10.8. Preventing a double `#include`.

```
#ifndef   SOME_VALUE

(text of the file)

#define   SOME_VALUE
#endif
```

Everything between the `#ifndef` and the `#endif` is processed if `SOME_VALUE` has not been defined. This includes processing the line that defines `SOME_VALUE`. If the header file appears twice in the compilation for any reason, it is ignored the second time because `SOME_VALUE` was defined the first time the file was processed.

At first glance, this doesn't seem to be a problem—until you realize that `#include` files can be nested. An `#include` file can itself contain a command to `#include` another file. This nesting could get messy if a file included a file which in turn included the original file. This situation would normally cause a major headache for the compiler, but is avoided by using this exclusion trick.

Listing 10.9 is the header file for screenlo.c. The first line of the file is a line containing an `#ifndef` exclusion method.

Listing 10.9. screenlo.h—the header file for screenlo.c.

```
#ifndef _SCREENLO_H
#define _SCREENLO_H
#include <stdio.h>

/*-----------------
Screen size in rows
-----------------*/
#define   SCREEN_ROWS    25

/*--------
prototypes
--------*/
```

continues

Listing 10.9. continued

```
void scroll_up(int), cls(void), scroll_message(char *),
          message_at_row(int, char *), message_at_center(char *);

int       get_one_char(void);
char *getstr(char *, int);


#endif     /* _SCREENLO_H */
```

The screenlo.h file itself includes <stdio.h> rather than including it in screenlo.c. This is a matter of preference. If double inclusion is prevented within stdio.h, it is handy to have everything that is needed for screenlo.c in one header file.

The rest of the file is fairly straightforward. `SCREEN_ROWS` which appeared in screenlo.c is defined as 25 and prototypes for all the functions are declared.

Menuing

Listing 10.10 is `menu9()` and support routines. The `menu9()` function can be passed an array of up to nine pointers to strings. These will be displayed in a menu on the screen numbered `1` through `9` along with a `0. Exit` line. The `menu9()` routine accepts a single value from the user and translates it to a numeric value. If the selection is within the range of picks, it returns the value, otherwise it provides an invalid entry message. Listing 10.11 is the header file for menu9.c.

Listing 10.10. menu9.c.

```
#include "menu9.h"

static char menu_message[79];
static int npicks;

/*------------------------------------------
Prototypes for local functions in this module.
------------------------------------------*/
static void display_menu (char *[]);
```

```
static int get_pick(void);

/*--------------------------------------------------
Displays up to 9 menu entries numbered 1 through 9 and
accepts user input and returns the number entered.
Array of pointers to strings must end with a NULL value.
--------------------------------------------------*/
int menu9(char *menu[])
{
     int pick;

     strcpy(menu_message,"");
     while(1)
          {
          display_menu(menu);
          strcpy(menu_message,"");
          pick = get_pick();
          if(pick == 0)
               return(0);
          if( (pick > npicks) || (pick < 1) )
               strcpy(menu_message, "Invalid selection");
          else
               return(pick);
          }
}

/*----------------------------------------------
Display the menu message and up to 9 lines of menu
followed by 0. Exit
----------------------------------------------*/
static void display_menu( char *menu[])
{
     int index;
     char buf[81];

     cls();
     scroll_message(menu_message);
     scroll_up(3);
     scroll_message("\tPlease Select:");
     scroll_up(1);
     for(index = 0; (menu[index]) && (index < 9); ++index)
          {
          sprintf(buf, "\t\t%d. %s", index + 1, menu[index]);
          scroll_message(buf);
          }
     scroll_up(3);
     message_at_row(20, "\t\t0. Exit");
     npicks = index;
```

continues

Listing 10.10. continued

```
}

/*------------------------------------------------------
Get a user key and pull all remaining characters up to and
including the newline. Return -1 if the entry is not
numeric, otherwise return the numeric value of the entry.
Pick is left set to the last character entered before the
newline.
------------------------------------------------------*/
static int get_pick(void)
{
     int pick;

     pick = get_one_char();

     if( !(isdigit(pick) ) )
          return(-1);
/*
 * Convert pick to a numeric value by subtracting
 * the ASCII value for the character '0' and return it.
 */
     pick -= '0';
     return(pick);
}
```

Listing 10.11. menu9.h.

```
#ifndef _MENU9_H
#define _MENU9_H

#include <stdio.h>
#include <ctype.h>
#include <string.h>

#include "screenlo.h"

/*-------------------------------
Prototypes for routines in menu9.c
-------------------------------*/

int menu9(char *text[]);

#endif /* _MENU9_H */
```

Listing 10.12 is a simple program to test `menu9()` and some of the routines in screenlo.c. Compile and link this with

```
cl test9.c menu9.c screenlo.c
```

or the equivalent for your C compiler. The resulting test9.exe can be used to check what happens when an invalid entry is entered, and that correct values are returned.

Listing 10.12. test9.c—testing `menu9()`.

```
/*-----------
Tests menu9()
-----------*/

#include "menu9.h"

static void say_what(char *msg);

char *main_menu[]={
     {"Line 1"},
     {"Line 2"},
     {"Line 3"},
     {NULL}};

int main()
{
     int pick;

     while(1)
          {
          pick = menu9(main_menu);
          switch(pick)
               {
               case 1:
                    say_what("1");
                    break;
               case 2:
                    say_what("Picked 2");
                    break;
               case 3:
                    say_what("Picked 3");
                    break;
               case 0:
                    say_what("Exiting");
                    cls();
                    return(0);
```

continues

Listing 10.12. continued

```
                }
            }
}


/*-------------------------------------------
Display the users pick and wait for ENTER key
-------------------------------------------*/
static void say_what(char *msg)
{
     char buf[81];

     sprintf(buf, "Picked %s", msg);
     scroll_message(buf);
     scroll_message("Press ENTER . . ");
     get_one_char();
}
```

Utility Routines

There are a couple of utility routines that will be needed for this project that have appeared in earlier chapters in one form or another. They are included in Listing 10.13, util.c, and 10.14, util.h, the associated header file. As I've said before, the advantage of designing after the program is written is that all this looks so well planned out.

Listing 10.13. util.c.

```
/*---------------------
General purpose routines
---------------------*/

#include "util.h"

/*-------------------------------
Truncate to last non blank character
-------------------------------*/
void trunc(char *str)
{
```

```
     int len;

     while( len = strlen(str))
          {
          --len;
          if(isspace(str[len]))
               str[len] = 0;
          else
               break;
          }

}

/*-----------------------------------------------------------------
Test each character for a space. Stop when a NUL is encountered
or a non-space.
If a non-space is encountered, return 0, otherwise return TRUE
----------------------------------------------------------------*/

int field_is_blank(char *str, int len)
{
     while( (len) && (*str))
          {
          if( !(isspace(*str)) )
               return(0);
          --len;
          ++str;
          }
     return(1);
}
```

Listing 10.14. util.h.

```
#ifndef _UTIL_H
#define   _UTIL_H

#include <ctype.h>
#include <string.h>

int field_is_blank(char*, int);
void trunc(char*);

#endif     /* _UTIL_H */
```

These three files could be combined into a library for use in other maintenance modules or menuing programs.

Summary

Encapsulation is important in C. Modules such as those in this chapter can be written independently of file-specific information and saved in their own library. If a program needs a nine-pick menu, even if it is not a maintenance module, it can be linked to `menu9()` without having to rewrite the code for the menu.

You've got a good start on maintenance in C, and in the next chapter you'll wrap up the whole project.

11

Phone Book Maintenance

Here we continue the work started in the previous chapter.

In this chapter you will learn about:

- Mid-level screen I/O
- Add, change, and delete
- Record layout
- File I/O
- The phone book maintenance module
- Modular maintenance

The first two sections are a continuation of the generic sections begun in the previous chapter.

Mid-Level Screen I/O

The screenmd.c module incorporates routines from the `MID-LEVEL-SCREEN` section in phonemnt.cob (Listing 10.1) but also includes the new routines `get_entries()`, `get_entry()`, and `display_entries()`. If you check phonemnt.cob, you will find that these routines were incorporated in the `PHONE-MAINTENANCE` section because they depended on displaying and accepting specific variable fields.

You may notice that `get_entries()` and `print_entries()` are variations on the routines developed in Listing 8.15 that are passed arrays of pointers to strings. Because these routines can be separated from the shape of the data, they are encapsulated as mid-level screen routines.

Listing 11.1. screenmd.c.

```
#include <stdio.h>
#include "screenmd.h"

/*--------------------------------------------------
               Data Entry and Display Routines
--------------------------------------------------*/


void get_entries(char *string[], char *receiver[], int width[])
{
     int index;

     for(index = 0; string[index][0] != 0; ++index)
          {
          get_entry(string[index],
               receiver[index], width[index]);
          }
}

/*--------------------------------------
Input a single string for specified width.
Truncate to last non-blank character
--------------------------------------*/
void get_entry(char *string, char *receiver, int width)
{
     char buf[81];

     sprintf(buf, "%s ?", string);
     scroll_message(buf);
```

```
     getstr(receiver, width);
     trunc(receiver);
}

/*-----------------------------------
Display a list of prompts and receivers
-----------------------------------*/
void display_entries(char *string[], char *receiver[])
{
     int index;
     char buf[81];

     for(index = 0; string[index][0] != 0; ++index)
          {
          sprintf(buf, "%s: %s",
               string[index], receiver[index]);
          scroll_message(buf);
          }
}

/*-----------------------------------------
               General Messages
-----------------------------------------*/

/*-------------
An error message
-------------*/
void error_msg(void)
{
     cls();
     scroll_message("An error occurred during entry.");
     scroll_up(1);
     press_enter();
}

void press_enter(void)
{
     message_at_center("Press ENTER to continue. . . .");
     getchar();
}

void record_not_found(void)
{
     cls();
     scroll_message("Record not found.");
     scroll_up(1);
     press_enter();
```

continues

Listing 11.1. continued

```
}


void please_wait(void)
{
     cls();
     message_at_center("\t\tPlease Wait . . . .");
}
```

Listing 11.2 is the rather simple header file for screenmd.c.

Listing 11.2. screenmd.h.

```
#ifndef _SCREENMD_H
#define  _SCREENMD_H

#include "screenlo.h"
#include "util.h"

/*-------------------------------------------------------
Prototypes for data entry routines and utility messages.
-----------------------------------------------------*/

void get_entries(char *[], char *[], int []);
void get_entry( char *, char *, int);
void display_entries(char *[], char *[]);

void     error_msg(void), press_enter(void),
     record_not_found(void), please_wait(void);

#endif     /* _SCREENMD_H */
```

Add, Change, and Delete

Listing 11.3 is maintain.c. This incorporates the high-level maintenance logic in the `BASIC-MAINTENANCE` section. It includes an extra routine for file compression, which you will see is needed once you get into file I/O. There is also a routine for printing the file

which is not implemented in this version, but it gives you an idea of the extendibility of the menu routine.

Listing 11.3. maintain.c.

```
/*---------------------------------
Front end for a maintenance module.
---------------------------------*/

#include "maintain.h"

/*-----------------------------
The main menu for maintenance.
-----------------------------*/

char *main_menu[]={
     "Add Record",
     "Change Record",
     "Delete Record",
     "Look up a Record",
     "Display Records",
     "Print Records",
     "Compress File",
     NULL};


/*-------------
Local functions
-------------*/

static void    add_record_init(void), add_record_entry(void),
               chg_record_init(void), chg_record_entry(void);

static int     enter_key(char *), enter_key_entry(void),
               this_one(char*);

/*-------------
Local Variables
-------------*/

static int screen_error_status;
#define    screen_entry_error (screen_error_status == 1)


int maintain(void)
```

continues

Listing 11.3. continued

```
{
     int pick;

     while(1)
          {
          pick = menu9(main_menu);
          switch(pick)
               {
               case 1:
                    add_record();
                    break;
               case 2:
                    change_record();
                    break;
               case 3:
                    delete_record();
                    break;
               case 4:
                    lookup_record();
                    break;
               case 5:
                    display_records();
                    break;
               case 6:
                    print_records();
                    break;
               case 7:
                    compress_file();
                    break;
               case 0:
                    cls();
                    return(0);
               }
          }
}


/*------------------------------------
               ADD RECORD
------------------------------------*/

/*----------------------------
1.  Open Append Mode
2.  Initialize for adding
3.  Enter the record and add it
4.  Close the data file
----------------------------*/
```

```
void add_record(void)
{
     open_append_data_file();
     add_record_init();
     add_record_entry();
     close_data_file();
}

/*--------------------------------------------
Initialize for add mode by clearing all of the
data entry fields.
--------------------------------------------*/
static void add_record_init(void)
{
     clear_scr_receivers();
}

/*------------------------------------------------
1.   Clear the error flag
2.   Enter all fields
3.   Test needed fields for validity
4.   If there is an error, then repeat 1 through 3
5.   If all OK, then load the record and write it.
------------------------------------------------*/
static void add_record_entry(void)
{
     while(1)
          {
          screen_error_status = 0;
          enter_fields();
          screen_error_status = validate_fields();
          if(screen_entry_error)
               {
               error_msg();
               }
          else
               {
               load_record();
               write_data_record();
               return;
               }
          }
}

/*------------------------------------
               CHANGE RECORD
------------------------------------*/
```

continues

Listing 11.3. continued

```
void change_record(void)
{
     open_io_data_file();
     if(enter_key("Change"))
          {
          chg_record_init();
          chg_record_entry();
          }
     else
          {
          record_not_found();
          }
     close_data_file();
}

static void chg_record_init(void)
{
     load_screen();
}

static void chg_record_entry(void)
{
     while(1)
          {
          screen_error_status = 0;
          enter_fields();
          screen_error_status = validate_fields();
          if(screen_entry_error)
               {
               error_msg();
               }
          else
               {
               reload_record();
               rewrite_data_record();
               return;
               }
          }
}

/*------------------------------------------------------------
          Enter the KEY for CHANGE, LOOKUP and DELETE mode
------------------------------------------------------------*/
static int enter_key(char *mode)
{
```

```
     if(enter_key_entry())
          {
          do{
               cls();
               load_screen();
               display_fields();
               if(this_one(mode))
                    return(1);
               }while(find_next_data_record());
          }
     return(0);
}

static int enter_key_entry()
{
     char *key;

     cls();

     while(1)
          {
          screen_error_status = 0;
          printf("Find Record.\n");
          key = get_key_entry();
          screen_error_status = validate_key();
          if(! screen_entry_error)
               break;
          else
               error_msg();
          }
     if(find_data_record(key))
          return(1);
     return(0);
}

static int this_one(char *msg)
{
     int ch;

     printf("\n%s this record?\n", msg);
     ch = get_one_char();
     if( (ch == 'Y') || (ch == 'y') )
          return(1);
     return(0);
}
```

continues

Listing 11.3. continued

```
/*------------------------------------
                DELETE RECORD
------------------------------------*/
void delete_record(void)
{
     open_io_data_file();
     if(enter_key("Delete"))
          {
          delete_data_record();
          }
     else
          {
          record_not_found();
          }
     close_data_file();
}

/*--------------------------------------------
                LOOK UP A RECORD
--------------------------------------------*/
void lookup_record(void)
{
     open_input_data_file();
     if(enter_key("Stop at"))
          {
          ;
          }
     else
          {
          record_not_found();
          }
     close_data_file();
}

/*---------------------------------------
                COMPRESS FILE
---------------------------------------*/
void compress_file(void)
{
     please_wait();
     compress_data_file();
}

/*-------------
Display Records
-------------*/
void display_records(void)
```

```
{
     open_input_data_file();
     while(read_data_record())
          {
          cls();
          load_screen();
          display_fields();
          press_enter();
          }
     close_data_file();
}

/*---------------------------------
               PRINT RECORDS
---------------------------------*/
void print_records(void)
{
     stub("Print Records");
}

/*---------------------------------------
          UTILITY and SUPPORT routines
---------------------------------------*/
static void stub(char *msg)
{
     char buf[81];

     cls();
     sprintf(buf, "\t\t%s", msg);
     scroll_message(buf);
     scroll_message("\t\tNot yet implemented");
     scroll_up(1);
     press_enter();
}
```

Listing 11.4, the header file for maintain.h, requires some explanation. It includes prototypes for all of the global routines in maintain.c, but also includes prototypes for two more sets of routines. These are the routines that are expected to be defined in the file I/O module and the file maintenance module. The reason for this is encapsulation. The normal process would be to create a file named phoneio.c for I/O to the phone file, and a phoneio.h header file for the module. The problem with this approach is that maintain.c would have to be modified for every maintenance module. It would have to include "phoneio.h" or "custio.h" depending on which file was to be maintained.

Creating a single header file makes it possible to leave maintain.c untouched and link it to other fileio.c and filemnt.c modules.

Listing 11.4. maintain.h.

```
/*--------
maintain.h
--------*/
#ifndef _MAINTAIN_H
#define _MAINTAIN_H

#include <stdio.h>

#include "menu9.h"
#include "screenmd.h"

/*----------------------------------
Prototypes for routines in maintain.c
----------------------------------*/

int maintain(void);
void add_record(void);
void change_record(void);
void delete_record(void);
void lookup_record(void);
void compress_file(void);
void print_records(void);
void display_records(void);

void stub(char *);

/*-----------------------------------------------------
The following routines are expected to be defined in the
fileio.c file specific IO module for the file that is
being maintained.
-----------------------------------------------------*/

int open_append_data_file(void);
int open_io_data_file(void);
int open_input_data_file(void);
void close_data_file(void);

int read_data_record(void);
int write_data_record(void);
int delete_data_record(void);
int rewrite_data_record(void);
void compress_data_file(void);

int find_data_record(char *), find_next_data_record(void);
```

```
/*-----------------------------------------------
The following routines are expected to be defined in
the filemnt.c file-specific maintenance modules.
-----------------------------------------------*/

void enter_fields(void), display_fields(void);
void clear_scr_receivers(void);
char *get_key_entry(void);
void load_record(void), load_screen(void), reload_record(void);
int validate_fields(void), validate_key(void);

#endif /* _MAINTAIN_H */
```

Record Layout

With the generic activity out of the way, it is possible to begin designing the file-specific maintenance. The first step in any such activity is to design the file record layout. The fields in the file will be last name, first name, and phone number.

There are three ways to approach stream record fields in C. First, the fields can be space delimited. This is a natural choice for C, as the `printf()` and `scanf()` families were designed to work on fields on the basis that spaces are skipped, and nonspaces are fields. A file designed this way would contain:

```
Jones Albert 5027951234
Arbuthnot Samantha 60892512345
```

With a file organized on a space-delimited basis, the fields could be read and written using

```
fscanf(file, "%s %s %s \n", last, first, number);
fprintf(file, "%s %s %s\n", last, first, number);
```

The problem with space delimiting is that in the real world some fields just insist on containing spaces. The following record would write successfully, but could never be read back in:

```
Baggins Bilbo R. (915) 555-1212
```

For the second choice, the fields can be variable length, and a unique character can be placed between each field that can be recognized during a read, and added during a write, such as

```
Jones,Albert,5027951234
```

or

```
Baggins¦Frodo T.¦5027951234
```

The vertical bar separator is probably better, as it is unlikely to come up in data entry. A variation on this uses a combined separator, in this case quoting the fields and separating them:

```
"Coyote","Wile E.","(905) 555-1212"
```

This file format is used a lot by databases and spreadsheets as a generic import/export format.

Character-delimited fields are slightly more difficult to process on a read, but fairly easy on a write. In the following example, the logic uses `"%[^¦]¦"` to indicate that `scanf()` is to pull all characters up to a vertical bar for the field, and then pull the vertical bar (to get it out of the way). Similarly `"%[^\n]\n"` pulls all characters up to a newline for the field, and then pulls a newline to clear it out of the way.

```
fscanf(file, "%[^¦]¦%[^¦]¦%[^\n]\n", last, first, number);
fprintf(file, "%s¦%s¦%s\n", last, first, number);
```

In the third method, the stream file can be converted into a pseudo-relative file by storing each field with a fixed number of characters. This has advantages later on when trying to add indexes or do binary searches as each record is a fixed length and it is possible to calculate distances for skipping around in the file. This first effort will not be attempting anything so complex, but the record layout will be fixed length anyway.

File I/O

Listing 11.5 is a header file that covers the phone record and some of the constants associated with the I/O to the phone file.

Listing 11.5. phoneio.h.

```
#ifndef _PHONEIO_H
#define _PHONEIO_H

#include <stdio.h>
#include <string.h>
#include <process.h>
#include <ctype.h>
#include "util.h"
```

```
#include "maintain.h"

/*------------------------------------------------------------
Phone record is three fields stored in a stream file (newline
terminated).

Field                Position       Length

LAST_NAME            1               20
FIRST_NAME           21              20
NUMBER               41              15

So we pre-define the format fields to be used by fprintf() and
fscanf() for input and output.
------------------------------------------------------------*/

#define   OUTPUT_FORMAT   "%-20s%-20s%-15s\n"
#define   INPUT_FORMAT    "%20c%20c%15c\n"

/*----------------------------------------
Constants:
     File Name on disk
     Work file name used during compression
     Record length
     Number of fields
----------------------------------------*/

#define   FILE_NAME      "phone.dat"
#define   COMPRESS_NAME  "phone.cmp"
#define   RECORD_LENGTH  56         /* Including newline */
#define   FIELD_COUNT       3

/*--------------------------------------------------------
Fields used for reading and writing to the file, and for
displaying on the screen.
--------------------------------------------------------*/

extern char    fname[], lname[], phone[];

#endif /* _PHONEIO_H */
```

The long list of standard header files contain the prototypes of routines that will be used in phoneio.c, the module that does I/O to the phone file. The util.h header file is also included because phoneio.c will need to call `field_is_blank()` and `trunc()` in util.c. The maintain.h header file, as previously mentioned, contains the prototypes for the functions in phoneio.c and phonemnt.c.

The next section of Listing 11.5 is a description of the record to be used and the formatting constants for input and output.

Several other constants are used in the I/O. The name of the physical file, the name of the work file used for compressing, and the record length and field count.

Deletion is done by rewriting a record using spaces in all fields, so a compression routine will be provided to squeeze the file, hence the name of the compression work file.

Finally phoneio.h makes reference to the global fields in phoneio.c that will be used for reading into and writing from. These fields must be accessible to routines outside of phoneio.c, so they are made globals and thereby available to other routines.

The `INPUT_FORMAT` is set up using a `"c"` specification to read characters regardless of content. This causes embedded spaces to be read in with the field if there are any.

The I/O module itself, phoneio.c, is quite long, and I have broken it into sections in Listings 11.6 through 11.9. There are actually five main sections. The first section in Listing 11.6 is variables used in the module. It includes the local variables used as `FILE` pointers, a long `fpos` used for storing the file position during a read, and the global string areas used to store the fields for a read or write.

Listing 11.6. phoneio.c (part 1).

```
/*----------------------------
phoneio.c

Does all IO to the phone file
----------------------------*/

#include "phoneio.h"


/*---------------------------------------------------------
               Local and Global VARIABLES
---------------------------------------------------------*/

/*----------------------
File names and pointers
----------------------*/

static FILE *iofile, *cmpfile;

static long fpos;
```

```
/*------------------------------------------------------------
These are globals into which values are read from the file, or
from which values are written to the file. They are global as
they must be available to other parts of the program.
------------------------------------------------------------*/

char lname[21],fname[21],phone[16];

/*------------------------------
Prototypes for the local functions
------------------------------*/

static void file_error(char *), clear_receivers(void);
static int fields_are_blank(void), write_a_record(FILE *);

/*-----------------------------------------------
                    OPEN and CLOSE
-----------------------------------------------*/

int open_append_data_file(void)
{
     if(iofile != NULL)
          {
          file_error("opening append an already open");
          }
     iofile = fopen(FILE_NAME, "a");
     if(iofile)
          return(1);
     file_error("opening append");
}

int open_input_data_file(void)
{
     if(iofile != NULL)
          {
          file_error("opening input an already open");
          }
     open_append_data_file();
     close_data_file();
     iofile = fopen(FILE_NAME, "r");
     if(iofile)
          return(1);
     file_error("opening input");
}

/*--------------------------------------------------------------
This opens the file for IO. It always opens the file append
first which automatically creates the file if it does not exist.
--------------------------------------------------------------*/
```

continues

Listing 11.6. continued

```
int open_io_data_file(void)
{
     if(iofile != NULL)
          {
          file_error("opening IO an already open");
          }
     open_append_data_file();
     close_data_file();
     iofile = fopen(FILE_NAME, "r+");
     if(iofile)
          return(1);
     file_error("opening IO");
}

void close_data_file()
{
     if(iofile == NULL)
          {
          file_error("closing an already closed");
          }
     fclose(iofile);
     iofile = NULL;
}
```

The second section, also in Listing 11.6, contains all the open and close logic. The file can be opened in three modes: input, append, and I/O. The first routine to open append is the simplest and includes some simple traps to capture unrecoverable errors. The routine checks if the `FILE` pointer is not `NULL` and exits through `file_error()`, because a file cannot be opened twice. The file is opened append, and if the open fails, an exit is again taken through `file_error()`. All access to the file is done by calling routines in this module, so the `FILE` pointer, `iofile`, is a local variable. It does not need to be accessed outside this module.

Opening input and I/O are similar to opening append with one difference. The file is first opened append and then closed again. This is a lazy way of ensuring that the file exists before it is opened. This takes care of creating the file the first time the program is run.

The close is simple, but sets the `FILE` pointer to `NULL`. This allows the three open routines to safely test, and assumes that if the `FILE` pointer is not `NULL`, the file is open.

The third section of phoneio.c in Listing 11.7 includes read, write, delete, and rewrite logic. Each of the I/O routines verifies that the file is open before attempting any I/O.

This logic will not catch errors such as writing to a file opened input, and an additional flag could be set up to signal the open mode and abort when the I/O and open mode are inconsistent. For now this simpler technique will do.

Listing 11.7. phoneio.c (part 2).

```
/*-------------------------------------------------------
                    READ WRITE REWRITE DELETE
-------------------------------------------------------*/

/*-------------------------------------------------------
Save the current file pointer.
Clear the receiving fields.
Check if we are at end of file and exit accordingly.

Scan in the fields.
Truncate each to last non-space character.

Use the return value from scanf() to establish if
the read was successful.
Returns 1 if successful and 0 if unsuccessful.
The only legal counts are FIELD_COUNT and EOF.
Anything else indicates the file has been corrupted and
the program exits.
-----------------------------------------------------*/

int read_data_record()
{
     int count;

     if(iofile == NULL)
          {
          file_error("reading a closed");
          }
     while(1)
          {
          fpos = ftell(iofile);
          if(feof(iofile))
               return(0);
          count = fscanf(iofile,
               INPUT_FORMAT, lname, fname, phone);

          trunc(lname);
          trunc(fname);
          trunc(phone);
```

continues

Listing 11.7. continued

```
          if(count == EOF)
               return(0);
          if(count < FIELD_COUNT)
               break;
          if(fields_are_blank())
               continue;
          else
               return(1);
          }
     file_error("reading");
}

/*---------------------------------------------------
Assumes the lname, fname, and phone are pre-filled with
values to write to the file. If less than RECORD_LENGTH
bytes are written, then an error has occurred.
---------------------------------------------------*/
int write_data_record(void)
{
     int count;

     if(iofile == NULL)
          {
          file_error("writing a closed");
          }
     count = write_a_record(iofile);
     if(count < RECORD_LENGTH)
          file_error("writing");
     return(1);
}

static int write_a_record(FILE *file)
{
     int count;

     count = fprintf(file, OUTPUT_FORMAT, lname, fname, phone);
     return(count);
}


/*-------------------------------------------
A delete is really a rewrite with blank fields.
-------------------------------------------*/
int delete_data_record(void)
{
```

```
     if(iofile == NULL)
          {
          file_error("deleting on a closed");
          }
     clear_receivers();
     return(rewrite_data_record());
}


/*--------------------------------------------
A rewrite is a write in which the file has been
repositioned to the point of the last read.
--------------------------------------------*/
int rewrite_data_record(void)
{
     if(iofile == NULL)
          {
          file_error("re-writing a closed");
          }
     fseek(iofile, fpos, SEEK_SET);
     return(write_data_record());
}
```

The read routine saves the current file pointer before the read and then uses `fscanf()` and the `INPUT_FORMAT` to collect the record into the three global string areas. The read routine truncates all fields to the last non-blank character and then checks if all fields are blank. This condition would occur if a record had been deleted. If all fields are blank, the read routine loops and reads another record. This continues until a valid record is found, or an end-of-file condition is met. Read uses the return value from `fscanf()` to test for validity of the I/O. The `fscanf()` function will return a field count of fields stored, or `EOF`. The routine checks for `EOF` to exit, or not enough fields read indicating some file corruption problem.

The write logic is broken into two functions, `write_data_record()` and a local function `write_a_record()`. The `write_a_record()` function is passed a `FILE` pointer, and you will see that it is used in the compress routine that appears in Listing 11.8. The write routine uses the output format to print to the file, and checks the return value from `fprintf()` to determine whether a problem exists. The `fprintf()` function will return the number of characters written to the file, and this should be equal to `RECORD_LENGTH` if all is well.

The rewrite logic assumes that it will be rewriting the record just read. It `fseeks()` to the saved value in `fpos` (saved during the last read operation), and then calls the write data record. This will overwrite the data at that position in the file. Delete clears the three string receivers and then calls the rewrite function.

You can see from this section that all the routines are built around read and write as the core routines. Delete and rewrite just do a write, but with some extra logic thrown in to get the file positioned and, if necessary, clear the fields.

Listing 11.8 contains some of the miscellaneous routines in phoneio.c. The compress logic is simple, given the groundwork done in earlier functions. The phone file is opened input and the compress file is opened output. The `read_data_record()` routine is used to read the phone file. This routine already skips blank (deleted) records so you need only to write to the compressed file. The `write_a_record` routine is called, passing the `FILE` pointer for the compressed file.

Listing 11.8. phoneio.c (part 3).

```
/*-------------------------------------------------------------
          Miscellaneous COMPRESS FIND FIND_NEXT
-------------------------------------------------------------*/

/*------------------------------------------------------------
1.    Open the phone file input and the compress work file
      for output.
2.    Read all records from phone file into the compress file.
3.    Delete the phone file.
4.    Rename the compress file to the data file name.
-------------------------------------------------------------*/

void compress_data_file(void)
{
      open_input_data_file();
      cmpfile = fopen(COMPRESS_NAME, "w");
      while(read_data_record())
           {
           write_a_record(cmpfile);
           }
      fclose(cmpfile);
      close_data_file();
      unlink(FILE_NAME);
      rename(COMPRESS_NAME, FILE_NAME);
}


/*-------------------------------------------------------
Rewind the file and then read all records comparing the
last name to the past key until record is found, or an
End of File condition is encountered.
-------------------------------------------------------*/
```

```
static char find_key[RECORD_LENGTH + 1];

int find_data_record(char *str)
{
     if(iofile == NULL)
          {
          file_error("searching a closed");
          }
     rewind(iofile);
     memcpy(find_key, str, RECORD_LENGTH);
     find_key[RECORD_LENGTH] = 0;
     return(find_next_data_record());

}

int find_next_data_record(void)
{
     if(iofile == NULL)
          {
          file_error("searching a closed");
          }
     while(read_data_record())
          {
          if(!(strcmp(lname, find_key)))
               return(1);
          }
     return(0);
}
```

The routine ends with two new and useful standard C library functions. The `unlink()` function deletes a file named in the passed string. The `rename()` function takes two arguments, `oldname` and `newname`. The old phone file is deleted, and the new compressed file is renamed so that it is now the phone file.

The find record routines work as a pair. `find_data_record()` is passed a string containing the key value for the search. The string is saved in a local static, and `find_next_data_record()` is called to locate the record. Once `find_data_record()` has been called with an initial key value, `find_next_data_record()` can be repeatedly called without a value and it will return subsequent occurrences of the same last name.

Listing 11.9 includes the support logic for the previous routines. The file error routine attempts to close up and prints an error message that includes the passed message that describes the I/O type that was being attempted when the error occurred. It also performs an `exit()` call to bail out of the whole program.

Listing 11.9. phoneio.c (part 4).

```
/*-----------------------------------------------------
            UTILITY ROUTINES to support IO
-----------------------------------------------------*/

/*-----------------------------------------------------

Close the file if it is open.
Provide a file error message and exit.
This is a general purpose routine for bailing out of
unrecoverable file errors.
-----------------------------------------------------*/
static void file_error(char *io)
{
     if(iofile != NULL)
          close_data_file();
     printf("An error occurred %s phone file.\n", io);
     printf("The file may be corrupted.\n");
     exit(0);
}

/*---------------------------------------
Test all fields for all characters = spaces.
---------------------------------------*/
static int fields_are_blank(void)
{
     if(  (field_is_blank(lname, sizeof(lname) - 1) ) &&
          (field_is_blank(fname, sizeof(fname) - 1) ) &&
          (field_is_blank(phone, sizeof(phone) - 1) )  )
          return(1);
     else
          return(0);
}

/*------------------------------------------------------
Clear all the fields used to read from or write to the file
------------------------------------------------------*/
static void clear_receivers(void)
{
     memset(lname, 0, sizeof(lname));
     memset(fname, 0, sizeof(fname));
     memset(phone, 0, sizeof(phone));
}
```

The `fields_are_blank()` routine checks and returns a nonzero value if all three of the record fields are blank. It uses `field_is_blank()` in util.c to test the fields. The

fields_are_blank() routine uses a new C command, sizeof(). This looks like a function, but is not; it is a compiler command that inserts the size of the requested data item. In this case,

```
field_is_blank(lname, sizeof(lname) - 1);
```

is compiled as

```
field_is_blank(lname, 31 - 1);
```

The sizeof() operator can take a variable, or a data type as an argument, and use it to establish the sizes of different data types on your machine, for example,

```
main()
{
     char message[12];

     printf("Size of an integer is %d.\n", sizeof(int));
     printf("Size of a float is    %d.\n", sizeof(float);
     printf("Size of a double is   %d.\n", sizeof(double));
     printf("Size of message is    %d.\n", sizeof(message));
}
```

This is similar to a preprocessor command, because it is translated by the compiler to an integer value representing the size of the item requested.

The clear_receivers() routine will set all three of the file fields to NUL.

Phone Book Maintenance Module

The last piece of the puzzle is phonemnt.c in Listing 11.10, which includes all of the phone file specific screen routines. These routines tend to act as an interface layer between the maintain.c module and the actual specifics of the data being processed.

Listing 11.10. phonemnt.c.

```
/*-----------------------------------
Screen routines for phone maintenance
-----------------------------------*/

#include "phonemnt.h"
```

continues

Listing 11.10. continued

```
/*---------------------
Fields for screen input.
---------------------*/
static char lname_field[21], fname_field[21], phone_field[21];

/*---------------------
Prompts for screen input.
---------------------*/
static char *prompt[] = {
     {"Last Name"},
     {"First Name"},
     {"Phone"},
     {NULL}
};

/*-----------------------------------------------
An array of pointers to input receivers, and their
lengths for get_entries.
-----------------------------------------------*/
static char *field[] = {
     lname_field,
     fname_field,
     phone_field
     };

static int length[] = { 20, 20, 15 };

/*--------------------------------------
Call straight into the maintain() routine
--------------------------------------*/
int main()
{
     maintain();
     return(0);
}


/*-------------
Input all fields
-------------*/
void enter_fields(void)
{
     get_entries(prompt, field, length);
}
```

```
/*-----------------------------------------------
Validate all fields. In this case only the key field
(last name) is tested for a valid entry
-----------------------------------------------*/
int validate_fields(void)
{
     return(validate_key());
}

/*---------------------
Validate last name field
---------------------*/
int validate_key(void)
{
     if(field_is_blank(lname_field, sizeof(lname_field) - 1))
          return(1);
     return(0);
}

/*----------------------------------------
Clear all screen receivers in preparation for
input.
----------------------------------------*/
void clear_scr_receivers(void)
{
     memset(lname_field, 0, sizeof(lname_field));
     memset(fname_field, 0, sizeof(fname_field));
     memset(phone_field, 0, sizeof(phone_field));
}

/*-------------------------------------------------
Accept entry of the "key" value, in this case the first
field.
-------------------------------------------------*/
char *get_key_entry(void)
{
     clear_scr_receivers();
     get_entry(prompt[0], field[0], length[0]);
     return(field[0]);
}

/*----------------
Display all entries
----------------*/
void display_fields(void)
{
     display_entries(prompt, field);
}
```

continues

Listing 11.10. continued

```
/*-----------------------------------
Load record fields from screen fields.
-----------------------------------*/
void load_record(void)
{
     strcpy(lname, lname_field);
     strcpy(fname, fname_field);
     strcpy(phone, phone_field);
}

/*-----------------------------------------------------
Load record fields from screen fields if they contain data.
-----------------------------------------------------*/
void reload_record(void)
{
     if(strlen(lname_field))
          strcpy(lname, lname_field);
     if(strlen(fname_field))
          strcpy(fname, fname_field);
     if(strlen(phone_field))
          strcpy(phone, phone_field);
}

/*---------------------------------------
Load screen fields from the record fields.
---------------------------------------*/
void load_screen(void)
{
     strcpy(lname_field, lname);
     strcpy(fname_field, fname);
     strcpy(phone_field, phone);
}
```

Listing 11.11 is the header file for phonemnt.c. It includes maintain.h, which contains the prototypes for the global routines in maintain.c, and phoneio.h, which allows access to `lname`, `fname`, and `phone` strings as globals.

Listing 11.11. phonemnt.h.

```
#ifndef _PHONEMNT_H
#define _PHONEMNT_H
```

```
#include "maintain.h"
#include "phoneio.h"

#endif /* _PHONEMNT_H */
```

There are two approaches to building this program. The first is to compile and link the separate modules. This could be done with a long single compile line.

```
cl phonemnt.c phoneio.c maintain.c menu9.c screenmd.c screenlo.c util.c
```

The second method would be to build a library out of the low-level routines, and then compile and link to the library.

```
cl /c maintain.c menu9.c screenmd.c screenlo.c util.c

lib maintain.lib +maintain +menu9 +screenmd +screenlo +util;
```

This will create a library named maintain.lib and you can link to it by just adding it to the cl command line as in:

```
cl phonemnt.c phoneio.c maintain.lib
```

Modular Maintenance

The beauty of this arrangement is the ease with which additional maintenance modules can be created. All that is needed is modules equivalent to phonemnt.c and phoneio.c but for the file being maintained.

Listings 11.12 through 11.15 are custio.c, custmnt.c, and their respective header files. These can be compiled and linked to the existing maintain.lib as follows:

```
cc custmnt.c custio.c maintain.lib
```

It takes only a few minutes to create these program modules, and, of course, you now have another maintenance module.

Listing 11.12. custio.h.

```
#ifndef _CUSTIO_H
#define _CUSTIO_H
```

continues

Listing 11.12. continued

```
#include <stdio.h>
#include <string.h>
#include <process.h>
#include <ctype.h>
#include "util.h"
#include "maintain.h"

/*-------------------------------------------------------------
Customer record is 5 fields stored in a stream file (newline
terminated).

Field               Position   Length

CUST_NAME           1          30
ADDRESS1            31         30
ADDRESS2            61         30
ADDRESS3            91         30
NUMBER              121        15

So we pre-define the format fields to be used by fprintf() and
fscanf() for input and output.
-------------------------------------------------------------*/

#define   OUTPUT_FORMAT   "%-30s%-30s%-30s%-30s%-15s\n"
#define   INPUT_FORMAT    "%30c%30c%30c%30c%15c\n"

/*-----------------------------------------
Constants:
     File Name on disk
     Work file name used during compression
     Record length
     Number of fields
-----------------------------------------*/

#define   FILE_NAME       "cust.dat"
#define   COMPRESS_NAME   "cust.cmp"
#define   RECORD_LENGTH   136        /* Including newline */
#define   FIELD_COUNT          5

/*-------------------------------------------------------
Fields used for reading and writing to the file, and for
displaying on the screen.
-------------------------------------------------------*/

extern char    name[], address1[], address2[],
               address3[], phone[];

#endif /* _CUSTIO_H */
```

Listing 11.13. custio.c.

```
/*----------------------------
custio.c

Does all IO to the customer file
----------------------------*/

#include "custio.h"

/*--------------------
File names and pointers
--------------------*/

static FILE *iofile, *outfile;

static long fpos;

/*------------------------------------------------------------
These are globals into which values are read from the file, or
from which values are written to the file. They are global as
they must be available to other parts of the program.
------------------------------------------------------------*/

char name[31], address1[31], address2[31],
          address3[31], phone[16];

/*------------------------------
Prototypes for the local functions
------------------------------*/

static void file_error(char *), clear_receivers(void);
static int fields_are_blank(void), write_a_record(FILE *);

/*---------------------------------------------
               OPEN and CLOSE
---------------------------------------------*/

/*--------------------------------------------------------------
This opens the file for IO. It always opens the file append
first which automatically creates the file if it does not exist.
--------------------------------------------------------------*/
int open_io_data_file(void)
{
     if(iofile != NULL)
          {
          file_error("opening io an already open");
          }
```

continues

Listing 11.13. continued

```
     open_append_data_file();
     close_data_file();
     iofile = fopen(FILE_NAME, "r+");
     if(iofile)
          return(1);
     file_error("opening io");
}

int open_append_data_file(void)
{
     if(iofile != NULL)
          {
          file_error("opening append an already open");
          }
     iofile = fopen(FILE_NAME, "a");
     if(iofile)
          return(1);
     file_error("opening append");
}

int open_input_data_file(void)
{
     if(iofile != NULL)
          {
          file_error("opening input an already open");
          }
     iofile = fopen(FILE_NAME, "r");
     if(iofile)
          return(1);
     file_error("opening input");
}

void close_data_file()
{
     if(iofile == NULL)
          {
          file_error("closing an already closed");
          }
     fclose(iofile);
     iofile = NULL;
}

/*-----------------------------------------------------
               READ WRITE REWRITE DELETE
-----------------------------------------------------*/
```

```
/*-----------------------------------------------------
Save the current file pointer.
Clear the receiving fields.
Check if we are at end of file and exit accordingly.

Scan in the fields.
Truncate each to last non-space character.

Use the return value from scanf() to establish if the read was
successful. Returns 1 if successful and 0 if unsuccessful.
The only legal counts are FIELD_COUNT and EOF.
Anything else indicates the file has been corrupted and
the program exits.
------------------------------------------------------------*/
int read_data_record()
{
     int count;


     if(iofile == NULL)
          {
          file_error("reading a closed");
          }
     while(1)
          {
          fpos = ftell(iofile);
          if(feof(iofile))
               return(0);
          count = fscanf(iofile,
               INPUT_FORMAT, name, address1,
               address2, address3, phone);

          trunc(name);
          trunc(address1);
          trunc(address2);
          trunc(address3);
          trunc(phone);

          if(count == EOF)
               return(0);
          if(count < FIELD_COUNT)
               break;
          if(fields_are_blank())
               continue;
          else
               return(1);
          }
```

continues

Listing 11.13. continued

```
     file_error("reading");
}

/*-------------------------------------------------
Assumes the fields are pre-filled with values to
write to the file. If less than RECORD_LENGTH bytes
written then an error has occurred.
-----------------------------------------------*/
int write_data_record(void)
{
     int count;

     if(iofile == NULL)
          {
          file_error("writing a closed");
          }
     count = write_a_record(iofile);
     if(count < RECORD_LENGTH)
          file_error("writing");
     return(1);
}

static int write_a_record(FILE *file)
{
     int count;

     count = fprintf(file, OUTPUT_FORMAT, name, address1,
                              address2, address3, phone);
     return(count);
}


/*-------------------------------------------
A delete is really a rewrite with blank fields.
-------------------------------------------*/
int delete_data_record(void)
{
     if(iofile == NULL)
          {
          file_error("deleting on a closed");
          }
     clear_receivers();
     return(rewrite_data_record());
}
```

```
/*-------------------------------------------
A rewrite is a write in which the file has been
repositioned to the point of the last read.
-----------------------------------------*/
int rewrite_data_record(void)
{
     if(iofile == NULL)
          {
          file_error("re-writing a closed");
          }
     fseek(iofile, fpos, SEEK_SET);
     return(write_data_record());
}


/*-----------------------------------------------------
          Miscellaneous COMPRESS FIND FIND_NEXT
---------------------------------------------------*/
/*-----------------------------------------------------
Open the file and the compress work file.
Read all records from the file into the compress file.
Delete the main file.
Rename the compress file.
---------------------------------------------------*/

void compress_data_file(void)
{
     open_input_data_file();
     outfile = fopen(COMPRESS_NAME, "w");
     while(read_data_record())
          {
          write_a_record(outfile);
          }
     fclose(outfile);
     close_data_file();
     unlink(FILE_NAME);
     rename(COMPRESS_NAME, FILE_NAME);
}


/*------------------------------------------------------------
Rewind the file and then read all records comparing the last
name until record is found, or an End of File condition is hit.
----------------------------------------------------------*/

static char find_key[31];

int find_data_record(char *str)
```

continues

Listing 11.13. continued

```
{
     if(iofile == NULL)
          {
          file_error("searching a closed");
          }
     rewind(iofile);

     strcpy(find_key, str);

     return(find_next_data_record());

}

int find_next_data_record(void)
{
     if(iofile == NULL)
          {
          file_error("searching a closed");
          }
     while(read_data_record())
          {
          if(!(strcmp(name, find_key)))
               return(1);
          }
     return(0);
}


/*---------------------------------------------------
          UTILITY ROUTINES to support IO
---------------------------------------------------*/

/*---------------------------------------------------
Close the file if it is open.
Provide a file error message and exit.
This is a general purpose routine for bailing out of
unrecoverable file errors.
---------------------------------------------------*/
static void file_error(char *io)
{
     if(iofile != NULL)
          close_data_file();
     printf("An error occurred %s customer file.\n", io);
     printf("The file may be corrupted.\n");
     exit(0);
}
```

```
/*---------------------------------------
Test all fields for all characters = spaces.
---------------------------------------*/
static int fields_are_blank(void)
{
     if(  (field_is_blank(name, sizeof(name) - 1) ) &&
          (field_is_blank(address1, sizeof(address1) - 1) ) &&
          (field_is_blank(address2, sizeof(address2) - 1) ) &&
          (field_is_blank(address3, sizeof(address3) - 1) ) &&
          (field_is_blank(phone, sizeof(phone) - 1) ) )
          return(1);
     else
          return(0);

}

/*-------------------------------------------------------
Clear all the fields used to read from or write to the file
-------------------------------------------------------*/
static void clear_receivers(void)
{
     memset(name, 0, sizeof(name));
     memset(address1, 0, sizeof(address1));
     memset(address2, 0, sizeof(address2));
     memset(address3, 0, sizeof(address3));
     memset(phone, 0, sizeof(phone));
}
```

Listing 11.14 custmnt.c

```
/*-------------------------------------
Screen routines for customer maintenance
-------------------------------------*/

#include "custmnt.h"

/*---------------------
Fields for screen input.
---------------------*/
static char     name_field[31], address1_field[31],
               address2_field[31], address3_field[31],
               phone_field[16];

/*---------------------
```

continues

Listing 11.14. continued

```
Prompts for screen input.
----------------------*/
static char *prompt[] = {
     {"Customer Name"},
     {"Address 1"},
     {"Address 2"},
     {"Address 3"},
     {"Phone"},
     {NULL}
};

/*------------------------------------------------
An array of pointers to input receivers, and their
lengths for get_entries.
-----------------------------------------------*/
static char *field[] = {
     name_field,
     address1_field,
     address2_field,
     address3_field,
     phone_field
     };
static int length[] = { 20, 20, 15 };

/*---------------------------------------
Call straight into the maintain() routine
--------------------------------------*/
int main()
{
     maintain();
     return(0);
}


/*-------------
Input all fields
-------------*/
void enter_fields(void)
{
     get_entries(prompt, field, length);
}

/*------------------------------------------------
Validate all fields. In this case only the key field
(last name) is tested for a valid entry
-----------------------------------------------*/
```

```
int validate_fields(void)
{
     return(validate_key());
}

/*---------------------
Validate last name field
---------------------*/
int validate_key(void)
{
     if(field_is_blank(name_field, sizeof(name_field) - 1))
          return(1);
     return(0);
}

/*-----------------------------------------
Clear all screen receivers in preparation for
input.
-----------------------------------------*/
void clear_scr_receivers(void)
{
     memset(name_field, 0, sizeof(name_field));
     memset(address1_field, 0, sizeof(address1_field));
     memset(address2_field, 0, sizeof(address2_field));
     memset(address3_field, 0, sizeof(address3_field));
     memset(phone_field, 0, sizeof(phone_field));
}

/*-----------------------------------------------------
Accept entry of the "key" value, in this case the first
field.
-----------------------------------------------------*/
char *get_key_entry(void)
{
     clear_scr_receivers();
     get_entry(prompt[0], field[0], length[0]);
     return(field[0]);
}

/*----------------
Display all entries
----------------*/
void display_fields(void)
{
     display_entries(prompt, field);
}
```

continues

Listing 11.14. continued

```
/*---------------------------------
Load record fields from screen fields.
---------------------------------*/
void load_record(void)
{
     strcpy(name, name_field);
     strcpy(address1, address1_field);
     strcpy(address2, address2_field);
     strcpy(address3, address3_field);
     strcpy(phone, phone_field);
}

/*----------------------------------------------------
Load record fields from screen fields if they contain data.
----------------------------------------------------*/
void reload_record(void)
{
     if(strlen(name_field))
          strcpy(name, name_field);
     if(strlen(address1_field))
          strcpy(address1, address1_field);
     if(strlen(address2_field))
          strcpy(address2, address2_field);
     if(strlen(address3_field))
          strcpy(address3, address3_field);
     if(strlen(phone_field))
          strcpy(phone, phone_field);
}

/*-------------------------------------
Load screen fields from the record fields.
-------------------------------------*/
void load_screen(void)
{
     strcpy(name_field, name);
     strcpy(address1_field, address1);
     strcpy(address2_field, address2);
     strcpy(address3_field, address3);
     strcpy(phone_field, phone);
}
```

Listing 11.15. custmnt.h.

```
#ifndef _CUSTMNT_H
#define _CUSTMNT_H

#include "maintain.h"
#include "custio.h"

#endif /* _CUSTMNT_H */
```

Summary

C stream I/O is simple to use, and the syntax is a lot less complicated than COBOL syntax of `SELECT`, `FD`, and `RECORD`, but it does require some planning.

A carefully planned program can become more than just a boilerplate; it can be incorporated into similar programs to reduce coding.

12

C Structures

C has a data type similar to the COBOL record. Structures are used like COBOL records, but can also be used in other ways. The structure and special operators for accessing structures are probably some of the most powerful features of the C language.

This chapter introduces the following topics:

- What is a C structure?
- Structure initialization
- Using `typedef` for structure shorthand
- Arrays of structures
- Passing structures
- Passing pointers to structures
- Using structures in programs

The correct use of structures in C tends to separate the pros from the dabblers.

What Is a C Structure?

Listing 12.1 is a COBOL record. A COBOL record can relate to a physical record on a disk file, or it could just be an area of reserved memory in WORKING-STORAGE. COBOL programmers tend to think of records as physically associated with a disk, but in fact any 01-level entry with data items below it is a record.

Listing 12.1. A COBOL record.

```
01  CUST-RECORD.
    05  CUST-NO                PIC 9(4).
    05  CUST-NAME              PIC X(30).
    05  CUST-BALANCE           PIC S9(5)V99.
```

So far anything like a record has been noticeably missing from the discussion of C. The C equivalent of a COBOL record is called a *structure.* Listing 12.2 is a C equivalent to the CUST-RECORD.

Listing 12.2. C cust record.

```
struct {
     long cust_no;
     char cust_name[31];
     double    cust_balance;
     } cust_record;
```

This reserves an area of memory with space for each of the members (elements of a structure) and names it cust_record. The members of the structure are accessed using the dot (.) operator. The cust_no member of cust_record is called

```
cust_record.cust_no
```

In COBOL you could access CUST-NO just by calling it CUST-NO, but C structure members must be accessed as *structure.member.* Because of this limitation, it is common to use shorter names for structures and members, as shown in Listing 12.3.

Listing 12.3. Usual structure naming.

```
struct {
     long no;
     char name[31];
     double    balance;
     } cust;
```

This allows the members to be accessed by variable names that still make sense, as shown in Listing 12.4, but are not as long-winded as they would be if each member were given a full COBOL-style name.

Listing 12.4. Accessing structure members.

```
void print_cust(void)
{
     printf("%d %s Balance = %f\n",
            cust.no, cust.name, cust.balance);
}
```

I want to be absolutely clear about the fact that the use of `structure.member` to reference a member does not change the nature of the member:

- `cust.no` is a `long` integer
- `cust.name` is a string
- `cust.balance` is a `double`

There are no special considerations in using structure members as variables other than to ensure that you provide the full name.

The following statement works as expected, copying a value into the name member of `cust`.

```
strcpy(cust.name, "Old Bailey");
```

One advantage of the naming convention for structure members is that the same member name may be used in different structures, as shown in Listing 12.5. The `cust.no`, `vendor.no`, `cust.name`, and `vendor.name` members are all unique and separate variables.

Listing 12.5. Using the same member name in different structures.

```
struct {
     int     no;
     char name[31];
     double due;
     }cust;

struct {
     int no;
     char name[31];
     double     last_payment_amt;
     double     balance;
     }vendor;
```

Structure Initialization

The initialization for a structure is somewhat similar to an array and is enclosed in braces. Listing 12.6 initializes the first three members of the vendor structure. The `balance` member is not initialized.

Listing 12.6. Initializing a structure.

```
struct {
     int no;
     char name[31];
     double    last_payment_amt;
     double    balance;
     }vendor =
          { 1007, "Healey and Sons", 22.95 };
```

A structure may contain any C data type including another structure, as shown in Listing 12.7. The part structure includes a vendor for the part. The listing also illustrates the method of initializing a nested structure with nested braces.

Listing 12.7. Structures within structures.

```
struct {
     int no;
     char description[31];
     struct {
                 int     no;
                 int lead_time;
                 double wholesale;
                 } vendor;
     double retail;
     long on_hand;
     }part ={
                 424,
                 "Loose Canon",
                 { 1007, 30, 27.15 },
                 59.95,
                 108
                 };
```

A nested structure is accessed with a second dot (.) operator. The following `if` statement accesses the `lead_time` member of the vendor member of the part structure. Notice again that `part.no` and `part.vendor.no` represent different variables:

```
if(part.vendor.lead_time > 45)
```

A C structure is more than just a record, or a convenient way to lump variables together. A C structure is in fact a user-defined data type. C contains a syntax for allowing a structure to be declared without being defined, as shown in Listing 12.8. This declares a structure called `_part_vendor` but does not reserve any storage for it. The `_part_vendor` identifier is called a *structure tag.*

Listing 12.8. Declaring a structure.

```
struct _part_vendor {
     int no;
     int lead_time;
     double wholesale;
     };
```

Once a structure is declared in this manner, you have in fact "created" a new data type that can be called `"struct _part_vendor"` within your program. You may now define different variables that have the same structure. Listing 12.9 declares the _part_vendor structure type, and then defines two variables that have this structure. Note that the structure members are accessed by the definition name, not by the structure tag.

Listing 12.9. Declaring and defining a structure.

```
struct _part_vendor {
     int no;
     int lead_time;
     double wholesale;
     };

struct _part_vendor vendor;
struct _part_vendor alt_vendor;

void rush_order()
{
     if( alt_vendor.lead_time < vendor.lead_time)
          {
          /* select alternate vendor */
          }
}
```

You may also create a user-defined data type (a structure) and define an instance simultaneously by combining the syntax for both. Listing 12.10 declares a _part_vendor structure and defines one instance of it all in one statement, and then defines a second instance.

Listing 12.10. Combined syntax.

```
struct _part_vendor {
     int no;
     int lead_time;
     double wholesale;
     }vendor;

struct _part_vendor alt_vendor;
```

Listing 12.11 contains examples of initializing these two different definitions. The initialization is identical for both styles.

Listing 12.11. Initializing.

```
struct _part_vendor {
     int no;
     int lead_time;
     double wholesale;
     }vendor = { 1007, 30, 27.15 };

struct _part_vendor alt_vendor = { 2217, 30, 27.29 };
```

You cannot initialize a structure declaration that does not define an instance of the structure. Listing 12.12 is an illegal initialization because the `_part_vendor` structure declaration only establishes the shape of the data, it does not define an instance, and therefore does not reserve any storage into which the values could be placed.

Listing 12.12. Illegal initialization.

```
struct _part_vendor {
     int no;
     int lead_time;
     double wholesale;
     } = { 1007, 30, 27.15 };
```

Declaring structures before defining them or while defining an instance is necessary when a structure is to be used for several different variables, and is very useful for nested structures. Listing 12.13 declares the `_part_vendor` and then two instances of it are defined within the part structure.

Listing 12.13. Using structure declarations.

```
struct _part_vendor {
     int no;
     int lead_time;
     double wholesale;
     };

struct {
     int no;
     char description[31];
```

continues

Listing 12.13. continued

```
     struct _part_vendor vendor;
     struct _part_vendor alt_vendor;
     double retail;
     long on_hand;
     }part;
```

Using *typedef* for Structure Shorthand

The `typedef` aliasing feature mentioned in Chapter 8, "Scope, Storage, and Prototyping," is very useful for creating a shorthand for structures. Most C programmers use it. You will recall that a `typedef` creates an alias for another data type as in the following:

```
typedef   int   AN_INTEGER;
```

which creates `AN_INTEGER` as an alias for `int`.

Using a `typedef` on a structure creates an alias for the keyword `struct` and the structure tag. In Listing 12.14, `PART_VENDOR` becomes a substitute way of saying `struct _part_vendor` within the part structure.

Listing 12.14. Using `typedef` with structures.

```
struct _part_vendor {
     int no;
     int lead_time;
     double wholesale;
     };

typedef struct _part_vendor PART_VENDOR;

struct {
     int no;
     char description[31];
     PART_VENDOR vendor;
     PART_VENDOR alt_vendor;
     double retail;
     long on_hand;
     }part;
```

A typedef may be placed directly in the structure declarations while omitting the structure tag, as shown in Listing 12.15.

Listing 12.15. Using typedef in a declaration.

```
typedef struct {
     int no;
     int lead_time;
     double wholesale;
     }PART_VENDOR;
```

A typedef may also be combined with a structure tag. In Listing 12.16, PART_VENDOR and struct _part_vendor both become ways of identifying this structure data type.

Listing 12.16. Using typedef in a declaration.

```
typedef struct _part_vendor{
     int no;
     int lead_time;
     double wholesale;
     }PART_VENDOR;
```

Arrays of Structures

Because a structure is a user-defined data type, it becomes a C data type and inherits other C data type properties. One of these is the ability to be used in array definitions. Listing 12.17 declares a VENDOR structure and a PART structure. The PART structure includes an array of three VENDOR structures. An array of 300 PART structures is defined as part. The program uses init_parts() to initialize the array of 300 parts with assorted values.

The initialization is a side issue. Normally such a table would be filled in from a file, but it is interesting. The two functions init_parts() and get_rand() at the end of the listing, are used for the initialization. The get_rand() function is passed a lo and hi value as a range, and get_rand() returns a random integer in range between the lo and hi values. The get_rand() function uses rand(), a standard C library function that generates and returns a pseudo-random integer. The logic in get_rand() first adjusts lo and hi to ensure that they are within limits (RAND_MAX is defined in <stdlib.h>), then extracts a pseudo-random number and adjusts it to ensure that it falls between lo and hi. The get_rand() function is used to generate random values to initialize the vendor number, price, and delivery days of the vendor member of the part structure.

The main work of the program is done in show_parts(). This function uses enter_part() which in turn uses getstr() to input a four-digit entry by the user. The input is converted to an integer using the atoi() function (converts a string to an integer). This part number is returned by enter_part(). The part number is passed to get_part_index() which searches the array for this part number and returns the index of the part if found, or -1 if the part is not found. If the part is found, it is printed using print_part().

Note the use of the structure name and index

```
structure[subscript].member
```

or, in the case of an array of structures within an array of structures,

```
structure[subscript].member_structure[subscript].member
```

For example,

```
part[idx].vendor[vidx].price
```

Listing 12.17. Arrays of structures.

```
/*-------------------------------------------
Creating and processing an array of structures

Must be linked to maintain.lib
-------------------------------------------*/

#include <stdio.h>
#include <stdlib.h>
#include <string.h>

#include "screenlo.h"

typedef struct {
     int no;
     int days;
     double price;
     }VENDOR;

typedef struct {
     int no;
     char description[31];
```

```
     VENDOR vendor[3];
     double retail;
     long on_hand;
     }PART;

/*-----------------
An Array of 300 parts
-----------------*/
#define     NUMBER_OF_PARTS   300
PART part[NUMBER_OF_PARTS];


/*----------------
Function prototypes
----------------*/
void init_parts(void), print_part(int), show_parts(void);

int  get_rand(int, int), enter_part(void),
     get_part_index(int);

/*---------------------------------
1.   Initialize the parts.
2.   Call the enter and display loop.
---------------------------------*/

void main()
{

     init_parts();
     show_parts();
}

/*----------------------------------------------
1.   Repeat until the part number entered is 0
2.   Get a part number from screen input
3.   If it's 0 then break out of the loop
4.   Look up the part
5.   If the returned index is -1 then display a part
     not found message
6.   Otherwise display data on the part
7.   Loop back to 2.
----------------------------------------------*/
void show_parts(void)
{

     int no, index;
```

continues

Listing 12.17. continued

```
     while(1)
          {
          no = enter_part();
          if(no == 0)
               break;
          index = get_part_index(no);
          if(index == -1)
               printf("Part not found. \n");
          else
               print_part(index);
          }
}

/*------------------------------------
1.   Initialize a buffer
2.   Print a message
3.   Get user input
4.   Convert to an integer using atoi()
5.   Return the integer
------------------------------------*/
int enter_part(void)
{
     char buf[5];
6p     strcpy(buf, "    ");
     printf("Enter part number? \n");
     getstr(buf, 4);
     return(atoi(buf));
}

/*----------------------------------------------
Search the array for the requested part number.
1.   Looping through all NUMBER_OF_PARTS entries
2.   If the past number matches the part number,
     return the index of the part that matches
3.   If there is no match, then return (-1).
----------------------------------------------*/
int get_part_index(int no)
{
     int idx;
6p     for(idx = 0; idx < NUMBER_OF_PARTS; ++idx)
          {
          if(no == part[idx].no)
               return(idx);
          }
     return(-1);
}
```

```
/*--------------------------------
Display the part information, and the
information on the three vendors
--------------------------------*/
void print_part(int idx)
{
     int vidx;
6p     printf(" Part %d is a %-30s retail=%6.2f On Hand=%04d\n",
               part[idx].no, part[idx].description,
               part[idx].retail, part[idx].on_hand);

     printf("Sold by: \n");
     for(vidx = 0; vidx < 3; ++ vidx)
          {
          printf(" Vendor %3d for %6.2f Delivery=%3d days. \n",
               part[idx].vendor[vidx].no,
               part[idx].vendor[vidx].price,
               part[idx].vendor[vidx].days);
          }
}

/*-------------------------------------------------------
                    INITIALIZE SECTION
This section sets up random values for the NUMBER_OF_PARTS
parts, numbering them from 1001 to 1000 + NUMBER_OF_PARTS.
The three vendors for each part are initialized as well
-------------------------------------------------------*/
/*-----------------------------------------------
Initialize NUMBER_OF_PARTS vendors with random data.
-----------------------------------------------*/
void init_parts(void)
{
     int idx, vidx;

     for(idx = 0; idx < NUMBER_OF_PARTS ; ++idx)
          {
          part[idx].no = idx + 1001;
          sprintf(part[idx].description, "Part %d", idx + 1001);
          for(vidx = 0; vidx < 3; ++vidx)
               {
               part[idx].vendor[vidx].no = get_rand(1, 100);
               part[idx].vendor[vidx].days = get_rand(15, 45);
               part[idx].vendor[vidx].price = get_rand(1000, 7500);
               part[idx].vendor[vidx].price /= 100;
               }
          part[idx].retail = part[idx].vendor[0].price * 2;
```

continues

Listing 12.17. continued

```
          part[idx].on_hand = get_rand(5, 50);
          }
}


#define     GET_RAND_MAX      RAND_MAX
#define     GET_RAND_MIN      (0 - RAND_MAX)

/*---------------------------------------------------------
1.    Reverse hi and lo if they are wrong way to.
2.    Force hi and lo to maximum and minimum values
3.    Force the difference between them to be within
      range by adjusting hi.
4.    Get a random number using the library rand() function
      and adjust it to fit within the range, and then add lo
      to so that it lies within the range.
---------------------------------------------------------*/
int get_rand(int lo, int hi)
{
     int range, num;

     if(hi < lo)
          {
          range = lo;
          lo = hi;
          hi = range;
          }

     if(hi > GET_RAND_MAX)
          hi = GET_RAND_MAX;
     if(lo < GET_RAND_MIN)
          lo = GET_RAND_MIN;6p
     while( (range = hi - lo) > RAND_MAX)
          hi -= (hi - RAND_MAX);

     num = rand();
     num %= range;
     num += lo;

     return(num);
}
```

Structures also respond to the `sizeof()` operator. Listing 12.18 prints the sizes in bytes of a vendor structure, and the size of a single part entry.

Listing 12.18. Using `sizeof()` with structures.

```
void how_big(void)
{
     printf("Size of a vendor = %d. \n", sizeof(VENDOR));
     printf("Size of a part =   %d. \n", sizeof(part[0]));
}
```

Note that `sizeof()` works on structures whether you use the structure `typedef` data type as in the first line, or an actual structure variable as in the second line.

If structures are of the same type, you may assign one structure to another using the = operator. Listing 12.19 overwrites all of the values in `vendor` with all of the values in `alt_vendor`.

Listing 12.19. Assigning structures using the = operator.

```
typedef struct {
     int no;
     int days;
     double price;
     }VENDOR;

VENDOR vendor;
VENDOR alt_vendor;

void change_vendors(int pidx)
{

     vendor = alt_vendor;
}
```

When an assignment of structures occurs, each member on the left is assigned the value of the corresponding member on the right of the equal sign. It is vaguely analogous to the COBOL verb `MOVE CORRESPONDING`, but the structures must be of the same type.

You may not compare structures. The following example is illegal as `part[pidx]` and `part[0]` are both structures. You can, of course, compare members of a structure as long as they are not structures.

```
if(part[pidx] == part[0])
```

The following example is legal because the members being compared are *atomic* (cannot be broken into smaller parts) C data types, in this case integers.

```
if(part[pidx].no == part[0].no)
```

Passing Structures

The C rules about passing data types to functions also apply to structures. Arrays are passed by reference; all other data types are passed by value. If you call a function with a structure as an argument, a complete copy of the structure is passed to the function. The called function receives its own copy of the structure and can modify it without affecting the structure in the calling function. Listing 12.20 repeats parts of 12.17 changing `print_part()` to a function that is passed a complete `PART` structure instead of an index in to the array. The `print_part()` function is called by passing a single array element, `part[index]`.

```
print_part(part[index]);
```

Remember that the part variable is an array, but the variable `part[index]` is a single occurrence of the `PART` structure. A complete copy of `part[index]` is passed to `print_part()`. Carefully compare the differences between `print_part()` in Listing 12.17 and `print_part()` in Listing 12.20. Listing 12.20 does not use subscripts on the passed `PART` as the value passed is a single `PART` structure, not an array.

Listing 12.20. Passing a structure to a function.

```
/* Changed declaration */
void print_part(PART);

/*------------------------------------------------
1.   Repeat until the part number is entered as 0
2.   Get a part number from screen input
3.   If it's 0 then break out of the loop
4.   Look up the part
5.   If the returned index is -1 then display a part
     not found message
6.   Otherwise display data on the part
7.   Loop back to 2.
------------------------------------------------*/

void show_parts()
{
```

```
     int no, index;
6p     while(1)
          {
          no = enter_part();
          if(no == 0)
               break;
          index = get_part_index(no);
          if(index == -1)
               printf("Part not found. \n");
          else
               print_part(part[index]);      /* Pass one PART */
          }
}

/*-------------------------------
Display the part information, and the
information on the three vendors
-------------------------------*/
void print_part(PART prt)
{
     int vidx;
6p     printf(" Part %d is a %-30s retail=%6.2f On Hand=%04d\n",
               prt.no, prt.description,
               prt.retail, prt.on_hand);

     printf("Sold by: \n");
     for(vidx = 0; vidx < 3; ++ vidx)
          {
          printf(" Vendor %3d for %6.2f Delivery=%3d days. \n",
               prt.vendor[vidx].no,
               prt.vendor[vidx].price,
               prt.vendor[vidx].days);
          }
}
```

A function may also return a complete copy of a structure. Listing 12.21 changes `get_part_index()` to a `get_part()` function that returns an entire copy of the `PART` structure that it finds. An extra copy of the `PART` structure is created called `bad_part`. This is the `PART` that is returned by `get_part()` if the passed part number cannot be located. The `bad_part` structure, is left uninitialized. The changes in Listing 12.21 from Listing 12.17 are in `show_parts()` and the new function `get_part()` that replaces `get_part_index()`.

Inside `show_parts()`, a local `PART` structure called `the_part` is created. When `get_part()` returns a `PART` structure it is assigned to `the_part`. Because `get_part()` returns a complete `PART` structure, the assignment

```
the_part = get_part(no);
```

works correctly, filling `the_part` in with all the part member values returned by `get_part()`.

Listing 12.21. Returning a structure from a function.

```
/*-----------------------------------------------
Creating and processing an array of structures.
Passing structures to functions, and
returning structures from functions.

Must be linked to maintain.lib
----------------------------------------------*/

#include <stdio.h>
#include <stdlib.h>
#include <string.h>

#include "screenlo.h"

typedef struct {
     int no;
     int days;
     double price;
     }VENDOR;

typedef struct {
     int no;
     char description[31];
     VENDOR vendor[3];
     double retail;
     long on_hand;
     }PART;

/*-------------------------------
An Array of NUMBER_OF_PARTS parts
------------------------------*/
#define   NUMBER_OF_PARTS    300
PART part[NUMBER_OF_PARTS];
/*----------------------------------------------
Dummy part to return when a part is not found.
---------------------------------------------*/
PART bad_part;


/*----------------
Function prototypes
```

```
----------------*/
void init_parts(void), print_part(PART), show_parts(void);

int  get_rand(int, int), enter_part(void);

PART get_part(int);

/*--------------------------------------
1.   Initialize the parts.
2.   Call part entry and display function
-------------------------------------*/
void main()
{
     init_parts();
     show_parts();
}

/*--------------------------------------------------
1.   Repeat until the part number is entered as 0
2.   Get a part number from screen input
3.   If it's 0 then break out of the loop
4.   Look up the part
5.   If the returned no member of the_part is 0 then
     display a part not found message
6.   Otherwise display data on the part
7.   Loop back to 2.
-------------------------------------------------*/

void show_parts()
{

     int no;
     PART the_part;
6p     while(1)
          {
          no = enter_part();
          if(no == 0)
               break;
          the_part = get_part(no);
          if(the_part.no == 0)
               printf("Part not found. \n");
          else
               print_part(the_part);
          }
}
```

continues

Listing 12.21. continued

```
/*-----------------------------------
1.    Initialize a buffer
2.    Print a message
3.    Get user input
4.    Convert to an integer using atoi()
5.    Return the integer
-----------------------------------*/
int enter_part(void)
{
     char buf[5];
6p     strcpy(buf, "    ");
     printf("Enter part number? \n");
     getstr(buf, 4);
     return(atoi(buf));
}

/*---------------------------------------------
Search the array for the requested part number.
1.    Looping through all NUMBER_OF_PARTS entries
2.    If the past number matches the part number,
      return a copy of the PART structure that
      matches.
3.    If there is no match, then return a copy
      of bad_part.
---------------------------------------------*/
PART get_part(int no)
{
     int idx;
6p     for(idx = 0; idx < NUMBER_OF_PARTS; ++idx)
          {
          if(no == part[idx].no)
               return(part[idx]);
          }
     return(bad_part);
}

/*---------------------------------
Display the part information, and the
information on the three vendors
---------------------------------*/
void print_part(PART prt)
{
     int vidx;
6p     printf(" Part %d is a %-30s retail=%6.2f On Hand=%04d\n",
               prt.no, prt.description,
               prt.retail, prt.on_hand);

     printf("Sold by: \n");
```

```
     for(vidx = 0; vidx < 3; ++ vidx)
          {
          printf(" Vendor %3d for %6.2f Delivery=%3d days. \n",
               prt.vendor[vidx].no,
               prt.vendor[vidx].price,
               prt.vendor[vidx].days);
          }
}

/*-----------------------------------------------------
                    INITIALIZE SECTION
This section sets up random values for the
NUMBER_OF_PARTS parts, numbering them from 1001
to 1000 + NUMBER_OF_PARTS. The three vendors
for each part are initialized as well
-----------------------------------------------------*/
/*-----------------------------------------------------
Initialize NUMBER_OF_PARTS vendors with random data.
-----------------------------------------------------*/
void init_parts(void)
{
     int idx, vidx;

     for(idx = 0; idx < NUMBER_OF_PARTS ; ++idx)
          {
          part[idx].no = idx + 1001;
          sprintf(part[idx].description, "Part %d", idx + 1001);
          for(vidx = 0; vidx < 3; ++vidx)
               {
               part[idx].vendor[vidx].no = get_rand(1, 100);
               part[idx].vendor[vidx].days = get_rand(15, 45);
               part[idx].vendor[vidx].price = get_rand(1000, 7500);
               part[idx].vendor[vidx].price /= 100;
               }
          part[idx].retail = part[idx].vendor[0].price * 2;
          part[idx].on_hand = get_rand(5, 50);
          }
}


#define   GET_RAND_MAX  RAND_MAX
#define   GET_RAND_MIN   (0 - RAND_MAX)

/*-----------------------------------------------------------
1.   Reverse hi and lo if they are wrong way to.
2.   Force hi and lo to maximum and minimum values
3.   Force the difference between them to be within
     range by adjusting hi.
```

continues

Listing 12.21. continued

```
4.    Get a random number using the library rand() function
      and adjust it to fit within the range, and then add lo
      to so that it lies within the range.
--------------------------------------------------------*/
int get_rand(int lo, int hi)
{
     int range, num;

     if(hi < lo)
          {
          range = lo;
          lo = hi;
          hi = range;
          }

     if(hi > GET_RAND_MAX)
          hi = GET_RAND_MAX;
     if(lo < GET_RAND_MIN)
          lo = GET_RAND_MIN;6p
     while( (range = hi - lo) > RAND_MAX)
          hi -= (hi - RAND_MAX);

     num = (rand() % range) + lo;

     return(num);
}
```

Passing Pointers to Structures

You will have noticed that because the `get_part()` function returns a `PART` structure, it was necessary to create an extra copy of `PART`, `bad_part`, to so that `get_part()` had a value that it could return if a part could not be found. This is one of the complications caused by passing structures back and forth between functions. Passing complete structures around is clumsy and usually slows programs down. Fortunately, it is unnecessary.

Listing 12.22 is a simple example of passing a complete structure to a print routine. The print routine doesn't need a full copy of the structure. It isn't going to change values, it just needs access to the members to print them.

Listing 12.22. Passing a structure.

```
#include <stdio.h>

typedef struct{
     int      no;
     char name[31];
     double   balance;
     }CUSTOMER;

CUSTOMER customer = { 1002, "Henry Higgins", 29.95};

/*prototype for print_cust()*/
void print_cust(CUSTOMER);

void main()
{
     print_cust(customer);
}

void print_cust(CUSTOMER cust)
{
     printf("%d %s Balance is %6.2f \n",
                    cust.no, cust.name, cust.balance);
}
```

C allows you to pass pointers to any data type by using the & (pass by address) to override the C default of pass by copy. It should be possible to call a function such as `print_cust` with a pointer to the `CUSTOMER` structure instead of a copy of the structure as in:

```
print_cust(&customer);
```

The real problem arises in the receiving function. The data that has been received is not a `CUSTOMER` structure:

```
void print_cust(CUSTOMER cust)
{
}
```

but is a pointer to a `CUSTOMER` structure:

```
void print_cust(CUSTOMER *cust)
{
}
```

How do you access the members of `cust`? When the value received by a function is a pointer to a structure, a special operator is used for accessing members of the structure. The operator is the pointer (->). It replaces the dot operator in structure-member access when the variable is a pointer to a structure rather than a structure. Listing 12.23 repeats the printing problem, but passes a pointer to a structure.

Listing 12.23. Passing a pointer to a structure.

```
#include <stdio.h>

typedef struct{
     int       no;
     char name[31];
     double    balance;
     }CUSTOMER;

CUSTOMER customer = { 1002, "Henry Higgins", 29.95};

/*
 * prototype for print_cust() receiving a pointer to
 * a CUSTOMER
 */
void print_cust(CUSTOMER*);

void main()
{
     print_cust(&customer);   /* pass a pointer*/
}

void print_cust(CUSTOMER *cust)
{
     printf("%d %s Balance is %6.2f \n",
               cust->no, cust->name, cust->balance);
}
```

The variables retain their type just as they did with the dot operator.

```
cust->no                  is an integer
cust->name                is a string
cust->balance             is a double
```

Passing pointers to structures is faster than passing copies of structures. However if you modify `cust->balance`, you are in fact changing the value in customer.balance. This is frequently what you want to do. Listing 12.24 modifies a customer balance because of a 10 percent overdue charge. The logic is simple.

Listing 12.24. Modifying members through a pointer.

```
#include <stdio.h>

typedef struct{
     int       no;
     char name[31];
     double    balance;
     }CUSTOMER;

CUSTOMER customer = { 1002, "Henry Higgins", 29.95};

/*
 * prototype for print_cust() and add_overdue()
 * receiving a pointer to a CUSTOMER
 */
void print_cust(CUSTOMER*), add_overdue(CUSTOMER*);

void main()
{
     printf("Before: \n");
     print_cust(&customer);
     add_overdue(&customer);
     printf("After: \n");
     print_cust(&customer);
}

void print_cust(CUSTOMER *cust)
{
     printf("%d %s Balance is %6.2f \n",
               cust->no, cust->name, cust->balance);
}

/*-------
Add 10 %
-------*/
void add_overdue(CUSTOMER *cust)
{
     cust->balance *= 1.10;
}
```

Compare this with Listing 12.25 which does the same task, but passes a copy of the structure.

Listing 12.25. Modifying through a copy.

```
#include <stdio.h>

typedef struct{
     int       no;
     char name[31];
     double    balance;
     }CUSTOMER;

CUSTOMER customer = { 1002, "Henry Higgins", 29.95};

void print_cust(CUSTOMER*);

CUSTOMER add_overdue(CUSTOMER);

void main()
{
     CUSTOMER new_cust;
6p     printf("Before call: \n");
     print_cust(&customer);
     new_cust = add_overdue(customer);
     printf("New cust: \n");
     print_cust(&new_cust);
     printf("After call: \n");
     print_cust(&customer);
     customer.balance = new_cust.balance;
     printf("After assigning balance: \n");
     print_cust(&customer);
}

void print_cust(CUSTOMER *cust)
{
     printf("%d %s Balance is %6.2f \n",
               cust->no, cust->name, cust->balance);
}

/*-------
Add 10 %
-------*/
CUSTOMER add_overdue(CUSTOMER cust)
{
     cust.balance *= 1.10;
     return(cust);
}
```

Since the copy of customer passed to add_overdue() is a local copy for add_overdue(), the copy must be returned to the calling function. The returned copy has to be assigned to a another CUSTOMER structure, new_cust, on the return, and then the new_cust.balance can be extracted and assigned to customer.balance.

Structure pointer logic is so convenient to use, that you will rarely see a structure passed by copy. Almost all work with structures is done by passing a pointer to the structure.

Structure work inside functions is sometimes converted to pointer logic, as pointer logic is easy to use.

A function may also return a pointer to a structure. Listing 12.26 repeats Listing 12.21, but get_part() has been changed to return a pointer to the located PART structure instead of a copy of the structure. The print_part() function is passed a pointer to the PART structure instead of a copy of it.

Listing 12.26. Returning a structure pointer.

```
/*---------------------------------------------
Creating and processing an array of structures.
Passing pointers to structures to functions, and
returning pointers to structures from functions.

Must be linked to maintain.lib
---------------------------------------------*/

#include <stdio.h>
#include <stdlib.h>
#include <string.h>

#include "screenlo.h"

typedef struct {
     int no;
     int days;
     double price;
     }VENDOR;

typedef struct {
     int no;
     char description[31];
     VENDOR vendor[3];
     double retail;
     long on_hand;
     }PART;
```

continues

Listing 12.26. continued

```
/*------------------------------
An Array of NUMBER_OF_PARTS parts
------------------------------*/
#define   NUMBER_OF_PARTS     300
PART part[NUMBER_OF_PARTS];

/*----------------
Function prototypes
----------------*/
void init_parts(void), print_part(PART *), show_parts(void),
          print_vendor(VENDOR *);

int  get_rand(int, int), enter_part(void);

PART *get_part(int);

/*---------------------------------------
1.   Initialize the parts.
2.   Call part entry and display function
---------------------------------------*/
void main()
{
     init_parts();
     show_parts();
}

/*--------------------------------------------------
1.   Repeat until the part number is entered as 0
2.   Get a part number from screen input
3.   If it's 0 then break out of the loop
4.   Look up the part
5.   If the returned no member of the_part is 0 then
     display a part not found message
6.   Otherwise display data on the part
7.   Loop back to 2.
--------------------------------------------------*/

void show_parts()
{

     int no;
     PART *prt;
6p     while(1)
          {
          no = enter_part();
          if(no == 0)
```

```
                break;
            prt = get_part(no);
            if(prt == NULL)
                printf("Part not found. \n");
            else
                print_part(prt);
            }
}

/*-----------------------------------
1.   Initialize a buffer
2.   Print a message
3.   Get user input
4.   Convert to an integer using atoi()
5.   Return the integer
-----------------------------------*/
int enter_part(void)
{
     char buf[5];
6p     strcpy(buf, "    ");
     printf("Enter part number? \n");
     getstr(buf, 4);
     return(atoi(buf));
}

/*-------------------------------------------
Search the array for the requested part number.
1.   Looping through all NUMBER_OF_PARTS entries
2.   If the past number matches the part number,
     return a pointer to the PART structure that
     matches.
3.   If there is no match, then return a NULL
-------------------------------------------*/
PART *get_part(int no)
{
     int idx;
6p     for(idx = 0; idx < NUMBER_OF_PARTS; ++idx)
          {
          if(no == part[idx].no)
               return(&part[idx]);
          }
     return(NULL);
}

/*---------------------------------
Display the part information, and the
information on the three vendors
---------------------------------*/
```

continues

Listing 12.26. continued

```
void print_part(PART *prt)
{
     int vidx;
6p     printf(" Part %d is a %-30s retail=%6.2f On Hand=%04d\n",
               prt->no, prt->description,
               prt->retail, prt->on_hand);

     printf("Sold by: \n");
     for(vidx = 0; vidx < 3; ++ vidx)
          {
          print_vendor(&prt->vendor[vidx]);
          }
}

void print_vendor(VENDOR *vendor)
{
     printf(" Vendor %3d for %6.2f Delivery=%3d days. \n",
               vendor->no,
               vendor->price,
               vendor->days);
}


/*-----------------------------------------------------
                    INITIALIZE SECTION
This section sets up random values for the
NUMBER_OF_PARTS parts, numbering them from 1001
to 1000 + NUMBER_OF_PARTS. The three vendors
for each part are initialized as well
---------------------------------------------------*/
/*-----------------------------------------------------
Initialize NUMBER_OF_PARTS vendors with random data.
---------------------------------------------------*/
void init_parts(void)
{
     int idx, vidx;

     for(idx = 0; idx < NUMBER_OF_PARTS ; ++idx)
          {
          part[idx].no = idx + 1001;
          sprintf(part[idx].description, "Part %d", idx + 1001);
          for(vidx = 0; vidx < 3; ++vidx)
               {
               part[idx].vendor[vidx].no = get_rand(1, 100);
               part[idx].vendor[vidx].days = get_rand(15, 45);
```

```
                part[idx].vendor[vidx].price = get_rand(1000, 7500);
                part[idx].vendor[vidx].price /= 100;
                }
            part[idx].retail = part[idx].vendor[0].price * 2;
            part[idx].on_hand = get_rand(5, 50);
            }
}


#define    GET_RAND_MAX    RAND_MAX
#define    GET_RAND_MIN    (0 - RAND_MAX)

/*----------------------------------------------------------
1.    Reverse hi and lo if they are wrong way to.
2.    Force hi and lo to maximum and minimum values
3.    Force the difference between them to be within
      range by adjusting hi.
4.    Get a random number using the library rand() function
      and adjust it to fit within the range, and then add lo
      to so that it lies within the range.
----------------------------------------------------------*/
int get_rand(int lo, int hi)
{
      int range, num;

      if(hi < lo)
           {
           range = lo;
           lo = hi;
           hi = range;
           }

      if(hi > GET_RAND_MAX)
           hi = GET_RAND_MAX;
      if(lo < GET_RAND_MIN)
           lo = GET_RAND_MIN;6p
      while( (range = hi - lo) > RAND_MAX)
           hi -= (hi - RAND_MAX);

      num = (rand() % range) + lo;

      return(num);
}
```

The coding change to `get_part()` is simply adding the address-of operator to the return value:

```
return(&part[index]);
```

instead of

```
return(part[index]);
```

You no longer need the bad_part variable. Since get_part() is returning a pointer, it may return a NULL to indicate that the part was not found. The test in show_parts() is simplified to testing for NULL as the return value from get_part().

Some additional changes in print_part() have been made to illustrate another issue on pointers. The print_part() function is passed a pointer to a PART structure and you will see that syntax similar to the print_cust() problem is used, up to the section of the function that prints vendors. Instead of printing the vendors, another function, print_vendor() is called to print each vendor. The print_vendor function is called with a rather unusual-looking argument.

```
print_vendor(&prt->vendor[vidx]);
```

This looks pretty complicated until you break it down. Ignoring for the moment that vendor is a member of the PART structure, vendor is an array of structures. To pass one element of an array of structures you would use:

```
do_something(vendor[index]);
```

or

```
do_something(part[index]);
```

To pass a pointer to one element of an array of structures, add the address-of operator:

```
do_something(&vendor[index]);
```

or

```
do_something(&part[index]);
```

In this case the vendor structure is an array of structures within a PART structure. To pass a single element of the vendor array:

```
do_something(part[pidx].vendor[vidx]);
```

To pass a pointer to a single element of the vendor array, simply add the address-of operator.

```
do_something(&part[pidx].vendor[vidx]);
```

In this case the & operator works out to be "the address of whatever the rest of this variable is about," and the C compiler is able to sort out the fact that what you want is the address of the vendor[vidx] element, not the part[pidx] element.

In print_part() in Listing 12.26, the PART structure has already been turned into a pointer. To pass a single element in the vendor array:

```
do_something(prt->vendor[vidx]);
```

To pass a pointer to this element, once again add the address-of operator:

```
do_something(&prt->vendor[vidx]);
```

or in the case of Listing 12.26,

```
print_vendor(&prt->vendor[vidx]);
```

Within print_vendor(), the vendor variable is used as a pointer to a VENDOR structure to access the members.

A Review of Pointers

Listing 12.27 is our old friend strcpy() (called stringcpy() in this example).

Listing 12.27.

```
#include <stdio.h>

char *stringcpy(char*, char*);
void print_strings();

char text[]= "Hello";
char receiver[50];

void main()
{
     print_strings();
     stringcpy(receiver, text);
     print_strings();
}

char *stringcpy(char *dest, char *src)
{
     char *temp;

     temp = dest;

     while(*src)
```

continues

Listing 12.27. continued

```
        {
        *dest = *src;
        ++dest;
        ++src;
        }
    *dest = 0;
    return(temp);
}

void print_strings(void)
{
    printf("Text=<%s>, Receiver=<%s> \n", text, receiver);
}
```

The two key lines I want you to look at are `++dest` and `++src`. This increment operator causes each pointer to be moved up one position to the next character in the `src` and `dest` arrays. This is not because `++` means increment by 1. It actually means increment by the appropriate amount. If `++` (or `--`) is applied to a number, it changes the number by 1. If `++` is applied to a pointer, the pointer is incremented by the number of bytes occupied by the data type that is pointed to by the pointer. In the case of a `char` data type, this happens to be 1, so `++` still adds 1 to the pointer.

The `stringcpy()` function copies an array of characters until a NUL character is encountered.

Listing 12.28 is `intcpy()`, a rather silly function, that copies an array of integers until a zero-valued integer is encountered. Note that the logic flow is identical to 12.27, yet this program works as expected, copying an array of integers into another array of integers.

The size of an integer will be either two or four bytes depending on the machine and compiler. The compiler knows that a pointer to an integer must be incremented by the size of the integer in order to ensure that it points to the next integer. So the logic generated by the compiler for `++src` in `stringcpy()` will be "Add 1 (size of a `char`) to the address in the `src` variable."

In `intcpy()`, `src` is declared as a variable containing the address of an `int`, The logic generated for `++src` in `intcpy()` will be "Add 2 or 4 (size of an `int`) to the address in the `src` variable."

In both cases, `src` ends up containing the address of the next element of the array and `*src` (what's pointed to by `src`) is that value, either a `char` or an `int`.

Listing 12.28. Copying an array of integers.

```
#include <stdio.h>

int *intcpy(int*, int*);
void print_ints();

int numbers[] = { 15, 24, 5057, 122, 0};
int receiver[10];

void main()
{
     print_ints();
     intcpy(receiver, numbers);
     print_ints();
}

int *intcpy(int *dest, int *src)
{
     int *temp;

     temp = dest;

     while(*src)
          {
          *dest = *src;
          ++dest;
          ++src;
          }
     *dest = 0;
     return(temp);
}

void print_ints(void)
{
     printf("numbers = %d %d %d %d %d \n",
          numbers[0], numbers[1],
          numbers[2], numbers[3],
          numbers[4]);
     printf("receiver = %d %d %d %d %d \n",
          receiver[0], receiver[1],
          receiver[2], receiver[3],
          receiver[4]);
}
```

Let's expand this principle to arrays of structures. Listing 12.29 is a repeat of the `get_part()` function. Instead of accessing the global part array directly, it is passed a pointer to the part array. It searches the array by using the passed pointer, and returns a pointer to the correctly identified part. Within the `get_part()` function, `++prt` is translated to increment the address in `prt` by the size of a `PART` structure. Once this is done, `prt` now points to the next element of the array. Note the call to `get_part()` is passed `"part"` with no qualifiers. Since `part` is an array, it is automatically passed as a pointer.

```
get_part(part, no);
```

Listing 12.29. Processing arrays of structures with pointers.

```
/*--------------------------------------------
Search the array for the requested part number.
1.   Looping through all NUMBER_OF_PARTS entries
2.   If the past number matches the part number,
     return a pointer to the PART structure that
     matches.
3.   If there is no match, then return a NULL
--------------------------------------------*/
PART *get_part(PART *prt, int no)
{
     int idx;
6p     for(idx = 0; idx < NUMBER_OF_PARTS; ++idx)
         {
         if(no == prt->no)
              return(prt);
         ++prt;
         }
     return(NULL);
}
```

One warning on pointers to arrays: It is possible to pass a function a pointer to a single instance of a data type. If the function is expecting to be passed a pointer to the first element of an array, the function will not be processing an array, but unpredictable values that will be lying around in memory. Listing 12.30 passes two values to `intcpy()`. The compiler will not warn you of a problem, because the data type being passed is correct, pointers to integers, but `intcpy()` will think that it has received pointers to the first elements of two arrays and will proceed as programmed causing unpredictable results.

Listing 12.30. Passing a non-array to `intcpy()`.

```
int one = 1;
int two = 2;

some_func(void)
{
     intcpy(&one, &two);
}
```

Summary

As pointers are used extensively when dealing with structures, it is important that you really understand them. The following simple rules help with this.

- Arrays are always passed as pointers by default.
- All other data types, including structures, are passed as copies of the value.
- You may override the pass-by-copy default, by using the address-of (`&`) operator. This may be used on any data type, but is most frequently used on structures.
- If a called function receives a pointer, the increment operator, when applied to the pointer, increases the pointer by a value equal to the number of bytes in the size of the underlying data type, in effect pointing to the next element in the array.
- Pointer increment and decrement operations work correctly if the passed value is a pointer to an element of an array (usually the first element). If a pointer to a single instance is passed, an increment or decrement operation on the pointer will cause the pointer to point into some other area of memory.
- The members of a structure pointed to by a pointer are accessed by using the `->` operator.

It should be possible to read and write structures directly to files so that they can be used in the same way as COBOL records. Structures can contain NUL characters, and stream I/O files tend to be based on ASCII text. Stream files are not comfortable with NUL characters embedded in the record, so it is necessary to resort to low-level file I/O, which is the subject of the next chapter.

13

Based Numbers and Bit Operators

In C you will work much more closely with bits and bytes than you do in COBOL, and it is time to get the hang of number bases and bit operators.

In this chapter you will learn about:

- Representing numeric constants
- Base conversions
- Bit maps
- Bit logic operators
- Bit masks
- Signed and unsigned characters
- Bit-level operators
- Converting packed fields

Representing Numeric Constants

C will allow you to represent a numeric constant in decimal, octal, or hexadecimal bases.

Numbers starting with `0` (other than the value zero) are compiled as octal constants. Numbers beginning with `0X` or `0x` (zero followed by *x*) are compiled as hexadecimal constants. Numbers starting with a decimal digit are compiled as decimal constants.

Listing 13.1 initializes three integer constants using this method.

Listing 13.1. Initializing constants.

```
#include <stdio.h>

int  int_1 = 15;          /* Decimal 15 */
int  int_2 = 027;         /* Octal 27 = 23 */
int  int_3 = 0x1f;        /* Hex 1F = 31 */

main()
{
     printf("Values are %d %d %d.\n", int_1, int_2, int_3);
}
```

Although the values are initialized in decimal, octal, and hexadecimal, they are all printed in decimal, and the output of the program will be:

```
Values are 15 23 31.
```

Binary Numbers

When you picked up this book, you might have had a premonition that you would have to deal with binary numbers. The time has come. They are indirectly related to low-level file I/O, but you will need to understand them and the methods used to represent binary numbers.

The binary system uses `1`s and `0`s to represent the bits stored in one or more bytes of data. The use of `1`s and `0`s to illustrate a byte is not too daunting, but short integers are

16 bits long, and long integers are 32 bits long. Eventually you just lose the ability to track this kind of information with your eye. The examples below start to become meaningless at a short `int`.

byte	`01101001`
short `int`	`0101000101101011`
long `int`	`01000100110011001010101000111001`

There had to be some easier way of representing long strings of bits.

Octal Numbers

Octal numbering, in base 8, is a system based on the eight digits 0–7. One of the advantages of octal is that conversions between octal and binary are very easy to do.

An octal digit represents three binary bits, as shown in Table 13.1

Table 13.1. Binary to octal conversion.

Binary	*Octal*
000	0
001	1
010	2
011	3
100	4
101	5
110	6
111	7

To convert binary to octal:

1. Add `0`s to the left of the binary number until the number of digits is evenly divisible by 3.

   `10110101` becomes `010110101`

2. Group the number into chunks of three bits starting from the right.

   ```
   010 110 101
   ```

3. Translate each set of three bits into a single octal digit using Table 13.1.

   `010 110 101` becomes `265`

4. C requires that an octal number starts with a zero, so you would use this value as

   ```
   int value = 0265;
   ```

To convert octal to binary, reverse the process by converting each octal digit into a three-bit group, starting from the right.

The ease of translation makes octal a logical choice for representing binary information.

Hexadecimal Numbers

Once the byte (8 bits) became the standard unit of data in computers (it wasn't always), it seemed more sensible to come up with something that more closely approximated byte storage.

Base-16 numbering, hexadecimal, uses 16 digits: 0–9 and A–F. It is unfortunate in some ways that letters were chosen to represent the digits that had the value of 10 through 15, as it causes some confusion. There weren't really any other convenient symbols. The digits A–F (or a–f) are just symbols representing the values 10 through 15 and shouldn't be confused with the letters of the alphabet.

Hexadecimal-to-binary conversions are easy, though not quite as easy as binary–octal conversions.

A hexadecimal digit represents four binary bits, as shown in Table 13.2.

Table 13.2. Hexadecimal to binary conversion.

Binary	*Hexadecimal*
0000	0
0001	1
0010	2

Binary	*Hexadecimal*
0011	3
0100	4
0101	5
0110	6
0111	7
1000	8
1001	9
1010	A
1011	B
1100	C
1101	D
1110	E
1111	F

To convert to hexadecimal, break the bits into four-bit groups starting from the right, and convert each group into the equivalent hexadecimal digit.

To convert hexadecimal to binary, start from the right and convert each digit into the four-bit groups.

Base Conversions

There are many tricks to convert between hexadecimal, octal and decimal, but it is probably easier to just let the computer do this work for you. Listing 13.2 is a program that will accept input in any base, and will display a table of the conversions to other bases. It uses the ability of `sscanf()`, using the `"%i"` format, to scan in any of the standard hexadecimal, decimal, or octal formats, and uses `printf()` formatting characters to print the results in different bases.

Listing 13.2 bases.c.—converting decimal/hexadecimal/octal.

```
/*----
bases.c converts input to octal, decimal and
hexadecimal bases.
------*/

#include <stdio.h>
#include <process.h>

static unsigned long cvt_value( char*);
static void usage(void);

unsigned long start, last;


/*----
Program must be started with at least one argument
on the command line representing a starting value.
If a second value exists it is taken as the ending value.
Program prints octal, decimal and hexadecimal values for
all numbers in range.
------*/
void main(int argc, char *argv[])
{
     if((argc < 2) || (argc > 3))
          usage();

     start = cvt_value(argv[1]);
     last = 0L;

     if(argc == 3)
          last = cvt_value(argv[2]);

     printf("%12s %10s %8s\n", "Octal", "Decimal", "Hex");
     do{
          printf("%12lo %10lu %8lx\n", start, start, start);
          }while( ++start <= last);
}

/*----
The "%i" specification will accept input in any of the
standard C conventions for numbers: octal numbers starting with
0, hex numbers starting with 0x, and decimal numbers starting
with a non-zero value. The "%li" format is the long integer
version of "%i".
------*/
```

```
static unsigned long cvt_value(char *str)
{
     unsigned long result;

     result = 0;

     sscanf(str, "%li", &result);
     return(result);
}

/*----
Display some helpful text and exit
------*/
void usage(void)
{
     printf("Syntax:\n\n");
     printf(" bases lo [hi]\n");
     printf("\n");
     printf("Converts lo or range of lo to hi and displays\n");
     printf("results in decimal, octal and hex bases.\n\n");
     printf("Formats for lo and hi are:\n");
     printf(" nnnnn  = decimal where n = a decimal digit\n");
     printf("          decimal number must not start with 0\n");
     printf(" 0oooo  = octal   where o = an octal digit\n");
     printf(" 0xffff = hex     where f = a hex digit\n");
     exit(0);
}
```

Listing 13.2 is fine as far as it goes, but it omits binary for either input or output. Binary is not one of the types supported by `scanf()` or `printf()`.

Listing 13.3 adds binary routines to bases.c by adding a `'b'` prefix to a binary string as one of the possible input types. If the `cvt_value()` routine detects a `'b'` or `'B'` as the first character of the string, it calls another routine to convert binary input, `cvt_binary()`.

Listing 13.3. bbases.c—adding binary to bases.c.

```
/*----
bbases.c converts input to octal, decimal, binary and
hexadecimal bases.
------*/

#include <stdio.h>
#include <process.h>
```

continues

Listing 13.3. continued

```
static unsigned long cvt_value( char *);
static unsigned long cvt_binary( char *);
static void usage(void);
static char *ltob(unsigned long, char *);

unsigned long start, last;

char start_str[33];


/*----
Program must be started with at least one argument
on the command line representing a starting value.
If a second value exists, it is taken as the ending
value. Program prints octal, binary, decimal and hexadecimal
values for all numbers in range.

Binary numbers must be entered with a leading 'b' or 'B'.
------*/
void main(int argc, char *argv[])
{
     if( (argc < 2) || (argc > 3) )
          usage();

     start = cvt_value(argv[1]);
     last = 0L;

     if(argc == 3)
          last = cvt_value(argv[2]);

     printf("%12s %10s %8s %32s\n",
          "Octal", "Decimal", "Hex", "Binary");
     do{
          printf("%12lo %10lu %8lx %32s\n",
               start, start, start, ltob(start, start_str));
          }while( ++start <= last );
}

/*----
The "%i" specification will accept input in any of the
standard C conventions for numbers: octal numbers
starting with 0, hex numbers starting with 0x,
and decimal numbers starting with a non-zero value.
The "%li" format is the long integer version.
------*/
static unsigned long cvt_value(char *str)
```

```
{
     unsigned long result;

     result = 0;

     if( (*str == 'b') || (*str == 'B') )
          {
          ++str;
          return(cvt_binary(str));
          }

     sscanf(str, "%li", &result);
     return(result);
}

/*----
Convert a long to a 32 byte string of 1's and 0's
------*/
static char *ltob(unsigned long value, char *str)
{
     int idx;

     str += 33;
     *str = 0;
     --str;

     for(idx = 0; idx < 32; ++idx)
          {
          if( value % 2)
               *str = '1';
          else
               *str = '0';
          --str;
          value /= 2;
          }
     return(++str);
}

static unsigned long cvt_binary(char *str)
{
     unsigned long result;

     result = 0;

     while(*str)
          {
          result *= 2;
```

continues

Listing 13.3. continued

```
          if(*str == '1')
               result += 1;
          ++str;
          }
     return(result);
}


/*----
Display some helpful text and exit
------*/
void usage(void)
{
     printf("Syntax:\n\n");
     printf(" bases lo [hi]\n");
     printf("\n");
     printf("Converts lo or range of lo to hi and displays\n");
     printf("results in decimal, octal and hex bases.\n\n");
     printf("Formats for lo and hi are:\n");
     printf(" nnnnn  = decimal where n = a decimal digit\n");
     printf("                  decimal number must not start with 0\n");
     printf(" 0oooo  = octal   where o = an octal digit\n");
     printf(" 0xffff = hex     where f = a hex digit\n");
     printf(" Bbbbbb = binary  where b = a binary digit.\n");
     exit(0);
}
```

The `cvt_binary()` function is passed a string and converts it by multiplying the result by 2 and then adding 1 if the byte in the string is a `'1'`. The `cvt_binary()` function has no error checking and treats any non-`'1'` digit as a zero. It would convert `1231` as `1001`.

The output of a binary "string" is handled by `ltob()`. The `ltob()` routine creates a 32-character string by starting at the right-hand end of the string. The passed unsigned long value is tested repeatedly with a remainder operator. If there is a remainder after dividing by 2, the rightmost binary digit must be `'1'`, otherwise it is `'0'`. The value is actually divided by 2 to shift all the bits to the right and the process is repeated 32 times, stepping backward through the string.

You should compile and link bbases.c and keep it in your arsenal as a quick way of checking values.

Bit Maps

Bit maps are usually not familiar to COBOL programmers. Only a few COBOL dialects support bit manipulation, and they are usually disguised with a syntax that prevents you from seeing what is actually going on. COBOL has two well-known bits maps, but they are not "known" as bit maps. `LOW-VALUES` is a bit map representing all bits off, and `HIGH-VALUES` represents all bits on.

A byte is composed of eight bits. A bit can be either on or off. Numerically, this is conveniently represented as `1` for on and `0` for off. An eight-bit byte is represented by eight `0`s or `1`s as in:

```
00000000
00000100
01011101
```

If you check out the possible combinations you will find that a byte can represent 256 possible combinations of `0`s and `1`s ranging from `00000000` to `1111111`.

Bits are usually numbered backwards from left to right:

Bit position	8 7 6 5 4 3 2 1
Bits	1 0 0 0 1 0 1 1

In the above example, bits 1, 2, 4 and 8 are on.

This is not the only method used to number bits, and you will also find such numbering schemes as shown below:

Bit Position	7 6 5 4 3 2 1 0
Bits	1 0 0 0 1 0 1 1
Bit Position	1 2 3 4 5 6 7 8
Bits	1 0 0 0 1 0 1 1
Bit Position	0 1 2 3 4 5 6 7
Bits	1 0 0 0 1 0 1 1

This can be very confusing, and it is important when reading about bit masks in any manual that you understand the numbering system that is being used.

The leftmost bit is also called the high-order bit, and the rightmost is the low-order bit. In this discussion, the high-order bit will be bit 8, and the low-order bit will be bit 1 as in the first numbering example.

Bit maps are frequently used in C programming as a method of flagging certain conditions or behavior. For example, you might decide that a single byte of information will be used to flag the behavior of a data entry field on the screen. You could specify that bit 1, when turned on, specifies that the field should be displayed underlined. Bit 2, when on, specifies that all alphabetic characters entered into the field will be converted to uppercase. Bit 3, when on, specifies that the field is to blink. In order to set this field control byte to an underlined field that blinks and converts alphabetic characters to uppercase, you would set the control byte to a value of:

```
00000111
```

A non-underlined version of the same field would be effected by setting the control byte to:

```
00000110
```

In an example like this, a single byte of control information is more economical than creating a special flag for each case. Underlining/non-underlining are mutually exclusive conditions, as are blink/steady and upper-/lowercase.

If you decided to create a numeric-only entry field, you could require that bit 4, when set on, will beep the terminal bell if the user attempted to enter any key that is not numeric, and the field will only accept the digits 1–9, the signs + and - and a decimal point. In the program, you would have to include logic that if bit 4 were set on, the state of bit 2 would be ignored (upper-/lowercase), because it makes no sense to honor this bit.

In C, using bit maps can be extended beyond eight bits. A short or long integer can be used as a bit map providing 16 or 32 bits respectively, or a complete character array could be devoted to bit-mapping, allowing a bit map of any number of bits.

Reading bit maps as a string of `1`s and `0`s is usually awkward, and C doesn't provide a direct way of assigning a constant in binary.

Bit maps in C are initialized and manipulated using either octal or hexadecimal constants. Octal was the "standard" in early C code, but hexadecimal is rapidly overtaking it because it is frequently easier to use to represent a map. Both are seen in modern C code, and you need to understand the hexadecimal and octal numbering systems to be able to read the values.

Bit Logic Operators

The bit logic operators allow you to combine two bit patterns in various ways. In the following examples, I use 8- and 16-bit values. The operators can also be used on 32-bit values.

An AND operation causes each pair of bits to be compared. If both bits are on, the resulting bit is set on; otherwise it is set off. The C bitwise AND operator is `&`. In the example below, `z` is set to a value of `65`, the result of ANDing two bit patterns.

```
unsigned short int x, z;

    x = 85;
    y = 227;

    z = x & y;

              x       0 0 0 0 0 0 0 0 0 1 0 1 0 1 0 1 (85)
    &         y       0 0 0 0 0 0 0 0 1 1 1 0 0 0 1 1 (227)
    ----------------------------------------------------------
    =         z       0 0 0 0 0 0 0 0 0 1 0 0 0 0 0 1 (65)
```

An OR operation (sometimes called inclusive OR) causes each pair of bits to be compared. If either bit is set on, the resulting bit is set on. The C bitwise OR operator is `¦`. In the example below `z` is set to the value `247`, the result of ORing two-bit patterns.

```
unsigned short int x, z;

    x = 85;
    y = 227;

    z = x ¦ y;

              x       0 0 0 0 0 0 0 0 0 1 0 1 0 1 0 1 (85)
    &         y       0 0 0 0 0 0 0 0 1 1 1 0 0 0 1 1 (227)
    ----------------------------------------------------------
    =         z       0 0 0 0 0 0 0 0 1 1 1 1 0 1 1 1 (247)
```

An exclusive OR operation (also called XOR) causes each pair of bits to be compared. If only one bit is on, the resulting bit is set on. If neither bits or both bits are on, the resulting bit is set off. The C bitwise XOR operator is `^`. In the example below, `z` is set to the value 182, the result of XORing two bit patterns.

```
unsigned short int x, z;

    x = 85;
    y = 227;

    z = x ^ y;

              x       0 0 0 0 0 0 0 0 0 1 0 1 0 1 0 1 (85)
    &         y       0 0 0 0 0 0 0 0 1 1 1 0 0 0 1 1 (227)
    ----------------------------------------------------------
    =         z       0 0 0 0 0 0 0 0 1 0 1 1 0 1 1 0 (182)
```

The NOT operator is a unary operator that is used to invert (reverse) the value of each bit in a bit map. The C bitwise NOT operator is ~. In the example below, `z` is set to the value `65450`, the result of inverting all the bits in a bit pattern.

```
unsigned short int x, z;

     x = 85;

     z = ~x;

          x = 0 0 0 0 0 0 0 0 0 1 0 1 0 1 0 1 (85)
     ______________________________________________
     z = ~x = 1 1 1 1 1 1 1 1 1 0 1 0 1 0 1 0 (65450)
```

One of the tricks to learning to work with bit operators is to stop thinking of values arithmetically. You can see from the above examples that AND, OR, XOR, and NOT produce values that make no sense arithmetically. When you are working with bit operators you are really working with 8, 16, or 32 on/off flags.

Bit Masks

A bit mask is a bit map that is used in an AND, OR, XOR, or NOT operation to manipulate or extract a value from another bit map.

Let's return to the previous example of controlling field display characters for an example of using bit masks. In Listing 13.4, a display routine has been set up in which the first byte of the string to be displayed contains field control information. The `display_it` routine is passed the entire string and uses the first byte to set underlining or blinking, and then displays from the next byte on. Hexadecimal constants are defined for the display attributes of `UNDERLINE` and `BLINK`, and for the data entry attributes of `UPPERCASE` and `NUMERIC`. This example only uses `UNDERLINE` and `BLINK`. The logic in main sets the first byte of `message[]` to `BLINK` ORed with `UNDERLINE`. This sets the first byte to a value having both the `BLINK` and `UNDERLINE` bits on (bits 4 and 3) as shown below:

```
          BLINK               0 0 0 0 1 0 0 0
OR        UNDERLINE           0 0 0 0 0 1 0 0
                              _______________
=                             0 0 0 0 1 1 0 0
```

Listing 13.4. Using bit masks.

```
/*----
Using bit masks
------*/

#include <stdio.h>

static char message[]= " Hello";

#define   BLINK         0x08 /* 00001000 */
#define   UNDERLINE 0x04 /* 00000100 */
#define   UPPERCASE 0x02 /* 00000010 */
#define   NUMERIC       0x01 /* 00000001 */

static void display_it(char *), underline_on(void),
               underline_off(void), blink_on(void),
               blink_off(void);

void main()
{
     message[0] = BLINK¦UNDERLINE;
     display_it(message);
}

static void display_it( char *msg)
{
     if(*msg & UNDERLINE)
          underline_on();
     else
          underline_off();
     if(*msg & BLINK)
          blink_on();
     else
          blink_off();

     ++msg;
     printf("%s\n", msg);
}

/*----
Pseudo routines
------*/
void underline_on(void)
{
     printf("Underline on  ");
}
```

continues

Listing 13.4. continued

```
void underline_off(void)
{
     printf("Underline off ");
}

void blink_on(void)
{
     printf("Blink on  ");
}

void blink_off(void)
{
     printf("Blink off ");
}
```

The `display_it()` routine tests the first byte of the passed message by ANDing it with the `UNDERLINE` bit. An AND produces a value only if bits are on in both bytes. The value of `UNDERLINE` represents only one bit on. In this case `(*msg & UNDERLINE)` produces a value (nonzero), so `if(*msg & UNDERLINE)` tests true.

```
          *msg              0 0 0 0 1 1 0 0
&         UNDERLINE         0 0 0 0 1 0 0 0
                            _______________
=                           0 0 0 0 1 0 0 0  (TRUE)
```

The `underline_on()` logic is called. The underline and blink routines are stubs that display messages rather than actually setting blinking or underlining on. Setting terminal attributes is beyond the scope of this book, but in designing such a screen handler, `underline_on()` would be a routine that actually turns on underlining before displaying the field. The logic for `BLINK` handling is identical, but works with bit 3.

Listing 13.5 takes this problem a little further and illustrates additional methods for manipulating bit maps. The `main()` function sets up blinking and displays the message. The first byte is ORed with `UNDERLINE` and the message is redisplayed. The OR turns on the `UNDERLINE` bit.

Listing 13.5. Using bit masks.

```
/*----
Using bit masks
------*/

#include <stdio.h>

static char message[]= " Hello";

#define   BLINK         0x08 /* 00001000 */
#define   UNDERLINE 0x04 /* 00000100 */
#define   UPPERCASE 0x02 /* 00000010 */
#define   NUMERIC       0x01 /* 00000001 */

static void display_it(char *), underline_on(void),
               underline_off(void), blink_on(void),
               blink_off(void);

void main()
{
     message[0] = BLINK;
     display_it(message);

     message[0] |= UNDERLINE;
     display_it(message);

     message[0] &= ~(BLINK);
     display_it(message);

     message[0] &= ~(UNDERLINE);
     display_it(message);
}

static void display_it(char *msg)
{
     if(*msg & UNDERLINE)
          underline_on();
     else
          underline_off();
     if(*msg & BLINK)
          blink_on();
     else
          blink_off();

     ++msg;
```

continues

Listing 13.5. continued

```
    printf("%s\n", msg);
}

/*----
Pseudo routines
------*/
void underline_on(void)
{
    printf("Underline on  ");
}

void underline_off(void)
{
    printf("Underline off ");
}

void blink_on(void)
{
    printf("Blink on  ");
}

void blink_off(void)
{
    printf("Blink off ");
}
```

Note that the `main()` function then uses an AND with a NOT. `BLINK` has a value of `00001000`. `~(BLINK)` inverts the value and the AND masks it against the current values of `message[0]` (which at this point in the logic happens to be `00001100`).

```
            BLINK           0 0 0 0 1 0 0 0

            ~(BLINK)        1 1 1 1 0 1 1 1
   AND      message[0]      0 0 0 0 1 1 0 0
                            _______________
   =                        0 0 0 0 0 1 0 0
```

This turns off bit 4, the blink bit, without affecting the `UNDERLINE` bit.

When you are using masks to turn bits on and off or to extract their values, it is useful to remember three standard methods for turning a bit on or off:

- ORing a value with a bit mask will turn ON the bit (or bits) in the value.
- ANDing a value with an inverted bit mask (~mask) will turn the bit or bits off in the value.
- ANDing a value with a bit mask tests if any of the bits in the mask are on in the value being tested.

`ON`	`value ¦= UNDERLINE;`	
`OFF`	`value &= ~(UNDERLINE)`	
	`value &= UNDERLINE`	TRUE if any of the bits in `UNDERLINE` are on in value.

Listing 13.5 continues by turning off the underline bit and displaying the message again. The output from Listing 13.5 will be:

```
Underline off Blink on  Hello
Underline on  Blink on  Hello
Underline on  Blink off Hello
Underline off Blink off Hello
```

The exclusive OR operator is used much less frequently than AND, OR and NOT. It tends to act like a toggle switch throwing a bit on or off with each application.

Listing 13.6 sets up the message with blinking and underlining, and then XORs the `UNDERLINE` bit several times.

Listing 13.6. Using XOR.

```
/*-------------
Using bit masks
-------------*/

#include <stdio.h>

static char message[]= " Hello";

#define   BLINK          0x08 /* 00001000 */
#define   UNDERLINE 0x04      /* 00000100 */
#define   UPPERCASE 0x02      /* 00000010 */
#define   NUMERIC        0x01 /* 00000001 */


static void display_it(char *), underline_on(void),
               underline_off(void), blink_on(void),
               blink_off(void);
```

continues

Listing 13.6. continued

```
void main()
{
     message[0] = BLINK¦UNDERLINE;
     display_it(message);

     message[0] ^= UNDERLINE;
     display_it(message);

     message[0] ^= UNDERLINE;
     display_it(message);

     message[0] ^= UNDERLINE;
     display_it(message);
}

static void display_it( char *msg)
{
     if(*msg & UNDERLINE)
          underline_on();
     else
          underline_off();
     if(*msg & BLINK)
          blink_on();
     else
          blink_off();

     ++msg;
     printf("%s\n", msg);
}

/*----
Pseudo routines
------*/
void underline_on(void)
{
     printf("Underline on  ");
}

void underline_off(void)
{
     printf("Underline off ");
}

void blink_on(void)
{
```

```
    printf("Blink on  ");
}

void blink_off(void)
{
    printf("Blink off ");
}
```

The output from Listing 13.6 will be:

```
Underline on  Blink on  Hello
Underline off Blink on  Hello
Underline on  Blink on  Hello
Underline off Blink on  Hello
```

The first XOR is applied to `message[0]`, containing a value of `00001100`. It turns the underline bit off resulting in a value of `00001000`.

```
          message[0]       0 0 0 0 1 1 0 0
XOR       UNDERLINE        0 0 0 0 0 1 0 0
                           ---------------
=                          0 0 0 0 1 0 0 0
```

The second XOR is applied to new value of `message[]`, `00001000`, which turns the underline bit back on.

```
          message[0]       0 0 0 0 1 0 0 0
XOR       UNDERLINE        0 0 0 0 0 1 0 0
                           ---------------
=                          0 0 0 0 1 1 0 0
```

There are times when a toggle action is needed, but they are much less frequent. With an OR or AND NOT, the resulting bit is known to have been switched on or off. With XOR, the resulting bit has been flipped to the opposite value.

Signed and Unsigned Characters

Listing 13.7 is a simple program with a surprising output. It initializes a single character to a hexadecimal value of 80 and then displays that value as a character, a decimal integer, and a hexadecimal value.

Listing 13.7. Unusual character behavior.

```
#include <stdio.h>

char one[1] = {0x80};
char two = 0x80;

void main()
{
     printf("%c %d %x\n", one[0], one[0], one[0]);
}
```

The output from this program is:

```
? -128 ff80
```

The first character will usually be something odd such as a black square or a foreign alphabet character. The `-128` is surprising enough, but the hexadecimal display of the character indicates that what was a one-byte character now contains two bytes.

I touched on this briefly earlier, but this is a good place to look at the problem in more detail. There are actually two separate actions by the C compiler combining to cause this problem.

The first action by the compiler is that of treating single characters as if they were signed eight-bit integers, a sort of tiny `int`. When treated as signed integers, they follow the pattern used in C of using the leftmost bit as a sign for any integer type. A `char` (tiny `int`) having the eighth bit on is considered to be a negative value. A short `int` with the sixteenth bit on is considered to be a negative value, and a long `int` with the thirty-second bit on is considered to be negative. This does not apply to unsigned `short` or unsigned `long`.

The sign issue is usually not a problem for characters. The ASCII code set extends from hexadecimal `00` (decimal `0`) to hexadecimal `7f` (decimal 127) which comprises the 128 eight-bit patterns from `00000000` to `01111111`. Printable characters and control characters from the ASCII set never have the eighth bit set on.

In Listing 13.7, I deliberately forced the eighth bit on, which changes all the rules. The value at `one[0]` is now treated as a signed tiny integer with the value of `-128`.

The second action by the compiler is the promotion of characters to integers when they are accessed as individual characters. The line below, taken from Listing 13.7, actually passes a pointer to a format string and three integers to `printf()`. Each time `one[0]` is accessed as a single character, it is converted to an integer before being passed to `printf()`.

```
printf("%c %d %x\n", one[0], one[0], one[0]);
```

Integers default to 16 or 32 bits depending on the machine and compiler, so the eight-bit value of `one[0]` becomes either a 16- or 32-bit value. The output from Listing 13.7 indicates that `one[0]` became a 16-bit value (two bytes), and `0xff80` is the hexadecimal representation of –128 for a 16-bit integer.

When dealing with values above `0x7f` in character fields, it is necessary to deal with this problem. The best method to get around this problem is to use an unsigned `char`. It behaves the way you expect a `char` to behave and does not become negative if values above `0x80` are stored in it. Listing 13.8 is the simple solution to the signed character problem.

Listing 13.8. Using unsigned characters.

```
#include <stdio.h>

unsigned char one[1] = {0x80};

void main()
{
     printf("%c %d %x\n", one[0], one[0], one[0]);
}
```

Bit-Shift Operators

There are two more bit-level operators that should be described, but you will probably rarely use them until you have been coding in C for a while. They are bit-shift operators, which shift bits left and right.

The right shift operator is >>, and the left shift operator is <<. The << operator left shifts the variable on its left by the number of places in the expression to the right of <<.

```
x = 2 << 1;
```

In the above example, a temporary variable is set to `2`. This is then left-shifted by one bit position and the result assigned to `x`. The leftmost bit is shifted out of the value. All bits are moved one position to the left, and the rightmost bit is filled with a `0`.

```
Value   0 0 0 0 0 0 0 0 0 0 0 0 0 0 1 0 << 1
  =     0 0 0 0 0 0 0 0 0 0 0 0 0 1 0 0
```

There is also a combined operator:

```
x = 2;
x <<= 1;
```

which left-shifts the value in x by 1 bit. Left-shifting is usually limited to a value within the number of bits in the variable. The example below doesn't make much sense, because there are only 16 bits in a short integer.

```
short int x;

     x = 3;
     x <<= 27;
```

Shifting 27 bit positions causes all information to roll off the end of the value.

Right-shifting is similar, in the opposite direction, but with a slight difference. Right-shifting is influenced by the sign of the value being shifted. If the value is unsigned, then all bits are shifted to the right, and the leftmost bit is filled with a 0. This is the exact reverse operation of a left shift.

```
unsigned short int x;

     x = 4;

     x >>= 2;
```

```
     Value    0 0 0 0 0 0 0 0 0 0 0 0 0 1 0 0 >> 2
       =      0 0 0 0 0 0 0 0 0 0 0 0 0 0 0 1
```

If the value is signed, the sign is preserved by the following procedure. All bits are right-shifted the number of bits specified. The leftmost bits are filled with a 0 or 1, matching the original value in the high-order bit position before the shift.

```
short int x;

     x = -119;

     x >>= 2;
```

```
     Value    1 1 1 1 1 1 1 1 1 0 0 0 1 0 0 1 >> 2
       =      1 1 1 1 1 1 1 1 1 1 1 0 0 0 1 0
```

It is unusual to use shift operators with signed values, but you should know the effects.

Converting Packed Fields

So far you have been patiently (or probably impatiently) wading through a lot of theory wondering if this is all leading up to something useful.

Even though bit maps and signed characters are a fact of life in C, a part of the language that you just have to learn (so there!), this is a good point to look at a COBOL data conversion problem.

The COBOL packed numeric field, usually called `COMP-3`, has no equivalent in C. A packed field contains one digit per half byte with the final byte holding a digit in the first four bits and a sign in the last four. The number `123` as a packed field would be contained in two bytes containing the hexadecimal values

```
0x12 0x3f
```

The number of bytes used by a packed field is calculated by adding the total number of digits plus 1 for the sign. 1 more is added if needed to make the number even, and then the result is divided by 2. A number such as `865334` creates six digit spaces plus 1 for the sign. Add 1 to bring this to the even number 8 and divide by 2. The hexadecimal values for this number would be

```
0x08 0x65 0x33 0x4F
```

Note that an extra `0` was added to the start of the number to pad it out so that a whole number of bytes is used. Packed fields do not contain half bytes.

The sign nybble (a half-byte is called a nybble) is the lower four bits of the last byte. It is `0x0d` for negative values and usually `0x0c` or `0x0f` for positive values.

The problem in dealing with a packed field is extracting the digits half a byte at a time. Bit-shifting logic and masking can be used effectively to do this.

Listing 13.9 contains a routine `cvt_packed()`, which converts a passed packed value to a C `double` and returns the `double` value. The auxiliary functions `lo_nybble_value()`, `hi_nybble_value()`, and `lo_nybble_sign()` are used to extract an integer (or sign) value from four bits. The logic in `main()` is used to set up a test condition to test the results from `cvt_packed()`. A pseudo-packed field is created with a value of `-780978` and is passed along with its length in bytes to `cvt_packed()`.

Listing 13.9. Converting COBOL packed fields.

```
/*---------------------------
Converting COBOL packed fields
---------------------------*/

#include <stdio.h>

double cvt_packed(unsigned char *, int);

static unsigned int hi_nybble_value(unsigned int),
                    lo_nybble_value(unsigned int);

static int          lo_nybble_sign(unsigned int);

unsigned char packed_val[] =
     {0x07, 0x80, 0x97, 0x8d};

/* -8356728.000000 */

void main()
{
     double work;

     work = cvt_packed( packed_val, 4);
     printf("%f\n", work);
}

/*------------------------------------------------
Extract hi nybble then low nybble until all but one
bytes are exhausted. This last byte will contain
a digit and a sign. Extract the digit from the hi
nybble and the sign from the low nybble.
------------------------------------------------*/

double cvt_packed( unsigned char *packed, int len)
{
     double result;
     int value;

     result = 0.0;

     for( ; len > 1; -- len)
          {
          result *= 10;
          result += hi_nybble_value(*packed);
          result *= 10;
```

```
            result += lo_nybble_value(*packed);
            ++packed;
            }
        result *= 10;
        result += hi_nybble_value(*packed);
        result *= lo_nybble_sign(*packed);
        return(result);
}

/*-----------------------------------------------------
Move the high four bits into the low four bits thereby
converting the bits into an integer
-----------------------------------------------------*/
static unsigned int hi_nybble_value( unsigned int byte)
{
        byte >>= 4;
        return(byte);
}

/*-------------------------------------------------
Return the integer in the lo 4 bits by masking off
the high order bits.
-------------------------------------------------*/
static unsigned int lo_nybble_value( unsigned int byte)
{
        byte &= 0x0f;
        return(byte);
}

/*-----------------------------------------------
Pick up just the sign using a low four bit mask
hex 0xd is negative, and treat any other value as
positive.
-----------------------------------------------*/
static int lo_nybble_sign( unsigned int byte)
{
        byte &= 0x0f;

        if(byte == 0x0d)
            return(-1);
        else
            return(+1);
}
```

A cvt_packed_dec() routine could be layered around cvt_packed() to include the number of decimals in the packed field. Listing 13.10 is an example of such a routine.

Listing 13.10. Converting with decimal places.

```
/*-------------------------------------------
Convert as a packed field, and then add decimals.
-------------------------------------------*/
double cvt_packed_dec(unsigned char *packed, int len, int dec)
{
     double result;

     result = cvt_packed(packed, len);

     while(dec--)
          result /= 10;

     return(result);
}
```

Summary

Bases and bit maps are probably some of the newest territory you have covered. There is little in COBOL that compares to them. They are very powerful, and allow you to deal with data problems at levels involving less than a byte of information as in the packed conversion problems.

In addition, bit masks are used in many of the standard C library functions, such as some of those we are about to deal with in low-level file I/O.

14

Low-Level File I/O

Low-level file I/O is somewhat closer to COBOL record-oriented I/O in that you are reading a number of bytes from a file. If the number of bytes is a consistent value, then you have something akin to record-oriented I/O.

In this chapter, you will learn about:

- What low-level I/O is
- Using `open()` and `close()`
- Using `read()` and write()
- Using `lseek()`, `tell()`, and `eof()`
- Low-level I/O in the phone book

This is the last major piece of the C language, and with it you can start putting some programming solutions together.

What Is Low-level I/O?

Low-level I/O is unfielded reading from and writing to a file. Much as you would expect, there are functions to open, close, read, and write a file. They are similar to the stream I/O functions.

Using *open()* and *close()*

The `open()` function is much more complicated than `fopen()`. The `open()` function is passed two or three arguments.

The arguments are a string pointer containing the name of the file and an integer containing a bit map that flags the open mode for the file. If the open mode is one that will result in a file being created, a third argument must be passed: an integer bit map containing flags for the protect mode of the newly created file.

The `open()` function usually requires that you `#include` at least two files: <fcntl.h> and <io.h>. The io.h file contains the function declarations for `open()`, `close()`, `read()`, and `write()`, while fcntl.h includes the constants to be used in `open()`.

The `open()` function returns an integer which is usually called a handle. An `open()` that fails returns a `-1`. This handle is used for I/O to the open file in the same way that the file pointer was used for stream I/O. Listing 14.1 is an example using `open()` and `close()`.

Listing 14.1. Using `open()` and `close()`.

```
#include <stdio.h>
#include <fcntl.h>
#include <io.h>

void main()
{
     int fil;

     fil = open("file.dat", O_RDWR);
     if(fil < 0)
          printf("File %s not found.\n", "file.dat");
     else
          close(fil);
}
```

The O_RDWR constant is defined in fcntl.h and will usually appear in that file as something like

```
#define    O_RDWR     0x0002
```

or

```
#define    _O_RDWR    0x0002
#define    O_RDWR     _O_RDWR
```

If you are using a Microsoft C/C++ compiler package or a Microsoft Visual C++ compiler, be sure to read the introduction to the run-time library reference. Microsoft has renamed many of its functions and constants. The open() function has become _open(), and the open() constants such as O_RDWR have become _O_RDWR. In practice this renaming makes little difference; programs are automatically linked with a library named oldnames.lib that resolves the old names into the new names. But if you start exploring the header files, you may be mystified as to why some of the names seem to be slightly wrong or contain an extra leading underscore.

The constants for opening a file are ORed together to create the open type that is wanted. To open a file for reading and writing, use

```
fil = open("file.dat", O_RDWR¦O_BINARY);
```

The flags and their effects in Microsoft C are listed in Table 14.1. If you are not using Microsoft C, be sure to check your run-time library reference for the comparable flags.

Table 14.1. Constants for open().

Constant	*Effect at* open() *Time*
O_APPEND	Repositions the file to the end of the file before each write. Each write() action adds to the end of the file.
O_BINARY	Opens the file in untranslated mode. CR-LF pairs are not modified, and Ctrl-Z is not treated as an end of file.
O_CREAT	Creates the file if it does not exist. It has no effect if it does exist.
O_EXCL	Used with O_CREAT. This means create and open a file only if it does not exist. Returns an error if the file does exist.
O_RDONLY	Open file for reading only. May not be used with O_RDWR or O_WRONLY.

continues

Table 14.1. continued

Constant	*Effect at* `open()` *Time*
O_RDWR	Opens file for reading and writing. May not be used with O_RDONLY or O_WRONLY.
O_TEXT	Opens file in text mode. CR-LF is translated to newline (LF), and Ctrl-Z is recognized as an end of file.
O_TRUNC	Opens and truncates an existing file to zero bytes. The user must have write permission on the file. Cannot be used with O_RDONLY.
O_WRONLY	Opens the file for writing. Cannot be used with O_RDONLY or O_RDWR.

The constants are actually three different groups of controls:

- The O_RDONLY, O_WRONLY, and O_RDWR flags control the read/write access to the file. One of these three flags must be specified for every open().
- The O_APPEND, O_TEXT, and O_BINARY values control character translation or file positioning during reads and writes.
- The O_TRUNC, O_EXCL, and O_CREAT flags control what to do at the open(), such as to create a new file or to cause an error if the file doesn't exist.

This set of flags provides all the standard opens as well as some useful new ones. Table 14.2 provides some idea of how to use the flags to create various types of open. All of these should be ORed with O_BINARY. If you get the urge to use the O_TEXT flag for an open, there is a strong possibility that you should use stream I/O and process the file as a text file. Stream I/O is more portable. For example, O_TEXT and O_BINARY do not exist as flags under UNIX, but UNIX has other flags for open.

Table 14.2. Some examples of combining open modes.

Open Flags	*Effect*
O_CREAT¦O_APPEND¦O_WRONLY	This is classic append mode. The file is created if it does not exist. Only writing is available, and writes are done at the end of the file.

Open Flags	*Effect*
`O_RDONLY`	Classic open input. An error occurs if the file does not exist.
`O_CREAT¦O_RDONLY`	Optional open input. The file is created if needed.
`O_CREAT¦O_TRUNC¦O_WRONLY`	Classic open output. File is created if needed, or truncated to zero bytes if it exists, and only writing is allowed.
`O_RDWR¦O_APPEND`	A read append mode. Reads can be done anywhere in the file, but writes are all done at the end of the file.
`O_RDWR`	Classic I/O mode. Reading and writing is allowed, and an error occurs if the file does not exist.
`O_RDWR¦O_CREAT`	Optional I/O mode. File is created if it does not exist.

Some combinations are meaningless, and may either be ignored by the `open()`, or may cause `open()` errors. For example, `O_RDONLY¦O_APPEND` is a meaningless combination.

The third argument is only required when `O_CREAT` is used as a flag. If the file exists, it is ignored. This third argument can be `S_IWRITE` or `S_IREAD`, or the two combined, `S_IWRITE¦S_IREAD`. Under MS-DOS there is no such thing as a write-only file, so `S_IWRITE` and `S_IREAD¦S_IWRITE` are equivalent. The `S_IREAD` and `S_IWRITE` flags are defined in yet another include file <sys\stat.h>. Listing 14.2 opens (and creates if needed) a file and then closes it.

Listing 14.2. `open()` and `close()`.

```
/*-----------------------------
Create a file and then close it.
-----------------------------*/
#include <stdio.h>
#include <fcntl.h>
#include <io.h>
#include <sys\stat.h>
```

continues

Listing 14.2. continued

```
void main()
{
     int fil;

     fil = _open("file.dat", O_CREAT¦O_RDWR, S_IREAD¦S_IWRITE);
     if(fil < 0)
          perror("file.dat");
     else
          close(fil);
}
```

This is a good point to learn a new standard library function. The `perror()` function is a handy tool for tracking down problems. C contains a global reference named `errno`. It is declared in <errno.h> along with a list of error codes. You can access this variable directly as shown in Listing 14.3. Listing 14.3 attempts to delete an illegal filename (illegal under MS-DOS) and then immediately displays the value of `errno`.

Listing 14.3. Using the `errno` value.

```
/*-----------------
Using the errno value
-----------------*/

#include <stdio.h>
#include <errno.h>

char file_name[] = "doodah.doodah";

void main()
{
     unlink(file_name);
     printf("Error = %d\n", errno);
}
```

The `errno` reference is a global value that contains a number representing the error code for the last call to a standard C library routine. Listing 14.3 will print something like

```
Error = 2
```

This is handy but awkward. You still have to look up a 2 in errno.h to find out what it means. The `perror()` function does this for you and prints an English message for the

error. The `perror()` function requires one argument, a string containing the first part of the message that you want displayed. This string is printed with a trailing colon followed by the text of the error. Listing 14.4 prints the message

```
doodah.doodah: No such file or directory
```

Listing 14.4. Using `perror()`.

```
#include <stdio.h>
#include <errno.h>

char file_name[] = "doodah.doodah";

void main()
{
     unlink(file_name);
     perror(file_name);
}
```

The `errno` value always contains the error code of the last error created by a standard library call, so accessing `errno` directly or by using `perror()` must be done immediately after the error that you wish to check, as shown in Listing 14.2.

Using *read()* and *write()*

Once a file is opened you may read from it or write to it (depending on the open mode) using `read()` and `write()`. These functions exactly complement each other.

The `read()` function expects the integer file number or handle returned by an `open()`, a pointer to a buffer in memory into which the bytes will be read, and an integer count of bytes to be read. The `write()` function expects an integer file number or handle returned by an `open()`, a pointer to a buffer in memory from which the bytes will be written, and an integer count of bytes to be written.

Listing 14.5 is a handy hexadecimal display utility that will open a file and read it 16 bytes at a time using `open()`, `close()`, and `read()`. This is a good program to compile and keep available as you can use it to look at other files created and updated with binary values that cannot be displayed by an editor or file display utility. This program must be linked with maintain.lib, created in Chapters 11 and 12, or linked directly to the screenlo.c source file. It uses routines from that library.

Listing 14.5. hd.c.

```
/*-----------------
hd.c

A hex display utility
-----------------*/

#include <stdio.h>
#include <ctype.h>
#include <string.h>

#include <fcntl.h>
#include <io.h>
#include "screenlo.h"

static char file_name[80];

void hex_it(int), hex_a_line(char*, long, int);

#define   BYTES_PER_LINE 16

/*-----------------------------------------------
Open the named file is possible and display it in hex
-----------------------------------------------*/
void main()
{
     int input_file;

     printf("Input file name?\n");
     getstr(file_name, 80);
     input_file = open(file_name, O_BINARY¦O_RDONLY);
     if(input_file == -1)
          {
          perror(file_name);
          return;
          }
     hex_it(input_file);
     close(input_file);
}

/*-----------------
Display a file in hex
-----------------*/
void hex_it(int inf)
{

     long address;
```

```
    int lines, count;
    unsigned char buf[BYTES_PER_LINE + 1];

    address = 0;
    while(1)
        {
        for(lines = 0; lines < 22; ++lines)
            {
            memset(buf, 0, sizeof(buf));
            count = read(inf, buf, BYTES_PER_LINE);
            if(count == 0)
                break;
            hex_a_line(buf, address, count);
            if(count < BYTES_PER_LINE)
                break;
            address += BYTES_PER_LINE;
            }
        if(count < BYTES_PER_LINE)
            break;
        printf("Press Enter . . .\n");
        get_one_char();
        }
    printf("-END OF FILE-\n");
}


/*-----------------------------------------------
Is passed a pointer to bytes of data, a long address
and the number of bytes of data to display.

It displays the address followed by 16 bytes of
data in hex format followed by the sixteen bytes.

If a byte is printable, it is displayed as is, if it
is not, it is replaced by a '.' in the buffer. The
complete buffer is displayed at the end of the
hex display values.

If less than 16 bytes remain to be displayed, the
hex display and character display are filled with spaces.

This function uses the isprint() test from the standard
C library to determine if a character can be displayed.
-------------------------------------------------*/
void hex_a_line(char *buf, long address, int count)
{
    int byte;
```

continues

Listing 14.5. continued

```
    if(count == 0)
        return;
    printf("%06lX:", address);

    for(byte = 0; byte < BYTES_PER_LINE; ++byte)
        {
        if(count)
            {
            printf(" %02X", buf[byte]);
            if(!(isprint(buf[byte])))
                buf[byte] = '.';
            --count;
            }
        else
            {
            printf("   ");
            buf[byte] = ' ';
            }
        }
    printf(" %s\n", buf);
}
```

Using *lseek()*, *tell()*, and *eof()*

The `lseek()` function is the low-level counterpart to `fseek()`. The arguments are an integer file number returned by an `open()`, an offset, and a code for beginning of file, end of file, or current position. If you open low-level files using `O_BINARY`, `lseek()` can be used to correctly position you within a file using any starting position or offset.

The `tell()` function is the low-level counterpart to `ftell()`. It takes one argument, an integer file number returned by an `open()`, and it returns a long integer containing the file position.

The `eof()` function is the low-level counterpart to `feof()`. It takes one argument, an integer file number returned by an `open()`, and it returns a nonzero value of the file is at end.

Low-Level I/O in the Phone Book

Using low-level I/O and structures, it is possible to rewrite phonemnt.c and phoneio.c from Chapter 12 to use an I/O style that is much more like reading and writing a record.

Listing 14.6 is the new phoneio.h and Listing 14.7 is the new phoneio.c. Note the use of the `PHONE` structure as if it were a record. Reads and writes are done directly to and from the phone structure by using a pointer to the structure as in

```
read( file, &phone, sizeof(phone));
```

The use of `sizeof(phone)` makes it possible to modify the phone record at a later date with a minimum of change to the code.

Listing 14.6. phoneio.h.

```
#ifndef _PHONEIO_H
#define _PHONEIO_H

#include <stdio.h>
#include <string.h>
#include <process.h>
#include <ctype.h>

#include <fcntl.h>
#include <io.h>
#include <sys\stat.h>

#include "util.h"
#include "maintain.h"

/*-------------------------------------------
Phone record is three fields stored in a binary file
as part of a structure.

Field               Length

LAST_NAME            20
FIRST_NAME           20
NUMBER               15

-------------------------------------------*/
```

continues

Listing 14.6. continued

```
typedef struct {
     char lname[21];
     char fname[21];
     char no[16];
     }PHONE;

/*---------------------------------------
Constants:
     File Name on disk
     Work file name used during compression
     Record length
     Number of fields
---------------------------------------*/

#define   FILE_NAME      "phone.dat"
#define   COMPRESS_NAME  "phone.cmp"

/*---------------------------------------------
Struct used for reading and writing to the file,
and for displaying on the screen.
---------------------------------------------*/

extern PHONE phone;

#endif /* _PHONEIO_H */
```

Listing 14.7. phoneio.c.

```
/*---------------------------
phoneio.c

Does all IO to the phone file
---------------------------*/

#include "phoneio.h"

/*-------------------
File names and pointers
-------------------*/

#define   FILE_IS_CLOSED 9999

static int iofile = FILE_IS_CLOSED;
```

```
static int outfile = FILE_IS_CLOSED;

static long fpos;

/*-----------------------------------------------
This is the global struct into which values are read
from the file, or from which values are written to
the file. They are global as they must be available
to other parts of the program.
-----------------------------------------------*/

PHONE phone;

/*-------------------------------
Prototypes for the local functions
-------------------------------*/

static void file_error(char *), clear_receivers(void);
static int fields_are_blank(void), write_a_record(int);

/*-----------------------------
              OPEN and CLOSE
-----------------------------*/

/*-----------------------------------------------------------
This opens the file for IO. It always opens the file append first
which automatically creates the file if it does not exist.
-----------------------------------------------------------*/
int open_io_data_file(void)
{
     if(iofile != FILE_IS_CLOSED)
          {
          file_error("opening io an already open");
          }
     open_append_data_file();
     close_data_file();
     iofile = open(FILE_NAME, O_BINARY¦O_RDWR);
     if(iofile != -1)
          return(1);
     perror(FILE_NAME);
     file_error("opening io");
}

int open_append_data_file(void)
{
     if(iofile != FILE_IS_CLOSED)
          {
```

continues

Listing 14.7. continued

```
          file_error("opening append an already open");
          }

     iofile = open(FILE_NAME,
                    O_BINARY¦O_CREAT¦O_APPEND¦O_WRONLY,
                    S_IREAD¦S_IWRITE);

     if(iofile > -1)
          return(1);
     perror(FILE_NAME);
     file_error("opening append");
}

int open_input_data_file(void)
{
     if(iofile != FILE_IS_CLOSED)
          {
          file_error("opening input an already open");
          }
     open_append_data_file();
     iofile = open(FILE_NAME, O_BINARY¦O_RDONLY);
     if(iofile > -1)
          return(1);
     perror(FILE_NAME);
     file_error("opening input");
}

void close_data_file()
{
     if(iofile == FILE_IS_CLOSED)
          {
          file_error("closing an already closed");
          }
     close(iofile);
     iofile = FILE_IS_CLOSED;
}

/*-----------------------------------------
               READ WRITE REWRITE DELETE
-----------------------------------------*/

/*---------------------------------------------------
Save the current file pointer.
Clear the receiving fields.
Check if we are at end of file and exit accordingly.
```

```
Read in the record.
Truncate each to last non-space character.

Use the return value from scanf() to establish
if the read was successful.
Returns 1 if successful and 0 if unsuccessful.
The only legal counts are EOF and sizeof(phone).
Anything else indicates the file has been corrupted and
the program exits.
--------------------------------------------------*/
int read_data_record()
{
     int count;


     if(iofile == FILE_IS_CLOSED)
          {
          file_error("reading a closed");
          }
     while(1)
          {
          fpos = tell(iofile);
          if(eof(iofile))
               return(0);
          count = read( iofile, &phone, sizeof(phone));

          trunc(phone.lname);
          trunc(phone.fname);
          trunc(phone.no);

          if(count == EOF)
               return(0);
          if(count < sizeof(phone))
               break;
          if(fields_are_blank())
               continue;
          else
               return(1);
          }
     perror(FILE_NAME);
     file_error("reading");
}

/*--------------------------------------------------------
Assumes the lname, fname, and phone are pre-filled with values
to write to the file. If less than sizeof(phone) bytes are
written then an error has occurred.
-------------------------------------------------------*/
```

continues

Listing 14.7. continued

```
int write_data_record(void)
{
     int count;

     if(iofile == FILE_IS_CLOSED)
          {
          file_error("writing a closed");
          }
     count = write_a_record(iofile);
     if(count < sizeof(phone))
          {
          perror(FILE_NAME);
          file_error("writing");
          }
     return(1);
}

static int write_a_record(int file)
{
     int count;

     count = write(file, &phone, sizeof(phone));
     return(count);
}


/*-----------------------------------------------
A delete is really a rewrite with blank fields.
-----------------------------------------------*/
int delete_data_record(void)
{
     if(iofile == FILE_IS_CLOSED)
          {
          file_error("deleting on a closed");
          }
     clear_receivers();
     return(rewrite_data_record());
}


/*-------------------------------------------------
A rewrite is a write in which the file has been
repositioned to the point of the last read.
-------------------------------------------------*/
int rewrite_data_record(void)
```

```
{
     if(iofile == FILE_IS_CLOSED)
          {
          file_error("re-writing a closed");
          }
     lseek(iofile, fpos, SEEK_SET);
     return(write_data_record());
}


/*-----------------------------------------
          Miscellaneous COMPRESS FILE FIND_NEXT
---------------------------------------*/
/*---------------------------------------------
Open the phone file and the compress work file.
Read all records from phone file into the compress file.
Delete the phone file.
Rename the compress file.
---------------------------------------------*/

void compress_data_file(void)
{
     open_input_data_file();
     outfile = open(COMPRESS_NAME,
          O_BINARY¦O_CREAT¦O_TRUNC¦O_WRONLY,
          S_IREAD¦S_IWRITE);
     while(read_data_record())
          {
          write_a_record(outfile);
          }
     close(outfile);
     close_data_file();
     unlink(FILE_NAME);
     rename(COMPRESS_NAME, FILE_NAME);
}


/*--------------------------------------------------
Rewind the file and then read all records comparing the last
name until record is found, or an End of File condition is hit
--------------------------------------------------*/

static char find_key[55];

int find_data_record(char *str)
{
     if(iofile == FILE_IS_CLOSED)
```

continues

Listing 14.7. continued

```
          {
          file_error("searching a closed");
          }
     lseek(iofile, 0L, SEEK_SET);

     strcpy(find_key,str);

     return(find_next_data_record());

}

int find_next_data_record(void)
{
     if(iofile == FILE_IS_CLOSED)
          {
          file_error("searching a closed");
          }
     while(read_data_record())
          {
          if(!(strcmp(phone.lname, find_key)))
               return(1);
          }
     return(0);
}


/*-----------------------------------------------
          UTILITY ROUTINES to support IO
-----------------------------------------------*/

/*---------------------------------------------------
Close the file if it is open.
Provide a file error message and exit.
This is a general purpose routine for bailing out of
unrecoverable file errors.
---------------------------------------------------*/
static void file_error(char *io)
{
     if(iofile != FILE_IS_CLOSED)
          close_data_file();
     printf("An error occurred %s phone file.\n", io);
     printf("The file may be corrupted.\n");
     exit(0);
}
```

```
/*----------------------------------------
Test all fields for all characters = spaces.
----------------------------------------*/
static int fields_are_blank(void)
{
     if(  (field_is_blank(phone.lname, sizeof(phone.lname)-1)) &&
          (field_is_blank(phone.fname, sizeof(phone.fname)-1)) &&
          (field_is_blank(phone.no, sizeof(phone.no) - 1) )  )
          return(1);
     else
          return(0);

}

/*-----------------------------------------------------
Clear all the fields used to read from or write to the file
-----------------------------------------------------*/
static void clear_receivers(void)
{
     memset(&phone, 0 , sizeof(phone));
}
```

The original version of phoneio.c used a `NULL` value for a `FILE` pointer to indicate that a file was closed. A `0` is a valid value for a low-level file number, so a pseudo-value of `9999` is created for the file integer and used to indicate that the file is closed.

The new phoneio.c also takes advantage of `perror()` for file errors. You should study and compare this listing to phoneio.c in Chapter 12.

On the screen side of phone maintenance, you will find that phonemnt.h, shown in Listing 14.8, is little changed.

Listing 14.8 phonemnt.h.

```
#ifndef _PHONEMNT_H
#define _PHONEMNT_H

#include "maintain.h"
#include "phoneio.h"

#endif /* _PHONEMNT_H */
```

The screen fields in phonemnt.c, shown in Listing 14.9, are created by using a local copy of the `PHONE` structure called `fld`. This simplifies some of the logic, such as `load_screen()` and `load_record()`, which can now be done by assigning the value of one structure to another. Compare this logic to that used in phonemnt.c in Chapter 12.

Listing 14.9. phonemnt.c.

```
/*---------------------------------
Screen routines for phone maintenance
---------------------------------*/

#include "phonemnt.h"

/*----------------------
Fields for screen input.
----------------------*/
static PHONE fld;

/*----------------------
Prompts for screen input.
----------------------*/
static char *prompt[] = {
     {"Last Name"},
     {"First Name"},
     {"Phone"},
     {NULL}
};

/*----------------------------------------------
An array of pointers to input receivers, and their
lengths for get_entries.
----------------------------------------------*/
static char *field[] = { fld.lname, fld.fname, fld.no };
static int length[] = { 20, 20, 15 };

/*------------------------------------
Call straight into the maintain() routine
------------------------------------*/
int main()
{
     maintain();
     return(0);
}
```

```
/*-------------
Input all fields
-------------*/
void enter_fields(void)
{
     get_entries(prompt, field, length);
}

/*---------------------------------------------
Validate all fields. In this case only the key field
(last name) is tested for a valid entry
---------------------------------------------*/
int validate_fields(void)
{
     return(validate_key());
}

/*---------------------
Validate last name field
---------------------*/
int validate_key(void)
{
     if(field_is_blank(fld.lname, sizeof(fld.lname) - 1))
          return(1);
     return(0);
}

/*---------------------------------------
Clear all screen receivers in preparation for
input.
---------------------------------------*/
void clear_scr_receivers(void)
{
     memset(&fld, 0, sizeof(fld));
}

/*-----------------------------------------------
Accept entry of the "key" value, in this case the first
field.
-----------------------------------------------*/
char *get_key_entry(void)
{
     clear_scr_receivers();
     get_entry(prompt[0], field[0], length[0]);
     return(field[0]);
}
```

continues

Listing 14.9. continued

```
/*---------------
Display all entries
---------------*/
void display_fields(void)
{
     display_entries(prompt, field);
}

/*-----------------------------------
Load record fields from screen fields.
-----------------------------------*/
void load_record(void)
{
     phone = fld;
}

/*---------------------------------------------------
Load record fields from screen fields if they contain data.
---------------------------------------------------*/
void reload_record(void)
{
     if(strlen(fld.lname))
          strcpy(phone.lname, fld.lname);
     if(strlen(fld.fname))
          strcpy(phone.fname, fld.fname);
     if(strlen(fld.no))
          strcpy(phone.no, fld.no);
}

/*--------------------------------------
Load screen fields from the record fields.
--------------------------------------*/
void load_screen(void)
{
     fld = phone;
}
```

The new phonemnt.exe can be created by compiling phonemnt.c and phoneio.c and linking the results with maintain.lib. Notice that the code for the maintain side of the logic is unchanged.

Summary

Low-level file I/O combined with structures produces a file layout and I/O system that begin to approximate the COBOL record layouts. Low-level file I/O is very efficient when used in this way because it reduces the field separation logic. A record read straight into a structure allows the members of the structure to be accessed without further fielding or field separation.

You still have a few tricks to learn (which I'll cover in the next chapter), but you now have all the basics that you need to code in C, and to read and understand C listings.

The next chapter cleans up a lot of loose ends, but by now you should be thinking with C logic, and be able to plan and design some projects of your own.

15

Tips, Tricks, and Advanced Techniques

There are some great tricks available in the C language that you can use to cut down the amount of coding that you do, improve the readability of code, and generally increase the power of a program.

In this chapter, you will learn about:

- Typing constants
- How to undefine
- Macros with parameters
- Stringizing
- Casting data types
- Allocating extra memory
- Void pointers

You do not need these to work in the C language, but you will eventually come across them.

Typing Constants

You may have noticed the use of `L` after some constants in earlier listings. For example, in

```
fseek(file, 0L, SEEK_SET);
```

the `L` is used to force the data type of the constant `0` to a `long`.

In most assignment contexts, the compiler is able to identify the data type of a number:

```
long var;
var = 0;

double other_var;
var = 1.1;
```

If your functions are all declared in prototypes, the compiler is able to recognize that a conversion is needed:

```
void do_something(long);
do_something(15);
```

The use of forced typing, then, is usually a matter of documentation. An integer constant can be forced to become `long` by adding `L` or `l` as in the following example. The lowercase `l` is rarely used because it is very easy to confuse it with a `1`.

```
do_something(15L);
do_something(15l);
```

An integer constant can be forced to become unsigned by adding a `U` or `u`, or an unsigned `long` by adding both a `U` and `L`.

A floating-point constant defaults to a `double` type. A `double` constant can be coerced into becoming a `float` constant by using `f` or `F`, or a `long double` by using `l` or `L`.

There is a case for forcing `double` constants. In the following example, the compiler may produce a warning that conversion between `float` types is going on:

```
float do_something(float);
     do_something(1.17);
```

The `1.17` is supposed to be created as a `double` constant, and the compiler warns that creating it as a `float` constant may cause loss of data. The warning can be shut off by coercing the constant as in the following example:

```
do_something(1.17F);
```

How to Undefine

You are already familiar with the #define preprocessor directive, and the tests for a defined value, #ifdef, #ifndef, #else, and #endif.

One other directive is #undef, which cancels the effect of a #define. If a value is defined and you want to redefine it with a new value, you should #undef the value first.

In Listing 15.1, DEBUG_LEVEL is defined as 1 for part of the source code, and then defined as 2 for another portion. DEBUG_LEVEL must be undefined before it is redefined, or the compiler provides a warning that you are redefining a constant.

Listing 15.1 uses a fairly standard trick: using an #undef inside an #ifdef-#endif pair. For a long listing, this prevents compilation errors if you attempt to #undef a value that has never been defined.

Listing 15.1. Using #undef.

```
/*----------
Using #undef
----------*/

#include <stdio.h>

int x_2(int), x_x(int);

void main()
{
     printf(" Results are %d %d \n", x_2(10), x_x(10));
}

#ifdef DEBUG_LEVEL
#undef DEBUG_LEVEL
#endif

#define     DEBUG_LEVEL  1

int x_2( int value)
{
#if       (DEBUG_LEVEL == 1)
     printf(">> x_2()\n");
#endif
#if       (DEBUG_LEVEL == 2)
```

continues

Listing 15.1. continued

```
    printf(">> x_2(%d)\n", value);
#endif

    value *= 2;

#if       (DEBUG_LEVEL == 1)
    printf("<<return\n");
#endif
#if       (DEBUG_LEVEL == 2)
    printf("<<return(%d)\n", value);
#endif
    return(value);
}


#ifdef DEBUG_LEVEL
#undef DEBUG_LEVEL
#endif

#define   DEBUG_LEVEL    2

int x_x( int value)
{
#if       (DEBUG_LEVEL == 1)
    printf(">> x_x()\n");
#endif
#if       (DEBUG_LEVEL == 2)
    printf(">> x_x(%d)\n", value);
#endif

    value *= value;

#if       (DEBUG_LEVEL == 1)
    printf("<<return\n");
#endif
#if       (DEBUG_LEVEL == 2)
    printf("<<return(%d)\n", value);
#endif
    return(value);

}
```

Listing 15.1 uses something else you haven't seen before: `#if` to test for a specific value of a `#define`. Study Listing 15.1 carefully; it includes just about all there is about defining and undefining in one example, except for

```
#if  (DEBUG_LEVEL != 1)
```

which is also valid.

Macros with Parameters

The `#define` preprocessor is even more powerful than a straight text-substitution mechanism. You can also create macros that contain parameters or place holders.

Listing 15.2 defines `display(x)` as `printf(x)`. This is a very simple macro that causes the compiler to locate any occurrence of `display()` with a value in the parentheses, and replaces it with `printf()`, placing the found value in the parentheses. This macro does little more than illustrate how a macro with arguments works.

Listing 15.2. Using a simple parameterized macro.

```
/*------------------------
Using a parameterized macro
------------------------*/

#include <stdio.h>

#define   display(x)          printf(x)

void main()
{
     display("Hello\n");
}
```

When the compiler encounters `display("Hello\n")`, it replaces it with `printf("Hello\n")`.

Listing 15.3 creates a `display_advancing()` macro that uses `printf()` to display a line and then adds a newline by a second call to `printf()`.

Listing 15.3. A more complex parameterized macro.

```
/*-----------------------
Using a parameterized macro
-----------------------*/

#include <stdio.h>

#define   display_advancing(x)          printf(x); printf("\n")

void main()
{
     display_advancing("Hello");
}
```

When the compiler encounters

```
display_advancing("Hello");
```

it replaces it with

```
printf("Hello"); printf("\n");
```

It is important when designing macros to try to avoid side effects. Listing 15.4 is a macro that replaces `square_of(x)` with `x * x`. In the first line of `main()`,

```
value = square_of(12);
```

is replaced with

```
value = 12 * 12;
```

which is exactly what is wanted. However, in the second line of `main()`,

```
value = square_of( 3 + 1);
```

is replaced by

```
value = 3 + 1 * 3 + 1;
```

Because a macro is a text-substitution mechanism, it does not resolve `3 + 1` to equal `4` and then compile

value = 4 * 4;

Listing 15.4. Side effects in a macro.

```
/*----------
Side effects
----------*/

#include <stdio.h>

#define   square_of(x)        x * x

void main()
{

     int value;

     value = square_of(12);

     value = square_of( 3 + 1);

}
```

In a case like this, it is much safer to "overuse" parentheses, as shown in Listing 15.5. This new definition of `square_of(x)` causes the two lines to become

```
value = ( ( 12) * (12) );
```

and

```
value = ( ( 3 + 1 ) * ( 3 + 1 ) );
```

Although the first example seems like overkill, the parentheses in the second example nicely prevent the macro from doing the wrong thing.

Listing 15.5. Correcting side effects in a macro.

```
/*-------------------------------------
Correcting side effects with parentheses
-------------------------------------*/

#include <stdio.h>

#define   square_of(x)        ( (x) * (x) )

void main()
{
```

continues

Listing 15.5. continued

```
    int value;

    value = square_of(12);

    value = square_of( 3 + 1);

}
```

Stringizing

Although this sounds like something you might do in a mozzarella factory to get the cheese to come out right, it is an operation done with macros.

Stringizing is the process of turning a nonstring macro argument into a quoted string. The simplest example is in Listing 15.6. The compiler converts `say(hello)` to `printf("hello")`. Stringizing is done by the single pound sign (#) preceding the argument in the macro definition.

Listing 15.6. Stringizing.

```
/*--------
Stringizing
--------*/

#include <stdio.h>

#define   say(x)    printf(#x)

void main()
{
    say(hello);     /* becomes printf("hello"); */
}
```

Macros can be used anywhere: in data or in code. One of their strongest uses is to make code more readable. Listing 15.7 creates a structure that is intended to be used to hold an array of prompts to be displayed on the screen. The members of the structure are a pointer to the string to display the length of the string, the row, and the column. The program

creates and initializes an array of four of these structures, which includes a final array element containing a NULL string pointer and 0 values for the other members.

Listing 15.7. Complex macros.

```
/*------------
Screen prompts
------------*/

#include <stdio.h>

typedef struct{
     char *name;
     int len;
     int row;
     int col;
     }PROMPT;


PROMPT cust_prompt[]={
     {"Name", 4, 8, 20},
     {"Address", 7, 10, 20},
     {"Phone", 5, 12, 20},
     {NULL, 0, 0, 0}
     };

void display_prompts(PROMPT *);

void main()
{
     display_prompts(cust_prompt);
}

/*------------------
Dummy display routine
------------------*/
void display_prompts(PROMPT *prompt)
{
     while(prompt->name)
          {
          printf("Display %s at row %d col %d for %d bytes. \n",
               prompt->name, prompt->row,
               prompt->col, prompt->len);
          ++prompt;
          }
}
```

The initialization of this array is odd-looking and not easy to understand. You may even find it necessary to refer to the structure definition to figure out which constant initializes which member. A larger structure would be even less understandable. The `display_prompts()` routine is a dummy that just prints the information in the structure array.

Compare Listing 15.7 to Listing 15.8, which creates a set of macros that allows the structure to be initialized in something that is a lot easier to read.

Listing 15.8. Using macros to improve readability.

```
/*------------
Screen prompts
------------*/

#include <stdio.h>

typedef struct{
     char *name;
     int len;
     int row;
     int col;
     }PROMPT;

/*----------------------------------------------
Macros to convert array initialization to something
more readable.
----------------------------------------------*/
#define   PROMPTER(x)         {x, sizeof(x)- 1,
#define   ROW(x)              x,
#define   COL(x)              x},
#define   LAST_PROMPT     {NULL, 0, 0, 0}

PROMPT cust_prompt[]={
     PROMPTER("Name")         ROW(8)    COL(20)
     PROMPTER("Address")      ROW(10)   COL(20)
     PROMPTER("Phone")        ROW(12)   COL(20)
     LAST_PROMPT
     };

void display_prompts(PROMPT *);

void main()
{
     display_prompts(cust_prompt);
}
```

```
/*------------------
Dummy display routine
------------------*/
void display_prompts(PROMPT *prompt)
{
     while(prompt->name)
          {
          printf("Display %s at row %d col %d for %d bytes. \n",
               prompt->name, prompt->row,
               prompt->col, prompt->len);
          ++prompt;
          }
}
```

Typecasting Data Types

Typecasting is a method of getting the compiler to pretend that one data type is another. There are several reasons you might want to do this, but this example will be familiar to COBOL programmers.

Listing 15.9 accesses a control file that contains multiple record types. Two structures are defined, `DIV` and `DEPT`, for the two types. Each of the records starts with a three-byte string of either `"DV"` for division or `"DP"` for department. The program up to `read_data()` just creates test data by generating 15 departments and eight divisions.

At `read_data()`, a generic buffer is created that is large enough to hold the largest record. Three bytes are read in, and the file is immediately backed up three bytes by using `lseek()` to seek `-3` positions from the current position. These three bytes are tested for `"DV"` or `"DP"`. If `"DV"` is found, a `DIV`-sized record is read from the file. If `"DP"` is found, a `DEPT`-sized record is read. The typecasting is done in

```
print_div( (DIV*) buf);
```

and

```
print_dept( (DEPT*) buf);
```

The `print_div()` function expects to receive a pointer to a `DIV` structure. Similarly, the `print_dept()` function is expecting a pointer to a `DEPT` structure. The data has been read into a generic buffer and must be passed as a pointer to a `char` array. The use of `(DIV*)` or `(DEPT*)` causes the compiler to pretend the pointer to `buf` that is being passed to either of the functions is actually a pointer to a structure of the required type.

Listing 15.9. Typecasting.

```
/*--------
Type casts
--------*/

#include <stdio.h>
#include <string.h>
#include <fcntl.h>
#include <io.h>
#include <sys\stat.h>

typedef struct {
     char code[3];
     int no;
     int div;
     char name[31];
     }DEPT;

typedef struct {
     char code[3];
     int no;
     char name[21];
     }DIV;

DEPT dept;
DIV division;

void write_data(void), write_dept(int, DEPT*),
          write_div(int, DIV*), read_data(void),
          print_div(DIV*), print_dept(DEPT*);

#define   FILE_NAME      "control.dat"
#define   RECORD_LENGTH  sizeof(dept)

void main()
{

     write_data();
     read_data();
}

/*----------------------
Write out some test data
----------------------*/
void write_data()
{
     int file, idx;
```

```
    file = open(FILE_NAME, O_BINARY¦O_CREAT¦O_WRONLY¦O_APPEND,
                        S_IREAD¦S_IWRITE);

    strcpy(dept.code, "DP");
    for(idx = 1; idx < 15; ++idx)
         {
         dept.no = idx;
         dept.div = (idx / 2) + 1;
         sprintf(dept.name, "Department #%d", idx);
         write_dept(file, &dept);
         }
    strcpy(division.code, "DV");
    for(idx = 1; idx < 8; ++idx)
         {
         division.no = idx;
         sprintf(division.name, "Division #%d", idx);
         write_div(file, &division);
         }
    close(file);
}

void write_dept(int file, DEPT *dp)
{
    write(file, dp, sizeof(DEPT));
}

void write_div(int file, DIV *dv)
{
    write(file, dv, sizeof(DIV));
}


/*--------------------------------
Read the data back in and print it.
--------------------------------*/
void read_data()
{
    int file, count;
    char buf[RECORD_LENGTH];

    file = open(FILE_NAME, O_BINARY¦O_RDONLY);

    while(1)
         {
         count = read( file, buf, 3);
         if(count < 3)
```

continues

Listing 15.9. continued

```
                break;
            lseek( file, -3L, SEEK_CUR);
            if( !( strcmp( buf, "DV")))
                {
                read( file, buf, sizeof(DIV));
                print_div( (DIV*) buf);
                }
            else
                {
                read(file, buf, sizeof(DEPT));
                print_dept( (DEPT*) buf);
                }
            }
        close(file);
}

void print_div( DIV *dv)
{
        printf("Division %d is named %s. \n", dv->no, dv->name);
}

void print_dept( DEPT *dp)
{
        printf("Department %d in Division %d is named %s. \n",
                dp->no, dp->div, dp->name);
}
```

Allocating Extra Memory

Sometimes it is not always possible or prudent to allocate all the data storage that will be needed for a program within the data section of the program. In COBOL, you must declare everything in `WORKING-STORAGE`, but in C, data storage can be dynamically allocated. Under MS-DOS, dynamic allocation of memory is rarely an issue, because it is a single-tasking machine and all memory is available to your single task. Under Windows and multi-user operating systems such as UNIX, it is necessary to consider memory allocation because it affects performance.

Memory that is needed for only a portion of the program can be allocated and then freed again after it has served its purpose. The `malloc()` function is called passing the number of bytes wanted, and returns a pointer if the memory is successfully allocated. The `free()` function can be used to return the memory to the free memory pool. Listing 15.10 allocates memory to duplicate a string, copies the string, converts the copy to uppercase, prints both strings, and then frees the allocated memory.

Listing 15.10. Dynamic memory allocation.

```
/*--------------------------
Using dynamic memory allocation
--------------------------*/

#include <stdio.h>
#include <malloc.h>
#include <string.h>

char a_string[] = "Hello World";

void main()
{
     char *copy;

     copy = malloc(strlen(a_string) + 1);
     if(copy == NULL)
          {
          printf("Unable to allocate memory\n");
          return;
          }
     strcpy(copy, a_string);
     strupr(copy);
     printf("The original string is <%s> \n", a_string);
     printf("The copy is <%s> \n", copy);
     free(copy);
}
```

The `malloc()` function returns uninitialized memory. The `calloc()` function is similar to `malloc()`. It is passed a number and a size, and allocates *`number * size`* bytes. This allocated memory is cleared to `0`s. The `free()` function should only be used to free memory that has been allocated with `malloc()` or `calloc()`.

Void Pointers

You have already seen the void keyword used to declare a function that either returns no value or receives no passed arguments. The example below receives no arguments and returns no value.

```
void do_something(void);
```

A function can also be declared with a void pointer. A void pointer is completely different from void as a parameter. This is another case of C using too few keywords, causing some confusion in what things mean. The next example declares a function that returns an integer, that is passed a void pointer as an argument.

```
int do_something(void *);
```

A void pointer as a passed argument in a declaration basically means that the function can legally be called passing a pointer to anything. In Listing 15.11, do_something is called passing a pointer to an int, to a string, and to a structure. The compiler will not complain about these different types because they all qualify as pointers.

Listing 15.11. Passing a void pointer.

```
/*-------------------
Passing a void pointer
-------------------*/

#include <stdio.h>

void do_something(void*);


char stuff[8];

int value;

struct{
     char name[31];
     int result;
     }a_struct;

void main()
{
     do_something(stuff);
     do_something(&value);
```

```
     do_something(&a_struct);
}

void do_something(void *ptr)
{
     /* do something here */
}
```

The memcpy() function is usually declared in <string.h> as

```
void *memcpy( void *, void*, int);
```

which identifies it as a function that can be passed two pointers to anything, and an integer, and will return a pointer that can be assigned to any pointer variable.

You do not have to use void pointers to program in C as long as you understand what they are when you see them in a listing.

Summary

This wraps up C. By now you should be coding well and have ideas and projects of your own to try out. C is flexible enough and powerful enough that there always seems to be some newer and better way of skinning the same old cat. Use C, pick up books on advanced techniques, and keep banging away at the keyboard. I hope you find it as interesting as I do.

Program Development

A program development cycle consists of editing, compiling, linking, and sometimes library building.

This book is primarily targeted at MS-DOS systems, but it is worth knowing how to tackle these problems on other systems. This appendix describes the following procedures for MS-DOS, UNIX, and VAX VMS machines.

- Editing
- Compiling
- Linking
- Building libraries
- Using libraries

Editing

Editing is very much a matter of personal preference. The only note worth mentioning is that C is a free-form language. If you are using, or are used to using, an editor that is already structured for COBOL, you will need to change your editing style. C does not have line numbers or enforced column positions. If your editor is set up for that style of programming, check whether it has a free-form text mode, and switch over to it for your C programming.

Listings A.1 and A.2 are a main program and some service routines to be edited and linked together for the examples in this chapter. They take a heading and center it.

Listing A.1. title50.c—centering a string.

```
#include <stdio.h>

char title[] = Year End Report";

char work_buffer[51];

main()
{
     strcpy(work_buffer,title);
     strncenter(work_buffer,50);
     printf("%s\n",work_buffer);
}
```

Listing A.2. stringer.c—string routines.

```
#include <string.h>
#include <ctype.h>

/* Left justify a string */
strljust(str)
char *str;
{
     int len;

     len = strlen(str);
     while(isspace(*str) != 0)
```

```
            {
            memmove(str,str + 1,len);
            str[len] = ' ';
            }
}

/* Reverse a string */
strrev(str)
char *str;
{
      char ch;
      char *end;

      end = str + strlen(str) - 1;

      while(str < end)
            {
            ch = *end;
            *end-- = *str;
            *str++ = ch;
}

/* Right justify a string */
strrjust(str)
char *str;
{
      strrev(str);
      strljust(str);
      strrev(str);
}

/* Truncate to last non-white character */
strtrunc(str)
char *str;
{
      char *end;

      end = str + strlen(str) - 1;

      while( (*str != 0) && ( isspace(*end) != 0 ) )
            {
            *end-- = 0;
            }
}

/* Pad a string for len with spaces */
struntrunc(str,len)
char *str;
```

continues

Listing A.2. continued

```
int len;
{
     while( strlen(str) < len)
          strcat(str," ");
}

/* Center a string */
strcenter(str)
char *str;
{

     strncenter(str,strlen(str));
}

/* Center a string within width */
strncenter(str,width)
char *str;
int width;
{
     int non_blank_len,padding;

     strtrunc(str);
     strrev(str);
     strtrunc(str);
     non_blank_len = strlen(str);

     padding = (width - non_blank_len ) / 2;

     struntrunc(str,padding);
     strrev(str);
     struntrunc(str,width);
}
```

For MS-DOS, select your favorite editor and type these two files. There are so many editors that it would take a book just to list and briefly describe them. Originally, MS-DOS came with the editor EDLIN, a single-line editor. Recent versions of MS-DOS have been distributed with EDIT, a quite passable editor, and certainly up to creating C source code.

For UNIX, I highly recommend learning vi. It is a cranky editor, but available on every UNIX machine. Once you learn it, you can edit on all UNIX machines.

VAX VMS is supplied with an array of configurable editors. I haven't found one I didn't like, so take your pick and configure it any way you want to.

Compiling

Compiling the source code turns it into an unlinked object module. C compilers such as Microsoft C and UNIX's cc compiler are capable of compiling and linking in one step, but for these examples I'll stick to compiling only. Compile each file into an unlinked object.

- Under MS-DOS, compile each source code file into title50.obj and stringer.obj using the Microsoft C compiler by typing

  ```
  cl /c title50.c
  cl /c stringer.c
  ```

  The `/c` switch indicates that the compile will stop before linking takes place.

- Under UNIX create title50.o and string.o by typing

  ```
  cc -c title50.c
  cc -c stringer.c
  ```

  The `-c` flag serves the same purpose as `/c` under DOS Microsoft C.

- For VAX VMS build TITLE50.OBJ and STRINGER.OBJ by typing

  ```
  cc title50.c
  cc stringer.c
  ```

  The VAX C compiler does not automatically invoke the linker, so you do not need a switch to prevent linking.

If there are errors in your code, correct them now. Common errors are misspelling a variable name in the body of the function or omitting the semicolon at the end of statements, omitting a brace, and other punctuation problems. Once the corrections are complete, recompile until you have an error-free compilation.

- Under MS-DOS the output files will be named TITEL50.OBJ and STRINGER.OBJ.
- Under UNIX the output file will be named title50.o and stringer.o.
- Under VAX VMS the output file will be named TITLE50.OBJ and STRINGER.OBJ.

Linking

The next step is to link the two files together to produce a single executable image.

- Under MS-DOS Microsoft C, link to create title50.exe with the following command:

  ```
  cl title50.obj.c stringer.obj
  ```

- Under UNIX, you must specify the output file name with an `-o` switch, so link to create title50 with the following command:

  ```
  cc -o title50 title50.o stringer.o
  ```

- Under VAX VMS, link with the following command:

  ```
  LINK/EXE=TITLE50 TITLE50.OBJ, STRINGER.OBJ
  ```

Building Libraries

As an alternative to direct linking, use the librarian to create a library and add your object file to the library. In this example, the library will be called mylib.

- Under MS-DOS, type

  ```
  lib mylib +stringer.obj;
  ```

  This creates the library mylib.lib and adds stringer.obj to the library.

- Under UNIX, type

  ```
  ar rv mylib.a stringer.o
  ```

  This creates the archive library mylib.a and adds stringer.o to it. Some versions of UNIX require that you further process the library (check your manuals) by running

  ```
  ranlib mylib.a
  ```

- Under VAX VMS, type

  ```
  LIBR/CREATE MYLIB.OLB
  LIBR/INSERT MYLIB.OLB STRINGER.OLB
  ```

  This creates MYLIB.OLB and adds STRINGER.OBJ to it.

Using Libraries

Once you create a library, you can link it to a main module.

- Under MS-DOS Microsoft C, link to create title50.exe with the following command:

```
cl title50.obj mylib.lib
```

- Under UNIX you must specify the output filename with an `-o` switch, so link to create title50 with the following command:

```
cc -o title50 title50.o mylib.a
```

- Under VAX VMS, link with the following command:

```
LINK/EXE=TITLE50 TITLE50OBJ, MYLIB.OLB/LIB
```

Routines in mylib that are needed by title50 are extracted by the link step and included in the output file. You can create any other source code file that uses these routines. It can then be compiled and linked with mylib.

COBOL to C Cross-Reference

COBOL	C	Chapter
`ADD 1 TO VAR-A.`	`++var_a;`	2
`ADD 7 TO VAR-A.`	`var_a += 7;`	2
`AND`	`&&`	5
`CLOSE TEXT-FILE.`	`FILE *file_ptr;` `fclose(file_ptr);`	9
`COMPUTE VAR-A = VAR-B - 1.`	`var_a = var_b - 1;`	2
`DIVIDE VAR-A BY VAR-B.`	`var_a /= var_b;`	2
`DIVIDE VAR-A-BY VAR-B` `    GIVING VAR-C REMAINDER VAR-D.`	`var_c = var_a / var_b;` `var_d = var_a % var_b;`	2

continues

<table>
<tr><th>COBOL</th><th>C</th><th>Chapter</th></tr>
<tr><td>IF VAR-A = VAR-B
    PERFORM DO-SOMETHING
    PERFORM SOMETHING-ELSE
ELSE
    PERFORM ANOTHER-OPTION</td><td>if(var_a == var_b)
    {
    do_something();
    something_else();
    }
else
    another_option();</td><td>5</td></tr>
<tr><td>IS EQUAL</td><td>==</td><td>5</td></tr>
<tr><td>IS GREATER THAN</td><td>></td><td>5</td></tr>
<tr><td>IS LESS THAN</td><td><</td><td>5</td></tr>
<tr><td>IS NOT EQUAL</td><td>!=</td><td>5</td></tr>
<tr><td>IS NOT GREATER THAN</td><td><=</td><td>5</td></tr>
<tr><td>IS NOT LESS THAN</td><td>>=</td><td>5</td></tr>
<tr><td>LEVEL 88
 01   ERROR-FLAG   PIC 9.
      88   NO-ERROR   VALUE 0.
      88   AN-ERROR   VALUE 1.</td><td>int error_flag;
#define no_error (error_flag
== 0)
#define an_error (error_flag
== 1)</td><td>8</td></tr>
<tr><td>MOVE 1 TO NUM-VAR-A.</td><td>num_var_a = 1;</td><td>2</td></tr>
<tr><td>MOVE CHAR-VAR-A TO CHAR-VAR-B</td><td>strcpy(char_var_b,char_var_a)</td><td>3</td></tr>
<tr><td>MOVE NUM-VAR-A TO NUM-VAR-B.</td><td>num_var_b = num_var_a;</td><td>2</td></tr>
<tr><td>MOVE WITH CONVERSION ALPHA-A
    TO NUM-B.</td><td>num_b = atoi(alpha_a);</td><td>6</td></tr>
<tr><td>MULTIPLY VAR-A BY VAR-B.</td><td>var_a *= var_b;</td><td>2</td></tr>
<tr><td>NEXT SENTENCE</td><td>;</td><td>5</td></tr>
<tr><td>OPEN INPUT TEXT-FILE.
 (line sequential)</td><td>FILE *file_ptr;
file_ptr = fopen(text_file,"r");</td><td>9</td></tr>
<tr><td>OR</td><td>||</td><td>5</td></tr>
</table>

COBOL	C	Chapter

`PERFORM`
`    WITH TEST AFTER`
`    UNTIL condition`
`        statement`
`        statement`
`  END PERFORM.`
	`do{`
	`    statement;`
	`    statement;`
	`    }while(!(condition));`
		5

`PERFORM DO-IT-TO-IT.`	`do_it_to_it();`	1

`PERFORM UNTIL condition`
`    statement`
`    statement`
`  END PERFORM.`
	`while(!(condition))`
	`    {`
	`    statement;`
	`    statment;`
	`    }`
		5

`PERFORM VARYING VAR-A`
`    FROM 1 BY 1`
`    UNTIL VAR-A > 10`
`      statement`
`      statement`
`  END PERFORM.`
	`for(var_a=1;!(var_a>10);++var`
	`_a)`
	`    {`
	`    statement;`
	`    statement;`
	`    }`
		5

`READ TEXT-FILE RECORD INTO`
`    TEXT-RECORD.`
(line sequential)
	`FILE *file_ptr;`
	
	`fgets(text_record, length,`
	`        file_ptr);`
		9

`RECORD`
` 01  CUST-RECORD.`
`     05  CUST-NO     PIC 9999.`
`     05  CUST-NAME   PIC X(30).`
`     05  CUST-BAL    PIC S9(5)V99.`
	`struct{`
	`    int no;`
	`    char name[31];`
	`    double balance;`
	`    }cust_record;`
		12

`SUBTRACT 1 FROM VAR-A.`	`--var_a;`	2
`SUBTRACT 15 FROM VAR-A.`	`var_a -= 15;`	2

`WRITE TEXT-RECORD.`
(line sequential)
	`FILE *file_ptr;`
	
	`fputs(text_record, file_ptr);`
		9

The Standard C Library

A standard C library breaks down into functions that fall into broad general categories. C libraries differ from vendor to vendor, but the examples in this appendix cover some of the more usual routines that are available. This listing should only be used as a reference for this book. When using a library in compiled code, be sure to check the vendor's manual on the function.

String Handling Family

`strcpy()`	Copy one string into another
`strncpy()`	Copy one string into another for length
`strcmp()`	Compare two strings
`strncmp()`	Compare two strings for length
`stricmp()`	Compare two strings, independent of case
`strlen()`	Get length of a string
`strcat()`	Concatenate two strings
`strchr()`	Search a string for a character
`strrev()`	Reverse a string
`strupr()`	Convert a string to uppercase
`strlwr()`	Convert a string to lowercase
`tolower()`	Convert a character to lowercase
`toupper()`	Convert a character to uppercase
`atoi()`	Convert a string to an integer
`atol()`	Convert a string to a long
`atof()`	Convert a string to a float
`atod()`	Convert a string to a double
`itoa()`	Convert an integer to a string

Character Testing Family

`isalnum()`	Test if a character is alphanumeric
`isapha()`	Test if a character is alphabetic
`isascii()`	Test if a character is ASCII
`iscontrol()`	Test if a character is a control character
`isdigit()`	Test if a character is a digit
`islower()`	Test if a character is lowercase
`ispunct()`	Test if a character is punctuation
`isspace()`	Test if a character is space, tab, CR, LF, FF
`isupper()`	Test if a character is uppercase
`isxdigit()`	Test if a character is a hexadecimal digit

Memory Handling Family

`memcpy()`	Copy memory for length
`memcmp()`	Compare memory for length
`memmove()`	Direction independent memory copy
`memset()`	Set a value in memory for length

Stream I/O Functions

`fopen()`	Open a file for stream I/O
`fclose()`	Close a file for stream I/O
`fcloseall()`	Close all files for stream I/O
`fgets()`	Get a string from a stream file
`fputs()`	Write a string to a stream file
`ftell()`	Get current position in a stream file
`fseek()`	Move to a position in a stream file
`fscanf()`	Read formatted input from a stream file
`fprintf()`	Write formatted output to a stream file
`feof()`	Test if a stream file is at end
`fgetc()`	Get a character from a stream file
`fputc()`	Write a character to a stream file
`rewind()`	Restart a stream file from position 1

Low-Level I/O Functions

`open()`	Open a file for I/O
`create()`	Create a new file for I/O
`close()`	Close a file for I/O
`read()`	Read bytes from a file
`write()`	Write bytes to a file
`lseek()`	Get current position in a file

General I/O Functions

`getchar()`	Get a character from input
`putchar()`	Write a character to output
`gets()`	Get a string from input
`puts()`	Write a string to output
`printf()`	Write formatted data to output
`sprintf()`	Write formatted output to memory
`scanf()`	Get formatted data from input
`sscanf()`	Get formatted data from memory

Miscellaneous Functions

`unlink()`	Delete a file

Functions in Alphabetical Order

atoi()

Summary

```
#include <stdlib.h>
int atoi(str)
char *str;                    NUL terminated string
```

Description

The `atoi()` function converts an ASCII string containing digits that represent an integer to its integer value. Conversion will include a leading + or - and stops when the first non-digit is encountered. Leading white space will be skipped.

Return Value

The `atoi()` function returns the integer result of the conversion.

See Also

`itoa()`

Example

```
main()
{
     int x,y,z;
     char buffer[15];
     char *p

     strcpy(buffer," -17");

     x=atoi(buffer);
}
```

The program will assign the value `-17` to `x` based on the given conversion rules.

close()

Summary

```
#include <io.h>
#include <errno.h>
int close(handle)

int handle;                    File number to close
```

Description

The `close()` function closes a file that has been opened for system level I/O by the `open()` function.

Return Value

The `close()` function returns zero if the close is successful or `-1` (EOF) if the close fails.

Remarks

Low-level and stream level file I/O should not be mixed, and a file opened with `fopen()` should only be closed using `fclose()` or `fcloseall()`.

fclose()

Summary

```
#include <stdio.h>
int fclose(stream)

FILE *stream;                    File to close
```

Description

Closes the file pointed to by stream, thus freeing the file pointer for use by another file. If the file is open for output, any characters in the buffer will be flushed.

Return Value

Returns EOF (`-1`) if the close is not successful and zero if it succeeds.

See Also

`fopen()`

Example

To close the file pointed to by `outfp`, use

```
fclose(outfp);
```

fcloseall()

Summary

```
#include <stdio.h>
void fcloseall()
```

Description

The `fcloseall()` function closes all files opened for I/O. It is designed to close stream files only.

feof()

Summary

```
#include <stdio.h>
int feof(stream)

FILE *stream;                    Input file to test
```

Description

The `feof()` function returns EOF (`-1`) if the specified file is at the end.

Return Value

The `feof()` function returns EOF (`-1`) if the specified input file is at end, and zero if it is not.

The return value only has meaning for stream files opened in input mode.

fgetc()

Summary

```
#include <stdio.h>
int fgetc(stream)
FILE *stream;                   File from which to receive a char
```

Description

The `fgetc()` retrieves the next character from a stream file opened in input mode.

Return Value

The `fgetc()` function returns the retrieved character, or EOF (`-1`) if the file is at end.

Example

```
#include <stdio.h>

main()
{
     FILE *infile,*outfile;
     int c;

     infile=fopen("file1.do","r");
     outfile=fopen("file2.do","w");

     while((c=fgetc(infile)!=EOF)
          fputc(c,outfile);

     fclose(infile);
     fclose(outfile);
}
```

The program opens file1.do for reading, file2.do for writing, and copies everything in file1.do to file2.do. Both files are then closed.

fgets()

Summary

```
#include <stdio.h>
char *fgets(buf,len,stream)

char *buf;                    Receiving buffer
int len;                      Length to read
FILE *stream;                 File to read from
```

Description

The `fgets()` function reads a string from the input stream and stores it in `buf`. Characters are read up to and including the first newline character (`'\n'`) or until `len - 1` characters have been read. A terminating `NULL` is added to the end of `buf`.

Return Value

The `fgets()` function returns a pointer to `buf` if any characters were read, or `NULL` if none are available (the file is at the end condition).

Example

```
#include <stdio.h>
main()
{
     char buf[256];
     char *ptr;
     FILE *input;

     input=fopen("file1.do","r");
     while(fgets(buf,256,input)){
          *ptr=buf;
          while(*ptr)
               putchar(*p++);
     }
     fclose(input);
}
```

The program opens file1.do and reads it in line by line until the file is exhausted. Each line is displayed character by character.

fopen()

Summary

```
#include <stdio.h>
```

```
FILE *fopen(filename, mode)

char *filename;               Pointer to the filename
char *mode;                   "r", "w", or "a"
```

Description

Opens the file given by `filename` for buffered I/O. `filename` is a system filename which may include a device.

The mode is `"r"` to read, `"w"` to write, or `"a"` to append to the file. Append mode (`"a"`) will create the file if it does not exist. Mode specifications must be in lowercase. An additional `"+"` will modify the open mode.

The file will be treated as a buffered text file, which means that newline characters will be converted to carriage return/line feed (CR/LF) pairs, and ^Z will be treated as end-of-file.

Opening a text file in append mode (`"a"`) positions the file at the end-of-file (^Z), so the first character written is added at the end of the file.

Table C.1. Summary of `fopen()` modes

Open Mode	*Open Type*	*Effect on File*
`"r"`	read	The file must exist before the open.
"w"	write	Creates a new file, destroying any copy of the file that existed before the open.
`"a"`	append (write)	The file is created if it does not exist. The file is added to at the end if it existed before the open.
`"r+"`	read/write	The file must exist before the open.
`"w+"`	read/write	Creates a new file destroying any copy of the file that existed before the open.
`"a+"`	read/append	Creates the file if it doesn't exist. Appends to an existing file.

The open will fail if

- `filename` is not a valid filename.
- `filename` is opened for reading and can't be found.

- mode is not valid.
- The maximum number of buffered files is already open.
- The device is not a valid device name.

Return Value

The value returned is a file pointer for a successful open or NULL if any errors are found.

Example

```
#include <stdio.h>

main()
{
     FILE *libfp, *fopen();
     static char fnam[]="sub.txt";

     if ((libfp = fopen(fnam, "r")) == NULL)
          printf("File %s not found\n",fnam);
     else
          fclose(libfp);
}
```

The program tests for the existence of sub.txt by trying to open it in read mode and displaying a message if not found.

fprintf()

Summary

```
#include <stdio.h>

void fprintf(stream,format,[arg]....)
FILE *stream;                  Output file
char *format;                  Control string
[arg]                          Data type(s) matching the control string
```

Description

The `fprintf()` function works like the `printf()` function that sends formatted data to the screen. Instead of going to the screen, the formatted data is sent to an output stream file.

See the `printf()` function for a description of formatting characters and how to use them.

See Also

`printf()`, `sprintf()`

Example

```
#include <stdio.h>
main()
{
     FILE *testfile;
     int x;
     testfile=fopen("test.do","w");
     for(x=1;x<11;++x)
          fprintf(testfile,"This is line %d\n",x);
     fclose(testfile);
}
```

The program opens a file and writes 10 lines to it, as shown below:

```
This is line 1
This is line 2
.
.
.
This is line 10
```

fputc()

Summary

```
#include <stdio.h>

int fputc(c,stream)

int c;                    Character to output

FILE *stream;             Output file
```

Description

The `fputc()` function puts a character in a stream file opened for output.

Return Value

The `fputc()` function returns EOF if an error occurs (such as running out of memory), or the character if no error occurs.

Example

See the example for `fgetc()`.

fputs()

Summary

```
#include <stdio.h>

int fputs(buf,stream)
char *buf;                          String to write
FILE *stream;                       Output file
```

Description

The `fputs()` function writes all characters in `buf` up to but not including the terminating `'\0'`.

Return Value

Zero if no errors, nonzero if an error occurs.

Example

```
#include <stdio.h>

main()
{
     FILE *infile,*outfile;
     char buf[256];

     infile=fopen("file1.do","r");
     outfile=fopen("file2.do","w");

     while(fgets(buf,256,infile))
     fputs(buf,outfile);

     fclose(infile);
     fclose(outfile);
}
```

The program copies file1.do to file2.do line by line.

fscanf()

Summary

```
#include <stdio.h>

int fscanf(stream,format[,arg]....)
FILE *stream;                    Input file
char *format;                    Format string
```

Description

The `fscanf()` function reads data from an input stream into the arguments supplied. For a description of format and arguments for `fscanf()`, see `scanf()`, the keyboard input version of this routine.

Return Value

The `fscanf()` function returns the number of format items successfully matched and assigned to arguments.

Remarks

The arguments to `fscanf()` must be pointers, or you won't get back the values assigned. If no items are matched, the count returned is zero, which is different from EOF. If an end-of-file is found in the middle of the format, the return value is the number of items matched to this point. The next call to `fscanf()` will return EOF.

Example

You can read a person's name from a file as follows:

```
char firstname[10], initial[2], lastname[20];
fscanf(fp, "%s %1s. %s", firstname, initial,
     lastname);
```

With the input `"Brian W. Kernighan"`, `firstname` will contain `"Brian"`, `initial` will contain `"W"`, and `lastname` will contain `"Kernighan"`.

getchar()

Summary

```
#include <stdio.h>

int getchar()
```

Description

The `getchar()` function waits for a keypress and returns the key.

Return Value

The `getchar()` function returns the key pressed.

See Also

`putchar()`

Remarks

The getchar() function and its complement putchar() both do conventional C end-of-line translation. The carriage-return character, '\r', is returned as a newline, '\n'. The newline, when sent to the console using putchar(), is translated into a carriage return and newline combination.

Example

```
#include <stdio.h>

main()
{
     int c;
     while((c=getchar())!= EOF)
          putchar(c);
}
```

The program accepts keyboard input and prints characters on the screen until Ctrl-Z (decimal 26) is received.

isalpha–isxdigit

Summary

```
#include <ctype.h>

int isalnum(c);          Alphanumeric('A'-'Z','a'-'z','0'-'9').

int isalpha(c);          A letter('A'-'Z', 'a'-'z').

int isascii(c);          ASCII (0x00-0x7f).

int iscntrl(c);          Control characters(0x00-0x1f and 0x7f).

int isdigit(c);          Digit ('0'-'9').

int islower(c);          Lowercase ('a'-'z').

int ispunct(c);          Any of !"#$%&'()*+,-./:;<=>?@[\]^_'{¦}~ .

int isspace(c);          Space (0x09-0x0d or ' ').

int isupper(c);          Uppercase ('A'-'Z').

int isxdigit(c);         Hex digit('A'-'F','a'-'f','0'-'9').

int c;                   Integer (character) to test.
```

Description

The `isascii()` routine produces a valid return for all integer values; the other routines all assume the integer being tested is in the ASCII range, and results are not valid for integers larger than 0x7f.

Return Value

All of the above functions return a zero if the character being tested is not within the requested range, and a nonzero if the character satisfies the conditions.

Example

```
#include <ctype.h>

main()
{
     int c;
     char n[5];

     strcpy(n,"not ");

     for(c=0;c<=0x7f;++c)
     {
          printf("%d is %salphanumeric ",c,isalnum(c)?"":n);
          printf("and %sa letter\n",isalpha(c)?"":n);

          printf("It is %sASCII",isascii(c)?"":n);
          printf("and %sa control\n",iscntrl(c)?"":n);

          printf("It is %sa digit",isdigit(c)?"":n);
          printf("and %slowercase\n",islower(c)?"":n);

          printf("It is %spuntuation",ispunct(c)?"":n);
          printf("and %sa space\n",isspace(c)?"":n);

          printf("It is %suppercase",isupper(c)?"":n);
          printf("and %sa hex digit\n",c,isxdigit(c)?"":n);

          printf("Press any key for next char");

          getch();
     }
}
```

This program displays the status of all values from 0 to 0x7f against all 10 comparisons.

itoa()

Summary

```
#include <stdlib.h>

char *itoa(number,str,base)
int number;                   Number to convert.
char *str;                    String to store converted data.
int base;                     Radix for the conversion (2-36).
```

Description

The `itoa()` function converts an integer into an ASCII string using the base. If the base is `-10`, the resulting string will include a leading `'-'` if the passed number is negative. All other bases are unsigned.

Return Value

The `itoa()` function returns a pointer to the string containing the converted number.

See Also

`atoi()`

Example

```
#include <stdlib.h>

main()
{
     char buffer[7], *itoa();

     puts(itoa(0xffff,buffer,2));
     puts(itoa(0xffff,buffer,10));
     puts(itoa(0xffff,buffer,-10));
     puts(itoa(0xffff,buffer,8));
     puts(itoa(0xffff,buffer,16));
}
```

The program converts the same number to strings of various bases and displays them on the screen.

The display for this program will be

```
1111111111111111
65535
-1
177777
FFFF
```

memcmp()

Summary

```
#include <string.h>

int memcmp(mem1,mem2,count);
char *mem1;                    Pointer to memory 1.
char *mem2;                    Pointer to 2nd memory area.
int count;                     Number of bytes to compare.
```

Description

The `memcmp()` function compares count bytes of `mem1` and `mem2` and returns a value indicating their relationship.

Return Value

```
 < 0    =       mem1 < mem2
 = 0    =       mem1 = mem2
 > 0    =       mem1 > mem2
```

See Also

`strcmp()`

Example

```
#include <string.h>

testmem(mem1,mem2)
char *mem1, *mem2;
{
     if(!(memcmp(mem1, mem2, 10))
          printf("Memory match\n");
}
```

The function compares two areas of memory for 10 bytes and prints a message if they match.

memcpy()

Summary

```
#include <string.h>

void *memcpy(dest,src,count);
char *dest;                    New Memory
char *src;                     Memory to copy from.
int count;                     Number of bytes to copy.
```

Description

The memcpy() function copies count bytes from src to dest. The memcpy() function calculates the location of the source and destination fields, and copies backward or forward to avoid overwriting memory. If dest is less than src, src is copied to dest by incrementing through memory. If dest is greater than src, the pointers are moved to the ends of the fields and the copy is done by moving backward through memory.

Return Value

The memcpy() function returns a pointer to beginning of the destination memory for the copy.

Example

```
#include <string.h>

char dest[8];

main()
{
char *fn;
     memcpy(dest,"HELLO DO",8);

}
```

The program uses memcpy() to store a filename at dest without the NULL terminator associated with the string.

memset()

Summary

```
#include <string.h>

void *memset(mem,c,count);
char *mem;                    Pointer to memory
int c;                        Character to use to fill
int count;                    Number of bytes to fill
```

Description

The memset() function fills memory with the value in c for count bytes starting at mem.

Return Value

The memset() function returns a pointer to the beginning of the memory that was filled.

Example

```
#include <string.h>

main()
{
     char buffer[200];

     memset(buffer,0xff,200);
}
```

The program uses memset to fill an area of memory with hexadecimal FFs.

open()

Summary

```
#include <fcntl.h.h>
#include<io.h>

int open(name,mode)
char *name;                   Name of file to open
unsigned int mode;            Open mode
```

Description

The `open()` function opens a file for system level file I/O. The `mode` flag must carry information that is available as manifest constants in the header files.

O_APPEND	Open and position to the end of the file.
O_CREATE	Open the file if it exists; create a new one if it does not.
O_TRUNC	Delete the old file if it exists and start with a new one.
O_RDONLY	Open for reading only.
O_WRONLY	Open for writing only.
O_RDWR	Open for reading and writing.

These open types are roughly analogous to input, output and append in terms of what they return depending on whether they find the file.

Return Value

The `open()` function returns a file handle (`0`–`15`) if the open is successful and EOF (`-1`) if it is not.

Example

```
#include <fcntl.h>
#include <io.h>

char data[]={0xe5,0x3e,'H',0xcd,0x44,0x4b};

main()

{

     int handle,c,i;
     char *bufr;

     if((handle=open("file.x",O_WRONLY|O_TRUNC))==EOF)
          {
          puts("File not opened");
          return;
          }
     write(handle,data,sizeof(data));

     if(close(handle))
          puts("Error on close");
}
```

The program creates a file and writes some hexadecimal data to it.

printf()

Summary

```
#include <stdio.h>

void printf(format[,arg]....)
char *format;                 Format string
[arg]                         Data of the type specified in the format
string
```

Description

The `printf()` function converts formats and prints its arguments on the output device under the control of the format string. The control string may contain ordinary characters or conversion specifications. Each conversion specification is introduced by the

character % and is ended by the conversion character. Between the % and the conversion character the following may appear:

- (hyphen)	Causes left justification.
A digit string	Specifies a minimum field width. If the digit string begins with 0, the field is zero-padded if any leading space is left.
. (period)	Introduces a precision specification. A digit string following a '.' indicates that a string field is to be truncated to this length.

The conversion characters themselves are:

d	Converts the argument to decimal notation.
o	Converts the argument to unsigned octal notation.
x	Converts the argument to unsigned hexadecimal notation.
u	Converts the argument to unsigned decimal notation.
c	Converts the argument to a single character.
s	Converts the argument as a string.
f	Converts the argument as a float or double.

An l preceding a d, o, x, or u specification indicates a long integer, an h indicates a short integer.

Return Value

None.

Remarks

Study your vendor manual for complete details on printf().

See Also

sprintf(),fprintf()

Example

```
#include <stdio.h>

main()
{
     unsigned int x;

     x=63000;
```

```
    printf("%d %x %o %u\n",x,x,x,x);

}
```

The program displays x as a decimal, hexadecimal, octal, and unsigned value.

putchar()

Summary

```
#include <stdio.h>

int putchar(c)
int c;                          Character to display.
```

Description

The `putchar()` function prints the specified character on the output device. Any newline characters are translated to a carriage return and a newline.

Return Value

The `putchar()` function returns `c`.

See Also

`getchar()`, `puts()`, `cputs()`

Remarks

The `getchar()` function and its complement `putchar()` both perform conventional C end-of-line translation. The carriage-return character, `'\r'`, is returned as a newline, `'\n'`. The newline, when sent to the console using `putchar()`, is translated into a carriage return and newline combination.

Example

```
#include <stdio.h>

main()
{
    int c;

    while((c=getchar())!= EOF)
        putchar(c);
}
```

The program accepts keyboard input and prints characters on the screen until Ctrl-Z (decimal 26) is received.

puts()

Summary

```
#include <stdio.h>

char *puts(str)
char *str;                    Null-terminated string to display
```

Description

The `puts()` function prints the specified character string on the standard output device. Any newline characters are translated to a carriage return and a newline. When the terminating `'\0'` is encountered, a CR-LF is output.

Return Value

The `puts()` function returns a pointer to the string.

See Also

`putchar()`

Remarks

The `puts()` function does conventional C newline translation, in which `'\n'` is sent to the terminal as `'\r\n'`. In addition, a newline is appended to the end of the string, causing a `'\r'` and `'\n'` at the end of the display.

Example

```
#include <stdio.h>

char *msg[]={
     "This is line one of the message",
     "And this is line two",
     "",
     "Press any Key to continue",
     0
     };

main()
{
     int i;

     i=0;
     while(msg[i])
          puts(msg[i++]);
     getchar();
}
```

The program will display four strings (one is empty), execute a CR-LF pair at the end of each string, and then wait for a single keystroke.

read()

Summary

```
#include <io.h>

int read(handle,buffer,count)

int handle;                    Low-level file number to read from

char *buffer;                  Receiver for read bytes
int count;                     Maximum number to read
```

Description

The `read()` function reads up to `count` bytes from a file opened for system level I/O and places them in `buffer`. The `read()` function assumes binary input and does no data conversions, and does not add a NULL to the buffer.

Return Value

The `read()` function returns the number of bytes read into the buffer.

scanf()

Summary

```
#include <stdio.h>

int scanf(format[,arg]...)
char *format;                  Input control string.
[arg]                          Pointers to data types matching the format
specification
```

Description

Reads characters from `stdin`, interprets them according to the specifications given in format, and stores them in the pointer arguments `arg1`, `arg2`, and so on.

Format	*Type of Input*	*Receiving Argument*
`"%d"`	Integer characters	Pointer to `int`
`"%ld"`	Integer characters	Pointer to `long`
`"%hd"`	Integer characters	Pointer to `short`
`"%o"`	Octal characters	Pointer to `int`
`"%lo"`	Octal characters	Pointer to `long`
`"%ho"`	Octal characters	Pointer to `short`
`"%x"`	Hexadecimal characters	Pointer to `int`
`"%lx"`	Hexadecimal characters	Pointer to `long`
`"%hx"`	Hexadecimal characters	Pointer to `short`
`"%u"`	Unsigned integer characters	Pointer to unsigned `int`
`"%lu"`	Unsigned integer characters	Pointer to unsigned `long`
`"%hu"`	Unsigned integer characters	Pointer to unsigned `short`
`"%U"`	Unsigned integer characters	Pointer to unsigned `long`
`"%f"`	Sign, digits, and decimal point	Pointer to `float`
`"%lf"`	Sign, digits, and decimal point	Pointer to `double`
`"%c"`	A single character including any whitespace character	Pointer to `char`
`"%s"`	String of characters	Pointer to an array of characters large enough to hold the input field plus a terminating NUL.
`"%n"`	No input	Pointer to `int`. This `int` will receive the character count of the total number of characters processed to this point, since the call to `scanf()`.

If a format string starts with a number, it represents the maximum number of characters that will be read to satisfy the argument. An asterisk starting a format string indicates that the argument is to be read as if it were the requested data type, but is not to be stored in a corresponding argument.

If the input cannot be interpreted according to the format specification, the argument is not modified at all.

Return Value

The value returned is the number of format items matched and assigned to the arguments. EOF is returned upon end-of-file or error.

Remarks

The arguments to `scanf()` must be pointers, or you will not get back the values assigned. When your input is from the console, the only way that the end-of-file will be recognized is if the first character typed on the line is ^Z. If no items are matched, the count returned is zero, which is different from EOF.

See Also

`fscanf()`, `sscanf()`

Example

You might read a person's name from the console like this:

```
char firstname[10], initial[2], lastname[20];

scanf("%s %1s. %s", firstname, initial, lastname);
```

If you type `Dennis M. Ritchie` on the console, `firstname` will contain `"Dennis"`, `initial` will contain `"M"`, and `lastname` will contain `"Ritchie"`.

sprintf()

Summary

```
#include <stdio.h>

void sprintf(buffer,format,[arg]....)

char *buffer;                Receiving buffer
char *format;                Control string
[arg]                        Data type if the format specification
```

Description

The `sprintf()` function works like the `printf()` function, which sends formatted data to the screen. Instead of going to the screen, the formatted data is sent to a memory buffer. See the `printf()` function for a description of formatting characters and how to use them.

See Also

`printf()`, `fprintf()`

Example

```
#include <stdio.h>
main()
{
     char buffer[1024];
     char *bptr;
     int x;

     for(x = 1, bptr = buffer; x < 11; ++x)
          {
          sprintf(bptr,"This is line %d\n",x);
          bptr += strlen(bptr);
          }
}
```

The program writes a string 10 times to `buffer` using `bptr` to step through the buffer, as shown below:

```
This is line 1
This is line 2
.
.
.
This is line 10
```

sscanf()

Summary

```
#include <stdio.h>
int sscanf(buffer,format[,arg]....)

char *buffer;                 Input buffer
char *format;                 Format string
[arg]                         Pointer to an argument matching the format
string
```

Description

The `sscanf()` function reads data from an input buffer into the arguments supplied. For information on format and arguments for `sscanf()`, see `scanf()`, the keyboard input version of this routine.

Return Value

The `sscanf()` function returns the number of format items successfully matched and assigned to arguments.

Remarks

The arguments to `sscanf()` must be pointers, or you will not get back the values assigned. If no items are matched, the count returned is zero.

Example

```
#include <stdio.h>

char buf[]= "19DFA8F7";

main(){
     int x,value,i;

     for(i=0,x=0;x<4;++x){
          sscanf(&buf[i],"%2x",&value);
          printf("Value = %d\n",value);
          i+=2;
     }
}
```

The program steps through the buffer two characters at a time and reads in the values as two hexadecimal digits. The values are then displayed in decimal format.

strcat()

Summary

```
#include <string.h>

char *strcat(str1,str2);
char *str1;                     Pointer to first string
char *str2;                     Pointer to string to concatenate
```

Description

The strcat() function copies characters from str2 to the end of str1 up to and including the terminating '\0' in str2. The receiver, str1, must be long enough to accommodate the combined lengths of the original str1 plus the additional characters from str2 and the '\0' terminator.

Return Value

The strcat() function returns a pointer to the beginning of str1.

Example

```
#include <string.h>

main()
{
     char filename[25];

     strcpy(filename,"A:");
     strcat(filename,"newfile.dat");

     open_file(filename);
}
```

The function uses strcpy() and strcat() to create the filename A:newfile.dat in preparation for an open.

strchr()

Summary

```
#include <string.h>

char *strchr(str,ch)
char *str;                  String to search
int ch;                     Character to search for
```

Description

The strchr() function searches a string up to the '\0' terminator looking for an occurrence of character ch. The character ch may itself be '\0', causing strchr() to return a pointer to the end of the string. The passed integer ch is converted to a character before the search begins. Effectively, ch=ch&0xff, causing values above 255 to be converted to the range 0–255.

Return Value

The strchr() function returns a pointer to the ch character if found. If ch does not occur within str, the function returns NULL.

Example

```
ok_and_open(filename)
char *filename;
{

     static char do_ext[4]=".TXT";
     char *ptr,*strchr();

     if(ptr=strchr(filename,'.'))
          {
          if(strcmp(ptr,do_ext)
               {
               printf("Error in filename\n");
               printf("File must be .TXT file\n");
               printf("Press any key to exit\n");
               getchar();
               _exit();
               }
          }
     else
          {
          strcat(filename,do_ext);
          }
     open_file(filename);
}
```

The ok_and_open() function is passed a pointer to a string that is supposed to contain a filename. The function uses the strchr() function to locate the beginning of the file extension portion of the name and uses the strcmp() function to test that the extension is ".TXT". If it is not, an error message is displayed and the program aborts. If no extension character is located, then the strcat() function is used to append a ".TXT" extension to filename before calling the open_file() function.

strcmp()

Summary

```
#include <string.h>

int strcmp(str1,str2)
```

```
char *str1;                    Pointer to string 1
char *str2;                    Pointer to 2nd string
```

Description

The `strcmp()` function compares `str1` and `str2` to the first `'\0'` terminator and returns a value indicating their relationship.

Return Value

```
 < 0    =        str1 < str2
 = 0    =        str1 = str2
 > 0    =        str1 > str2
```

See Also

`memcmp()`

Example

See the example included under `strchr()`.

strcpy()

Summary

```
#include <string.h>

char *strcpy(dest,src)
char *dest;                    Target string
char *src;                     String to be copied to target string
```

Description

The `strcpy()` function copies string `src` to string `dest` up to and including the `'\0'` terminator. String space allocated for `dest` must be large enough to hold the string and the `'\0'` terminator.

Return Value

The `strcpy()` function returns a pointer to `dest`.

See Also

`memcpy()`

Example

See the example for `strcat()`.

strlen()

Summary

```
int strlen(str)
char *str;                    NUL terminated String to measure
```

Description

The `strlen()` function returns the number of characters (not including the `'\0'` terminator) in string `str`.

Return Value

The return for `strlen()` is the length of the string. A return of zero indicates an empty string (`""`).

Example

```
#define _MAX_NAME 13

test_name(filename)
char *filename;
{
     if(strlen(filename) > _MAX_NAME)
          prints("Filename too long");
}
```

The function `test_name()` is passed a pointer to a string containing a filename. If the length of `filename` is greater than the longest legal filename, a message is displayed indicating that the name is invalid.

strlwr()

Summary

```
#include <string.h>

char *strlwr(str)
char *str;                    NUL terminated string
```

Description

The function `strlwr()` converts any uppercase characters in `str` to lowercase.

Return Value

The function `strlwr()` returns a pointer to the string.

See Also

`strupr()`, `strnupr()`, `strnlwr()`, `toupper()`, `tolower()`.

Example

```
#include <stdio.h>
#include <string.h>

char *names[]={"BOB","ALICE","TED","HELEN",0};

main(){
     int i;

     for(i=0 ; names[i] ; ++i){
          strlwr(&names[i][1]);
          printf("%d. %s\n",i+1,names[i]);
     }
}
```

The program converts all but the first letter of each of a list of names to lowercase. The result of running this program would be the display

```
1. Bob
2. Alice
3. Ted
4. Helen
```

strnlwr()

Summary

```
#include <string.h>

char *strnlwr(str,count)
char *str;                    NUL terminated string
int count;                    Number of letters to convert
```

Description

The function `strnlwr()` converts str to lowercase for `count` characters or until a `'\0'` terminator is encountered.

Return Value

The function `strnlwr()` returns a pointer to the converted string.

See Also

`strupr()`, `strlwr()`, `strnupr()`, `toupper()`, `tolower()`.

strnupr()

Summary

```
#include <string.h>

char *strnupr(str,count)
char *str;                    NUL terminated string
int count;                    Number of letters to convert
```

Description

The function `strnupr()` converts `str` to uppercase for `count` characters or until a `'\0'` terminator is encountered.

Return Value

The function `strnupr()` returns a pointer to the converted string.

See Also

`strupr()`, `strlwr()`, `strnlwr()`, `toupper()`, `tolower()`.

Example

```
#include <stdio.h>
#include <string.h>


char *names[]={"bob","alice","ted","helen",0};

main()
{
     int i;

     for(i=0 ; names[i] ; ++i)
          {
          strnupr(names[i],1);
          printf("%d. %s\n",i+1,names[i]);
          }
}
```

The program converts the first character of each of a list of names to uppercase.

The result of running this program would be

```
1. Bob
2. Alice
3. Ted
4. Helen
```

strrev()

Summary

```
#include <string.h>

char *strrev(str)
char *str;                    NUL-terminated string
```

Description

The function `strrev()` reverses the order of characters in the string `str`.

Return Value

The function `strrev()` returns a pointer to the converted string.

Example

```
char *rjustz(str,width)
char *str;
int width;
{
     strrev(str);

     while(strlen(str) < width)
          strcat(str,"0");

     return(strrev(str));
}
```

The function `rjustz()` right-justifies and zero-fills a field. The string and width are passed to the function, for example, `"45"` and `5`. The initial string is reversed to `"54"` and `"0"` is concatenated to the string until the length of the string is equal to the width, resulting in `"54000"`. This string is reversed a final time and returned as `"00045"`.

strupr()

Summary

```
#include <string.h>
```

```
char *strupr(str)
char *str;                     NUL-terminated string
```

Description

The function `strupr()` converts any lowercase characters in `str` to uppercase.

Return Value

The function `strupr()` returns a pointer to the string.

See Also

`strlwr()`, `strnupr()`, `strnlwr()`, `toupper()`, `tolower()`.

Example

```
#include <stdio.h>
#include <string.h>


main()
{
     char buffer[20];

     printf("Enter File to Process\n");
     gets(buffer);
     strupr(buffer);
     process(buffer);
}
```

The user-entered string is converted to uppercase using `strupr()` before passing the resulting string on to the `process()` function.

tolower()

Summary

```
#include <ctype.h>

int tolower(ch)
int ch;                        Character
```

Description

The function `tolower()` converts the single character `ch` to its lowercase version if it is uppercase.

Return Value

The function `tolower()` returns the lowercase version of the character, or the character if it was not uppercase.

See Also

`toupper()`, `strupr()`, `strlwr()`, `strnupr()`, `strnlwr()`.

Example

```
yesno()
{
     int ch;

     ch = getchar();
     ch = tolower(ch);

     if(ch == 'y')
          return(1);
     return(0);
}
```

A single user-input character is converted to lowercase to avoid having to test for `'y'` or `'Y'` before the comparison is done, and TRUE is returned if the user entered `'Y'` or `'y'`.

toupper()

Summary

```
#include <ctype.h>

int toupper(ch)
int ch;                         Character
```

Description

The function `toupper()` converts the single character `ch` to its uppercase version if it is lowercase.

Return Value

The function `toupper()` returns the uppercase version of the character, or the character if it was not lowercase.

See Also

tolower(), strupr(), strlwr(), strnupr(), strnlwr().

Example

```
yesno()
{
     int ch;

     ch = getchar();
     ch = toupper(ch);

     if(ch == 'Y')
          return(1);
     return(0);
}
```

A single user-input character is converted to uppercase to avoid having to test for 'y' or 'Y' before the comparison is done; TRUE is returned if the user entered 'Y' or 'y'.

unlink()

Summary

```
#include <io.h>
#include <stdio.h>

int unlink(filename)

char *filename;                    File to delete
```

Description

The unlink() function deletes the specified filename and erases the directory entry for that file.

Return Value

The unlink() function returns zero if successful and EOF (-1) if not.

Example

```
#include <io.h>
#include <stdio.h>

main()
{
```

```
    static char workfile[]="temp.wrk";

    FILE *fn;

    fn=fopen(workfile,"w");
    process(fn);
    fclose(fn);
    unlink(workfile);
}
```

The program creates a `workfile` and passes it to a lower-level process. When the process is complete, the file is closed and deleted.

write()

Summary

```
#include <io.h>

int write(handle,buffer,count)

int handle;                    File to write to
char *buffer;                  Write from buffer
int count;                     Number of bytes to write
```

Description

The `write()` function writes `count` bytes from `buffer` to the current file position of a file opened for low-level file I/O.

Return Value

The `write()` function returns the number of bytes written.

Example

See the example for `open()`.

D

Filters, Pipes, and Redirection

One of the intriguing aspects of the MS-DOS operating system is its ability to allow the user to direct screen output to a file, another device, or a program, and to redirect standard keyboard input to come from a file, another device, or a program. Using this facility, it is possible to use existing programs and MS-DOS commands to create powerful procedures and commands that would normally be available only through a special program. Some examples of what you can do are:

- Set up the keyboard to send all characters typed directly to the printer.
- Create a batch process requiring minimal operator input to log a complete list of all files on a disk to the printer, and place a date and time stamp on the listing automatically.
- Create DIR-type commands that allow the display of directory listings by various parameters, such as file date, file size, and so on.

Many programs running under MS-DOS perform the basic function of taking input from the keyboard and putting some result on the screen as a display.

The simplest example of this is the keyboard routine itself. Every time you strike a key, an electronic signal is received from the keyboard. The signal is changed or filtered in some way and put on the screen as a character. MS-DOS refers to the keyboard as *standard input* and the screen as *standard output.*

Standard output is used all the time in programs, as almost all information ends up being displayed on the screen. The system commands DIR and TYPE use standard output (the screen) as their output. Programs such as editors and word processors use standard input (the keyboard) as well as standard output.

It is possible to change input and output for many programs to allow the character stream to come from something other than the keyboard and go to something other than the screen. Input may be redirected to come from another device, a file, or another program. Output may be redirected the same way.

Redirecting input or output to use a file or a device is called *redirection.* Redirecting input or output to use another program is called *piping.*

Redirection is done by using the symbols > or < to mean output or input respectively. Try a couple of examples and you'll get the hang of this.

The DIR command uses standard output to display a directory on the screen. To redirect the output, use the > symbol followed by the name of the file or device to which you are sending the output.

```
DIR > PRN
```

directs output to the printer.

```
DIR > JUNK.TXT
```

directs output to the file junk.txt. If you try redirecting to the printer, make sure your printer is turned on. After you type these commands, nothing will happen on the screen, and then the disk prompt will reappear. If you redirect to the printer, the printer fires up and starts printing. If you redirect to a disk file, you'll observe the disk drive starting up.

The printed version of the directory will look like the output you would have seen on the screen. If you direct output to a file, that file now exists as a text file, and it contains a copy of what would have been sent to the screen. If you want to look at the file, enter the following command:

```
TYPE JUNK.TXT
```

and the file will be displayed, containing what would have been the directory display.

The output of TYPE can also be redirected as in the following commands:

```
TYPE ANYFILE.TXT >JUNK.TXT
```

or

```
TYPE ANYFILE.TXT > PRN
```

If you think about it, however, you will realize that the first version of the TYPE command is equivalent to COPY ANYFILE.TXT JUNK.TXT. There is one advantage to redirection in a case like this. Normally, redirecting output to a file causes that file to be newly created, or the contents of any previous version of that file to be destroyed and overwritten with the new file. Redirection provides an additional output symbol, >>, which means, "Redirect the output and append it to the end of the file if the file is already there. If the file does not exist, it is created; but if it does exist, the output is just tacked on to the end."

The two commands

```
TYPE ANYFILE.TXT > JUNK.TXT
```

and

```
TYPE ANOTHER.TXT >> JUNK.TXT
```

will cause the two files ANYFILE.TXT and ANOTHER.TXT to be concatenated into one file, JUNK.TXT. If an append redirection symbol, >>, is used for a device such as PRN, the output proceeds as if you had typed > because the printer is not a file device, and the output cannot be appended to it.

The output of almost any program that puts data on the screen when run from the command processor can be directed to a file or device. One very useful one is CHKDSK. Enter the following command:

```
CHKDSK  /V
```

and you will see a complete listing of files and directories displayed on the screen. Enter

```
CHKDSK /V > PRN
```

and this very useful information will be printed out in hard copy.

Redirecting input is also possible, but there are few programs that come standard on an MS-DOS computer which allow for much in the way of input. One useful pair are the DATE and TIME twins. Enter the command DATE and the date will be displayed, and you will be prompted to input a new date. If you press Enter, the date will be left unaltered. TIME works the same way. DATE and TIME are commands that use standard input and standard output.

Now you will have to create a file that contains the response required, and use this file for input. Assume for the moment that date and time are correctly set, and all you want is to press Enter to acknowledge the message requesting that the new date (or time) be entered. Use an editor to create a file ENTER.TXT containing a single empty line. The file ENTER.TXT now contains the single keystroke (Enter).

Type:

```
DATE < ENTER.TXT
```

This command instructs the computer to run the date procedure, but when keyboard input is required, to take it from the file ENTER.TXT. When you run it, the date will be displayed. The prompt requesting the new date will appear briefly, and then the C:\> prompt reappears.

```
TIME < ENTER.TXT
```

will behave in the same way.

Now you can combine redirected input and output to produce something useful. Enter the following command:

```
DATE < ENTER.TXT > PRN
```

which means "Run the date procedure, take the input from ENTER.TXT, and send the output to the printer." The result is a date line on the printer.

```
TIME < ENTER.TXT > PRN
```

will add the time message, and finally

```
CHKDSK /V > PRN
```

redirects the output of CHKDSK to the printer. You now have a full hard copy listing of the disk contents with a date and time stamp. A batch process containing these commands could be set up that allows a log of the contents of the disk to be created on a regular basis.

The two main filters provided by MS-DOS are FIND.EXE and SORT.EXE. FIND is actually a program that will search a text file for a particular string of characters. The command

```
FIND "hello" ANYFILE.TXT
```

will search the text file ANYFILE.TXT for lines containing the string `"hello"`. FIND is case-sensitive, and in the above example would not match `"Hello"` or `"HELLO"`. When a record or line of text is found containing the string, it is displayed on the screen.

If no file is named in the command line, FIND expects the input to come from the keyboard, or rather from standard input. Try this to get the hang of it. Enter

```
FIND "abc"
```

The screen will just stare at you, as the FIND program is now running, and it is expecting some input from the keyboard. Type a few lines of text, ending each line with Enter. In some of the lines include "abc", and in others, don't. You will notice that any lines containing the string "abc" are printed twice on the screen. Each line appears once on the screen as you type it, but is displayed a second time on the screen by the FIND program, if it contains the string "abc".

Type Ctrl-Z and then press Enter to end FIND. Ctrl-Z is a standard MS-DOS end-of-file character. You want FIND to take its input from somewhere other than the keyboard.

You could use FIND by redirecting the output of one program to a temporary file, and then use that file as input to FIND, as shown in the following example:

```
DIR > TEMP.TXT
FIND "-84" < TEMP.TXT
ERASE TEMP.TXT
```

The string "-84" would appear as part of the date entry for a directory, as in "10-02-84", so this particular sequence of commands would cause a directory display of only those files containing a 1984 date. In fact, the sequence illustrated above is exactly what a pipe does. It causes output to be placed in a temporary file, and input to be pulled from that temporary file. The symbol for a pipe is ¦. On the IBM PC this key is the shifted \ key. The above sequence of DIR and FIND can be entered as

```
DIR¦FIND "84"
```

The temporary file that is created by the pipe symbol is destroyed automatically, and there is no need to enter an erase command. The output from FIND is displayed on the screen. The output from a pipe series may also be redirected, as in

```
DIR¦FIND "84" > ANYFILE.TXT
```

The output from FIND that would normally go to standard out (screen) is redirected to a file. In English, the above command is:

> "Output a directory and hand it to the FIND program. FIND passes only those lines of text containing the string "84" and sends its output to the file ANYFILE.TXT."

Piped traffic may also be piped to another program.

The other filter available with MS-DOS is SORT. SORT takes its standard input and sorts it by a position in the record. If no position is specified, the program sorts from position 1 (the first character in the record). The command

```
DIR¦SORT
```

will produce a sorted list of the output from DIR.

Check the screen display of a DIR command, and you will observe that the date of the file starts in column 24 on the screen. The following illustrates a full use of pipes:

```
DIR¦FIND "84"¦SORT /+24>ANYFILE.TXT
```

The SORT command is a little confusing at first. The / after SORT is called a switch character, and to SORT it means the next characters are a parameter for the SORT program. In this case the parameter is the column number where the sort is to begin.

In English again:

> "Output a directory and hand the output to FIND. FIND passes only those records containing "84" and hands the results to SORT. SORT sorts all records that it receives starting at position 24 in the records, and its output finally comes to rest in the file ANYFILE.TXT. ANYFILE.TXT will contain a listing of files created in 1984 sorted in date order. Column 24 is the starting position of the date in the output from a DIR command."

SORT can also be used with redirected input and output. A text file containing a list of employees with each record arranged last name, first name could be sorted in last-name order with the command

```
SORT <EMPLOYEE.TXT >NEWFILE.TXT
```

If the last name began in column 40, the sorted output could be obtained with

```
SORT /+40<EMPLOYEE.TXT>NEWFILE.TXT
```

Remember that a pipe connects a program to a program, while a redirection connects a program to a file or device. In the above example, the following would not work even though it looks like a logical piping sequence, because EMPLOYEE.TXT and NEWFILE.TXT are not programs.

```
EMPLOYEE.TXT¦SORT /+40¦NEWFILE.TXT      (wrong)
```

One final note on the brotherhood of devices and files. MS-DOS supports several devices of which only two are of interest at the moment. PRN is the printer device and CON is the console device. PRN is an output device only. CON is composed of the keyboard and the screen.

When CON is used as a device for input it refers to the keyboard, and when used for output it refers to the screen. For many of the commands that relate to files, a device may be substituted. The most useful of these is the COPY command. Normally a copy is issued as:

```
COPY FILE1.TXT FILE2.TXT       (copy file1 into file2)
```

However, if you think of COPY as a command to COPY INPUT to OUTPUT, some variations on this are

`COPY FILE1.TXT CON`	(copy FILE1.TXT to the screen)
`COPY FILE1.TXT PRN`	(copy FILE1.TXT to the printer)
`COPY CON FILE2.TXT`	(copy keyboard input to FILE2.TXT)
`COPY CON PRN`	(copy keyboard entry to printer)
`COPY CON CON`	(copy keyboard entry to screen)

The last example is silly, but is included to illustrate the point. It will work. Wherever CON is being used as input (the keyboard), input is terminated by typing Ctrl-Z followed by Enter.

One final example is relevant and useful:

```
TYPE CON >> FILE2.TXT
```

The command is to type the file CON but redirect the output and append it to the end of FILE2.TXT. CON is not a file; therefore TYPE must wait for input from the keyboard. The effect is that whatever is typed at the keyboard is appended to the end of FILE2.TXT until you enter Ctrl-Z.

E

Screen Handling and Indexed Files

Screens and Keyboards

C was developed on a DEC PDP-11 running UNIX. UNIX grew up "supporting" all types of terminals—from dumb glass TTY devices with no screen controls beyond scrolling the screen up, to full-blown color graphics terminals with function keys, editing keys, arrows, and cursor positioning. C reflects the fact that there is no such thing as a standard terminal. The standard C library functions support dumb glass TTYs, the irreducible minimum for a terminal.

This is unfortunate because there is no standard library for smarter terminals. A UNIX package called Curses tried to resolve this by providing an interface that identifies the characteristics of the underlying terminal through a terminal data base. A series of routines allow cursor positioning, screen overlays, and the ability to recognize some of the more esoteric function and editing keys.

Curses is limited, but is possibly the critter that comes closest to being a standard library for terminal I/O. Versions of the Curses library exist for IBM PCs and clones running MS-DOS and for other operating systems. This allows you to create a program that could run on a UNIX or an MS-DOS PC and appear to be much the same program on either system.

For MS-DOS machines, several companies have released terminal libraries allowing you to create scrolling menus, mouse responsive screens, and validated field entry in multiple colors.

Then came Windows and the game totally changed. If you are working in C/C++ 7.0 or Visual C++ under Windows, you will find a wealth of routines for formatted output to windowed screens.

You will also find libraries for X Motif and The X Window System, which start to provide some portability across UNIX graphical interfaces.

Screen libraries for MS-DOS (aside from Curses, which was ported from UNIX) are not portable to other systems.

Indexed Files

Indexed files are not nearly in the same desperate state of affairs as screen handlers. Files are much simpler: "There's these bytes, see, and you put 'em on a disk in some sort of order."

The most popular indexed file library seems to be C-ISAM by INFORMIX Software. There are numerous flavors of C-ISAM on the market:

- C-ISAM itself is the progenitor of the many flavors, described below. It has been around quite awhile and has proven the test of time. It is the indexed file handler that lies under the INFORMIX data base, but is available as a package by itself. It is a library of routines that allows the creation, opening, reading, and writing of indexed files with multiple indexes (a primary and several alternates). When a file is created with an index, it creates a file with a .dat extension containing the data records, and another with an .idx extension that contains the index. This dual file arrangement is invisible to the programmer, who opens a file named cust. C-ISAM takes care of opening and/or creating a cust.dat and a cust.idx file.

- D-ISAM by Byte Designs in Canada is a work-alike clone of C-ISAM. It is provided with source code that you compile into your own library. The source code is MS-DOS- and UNIX-compatible and D-ISAM libraries access C-ISAM files with no trouble.
- Micro Focus ISAM is a version of C-ISAM that omits the .dat extension from the data file, creating files named cust and cust.idx. This ISAM handler is one of the handlers used by Micro Focus COBOL. C-ISAM is a fixed length record ISAM, and Micro Focus created another ISAM handler for variable length records. The C-ISAM libraries cannot access Micro Focus ISAM files and vice versa, because of the file extension changes, but internally the files are the same. I modified a version of D-ISAM source code to omit the .dat extensions, and this library had no trouble accessing Micro Focus ISAM files.
- IBM has included a version of C-ISAM on the R/S 6000 AIX (UNIX) machines. This appears to be vanilla C-ISAM with only a few changes. Unfortunately the changes are enough to make C-ISAM libraries unable to handle IBM ISAM files.
- SCO has included yet another version of C-ISAM on their 386 and 486 UNIX machines. They've followed the same philosophy as IBM: everything looks like C-ISAM files, but you cannot access files with C-ISAM or D-ISAM routines.

How ISAM Libraries Work

An ISAM library is a library of routines that allows you to open, close, read, and write indexed records. Code your program using these function calls, and then compile and link it with an ISAM library such as isam.lib or disam.lib.

Here is a sampling of some of the routines available. There are many more.

isopen

```
#include "isam.h"

int isopen(char *filename, int mode)
```

Where:

`filename`	The name of the file.

`mode`	A combination of an access mode parameter and a locking mode. Access mode and locking mode are added together to form the open mode.
`ISINPUT`	Open for input
`ISOUTPUT`	Open for writing
`ISINOUT`	Open for I/O
`ISMANULOCK`	Use manual locking
`ISAUTOLOCK`	Use automatic locking

Return Code

The function returns an integer handle for a file to be used for subsequent I/O to that file, or `-1` if an error occurred during the open.

Example

```
isam_file = isopen("cust", ISINOUT + ISAUTOLOCK);
```

isclose

```
#include "isam.h"

int isclose(int isam_file)
```

Where:

`isam_file`	The file handle returned by a successful call to `isopen()`.

Return Code

The function returns `0` if successful, and `-1` for an error.

isread

```
#include "isam.h"

int isread(int isam_file, char *record, int mode)
```

Where:

`isam_file`	A file handle returned by a successful open.	
`record`	A pointer to a memory area that contains the key value and receives the record after the read.	
`mode`	One of the following values:	
	`ISCURR`	Read the current record.
	`ISFIRST`	Read the first record.
	`ISLAST`	Read the last record.
	`ISNEXT`	Read the next record.
	`ISPREV`	Read the previous record.
	`ISEQUAL`	Read the record whose key value is contained in the record.
	`ISGREAT`	Read the first record with a key value greater than the key value contained in the record.
	`ISGTEQ`	Read the first record greater than or equal to the key value in the record.

Return Code

The function returns `0` if successful and `-1` if there is an error.

iswrite

```
#include "isam.h"

int iswrite(int isam_file, char *record)
```

Where:

`isam_file`	A file handle returned by a successful open.
`record`	A pointer to a memory area that contains the record to write to the file.

Return Code

The function returns `0` if successful, and `-1` if there is an error.

iserrno

```
extern int iserrno;
```

The `iserrno` variable contains the error code of the last error that occurred during a file I/O request through one of the ISAM library functions.

These errors have manifest constant names defined in isam.h. Table E.1 provides examples of `iserrno` errors.

Table E.1. `iserrno` error codes.

Name	*Number*	*Description*
EDUPL	100	An attempt to write a record that would have caused a duplicate primary key or a duplicate key value on an alternate key that does not allow duplicates.
ENOTOPEN	101	I/O attempted on an unopened file.
EBADARG	102	Invalid number of arguments or content of arguments in a call to an ISAM function.
EBADKEY	103	Key description is invalid when creating a new file with `isbuild()`.
ETOOMANY	104	The maximum number of files is already open.
EBADFILE	105	The ISAM file is corrupt.
ENOTEXCL	106	An attempt to add an index to or delete an index from an ISAM file when the file has not been opened for exclusive access.

Table E.1 provides only a short selection of the error codes that appear in `iserrno`, but should give you an idea of the thoroughness of the package.

Other ISAM Libraries

There are other ISAM libraries on the market. B-Trieve is one popular package. They all function in approximately the same way: they provide a library of routines that you can call to create and access an indexed file.

When selecting a library, you should consider two questions if you want to be portable and work out their relative importance:

- How portable is the library itself? Can this ISAM package be moved to more than one target machine?
- Are the data files created by the package portable, and do they need to be?

An indexed file package that is itself portable, and creates files that can be moved to other systems is ideal, but not always necessary.

GLOSSARY

address A numeric value representing a location in a computer's memory.

aggregate A C data type composed of one or more basic C data types. Arrays and structures are both aggregates. *Aggregate* is the opposite of *atomic* when applied to C data types.

array A variable that contains a repeated occurrence of the same type of data. For example,

```
int values[6];
```

defines an array of six integers.

ASCII American Standard Code for Information Interchange. A code uscd by computers to represent the letters of the alphabet, spaces tabs and other control information for terminals and printers. See Chapter 3, "C Characters and Strings."

atomic Generally referring to something that cannot be broken into smaller parts. In C data types, `int`, `float`, `double`, `long`, and `char` are some examples of atomic data types. They cannot be reduced to smaller parts. Arrays and structures are not atomic as they are composed of smaller data types. *Atomic* is the opposite of *aggregate* when applied to data types.

auto The default storage class for variables defined inside a function. These variables are created temporarily when the function is entered, and destroyed when the function exits. The `auto` storage class is rarely used explicitly in C code.

The two definitions of `func()` below are identical.

```
func(x)
int x;
{
    int y;
    y = 2;
    return(y * x);
}
func(x)
int x;
{
    auto int y;
    y = 2;
    return(y * x);
}
```

binary A base-2 numbering system using only 0 and 1 as digits. See Chapter 13, "Based Numbers and Bit Operators."

bit map A byte, short integer, long integer, or area of memory in which the bits of each byte in the variable or memory area are used as flags to signify on/off or true/false states. In communications programs, a single byte might be used to hold a set of flags to signify the current state of the communications line.

The following bit map indicates that the remote end has sent a "ready to receive" signal, and the local end is in fact transmitting data. The local end has not indicated a readiness to receive, and the remote end is not sending data.

Bit Position	8 7 6 5 4 3 2 1
Bits	0 0 0 0 1 1 0 0

Bit 4, when on, means the remote end of the line has sent a "ready to receive" signal, and bit 3 indicates that the local end is transmitting. Bit 2, when on, indicates that the local end of the line is ready to receive, and bit 1, when on, indicates that data is being received from the remote end.

bit mask A bit map (see *bit map*) used to set, clear, or retrieve the values in another bit map. Assuming a character variable called `state` containing the following

value:

Bit Position 8 7 6 5 4 3 2 1

Bits 0 0 0 0 1 0 1 0

a bit mask of 00000010 could be defined as

```
#define TEST_STATE 0x02
```

This could be applied to state to determine if bit 2 is on, as follows:

```
    if(state & TEST_STATE)
        printf("Bit 2 is on\n");
```

In this example, `0x02` defined by `TEST_STATE` is a bit mask.

For more information about bit masks and bit maps, see Chapter 13, "Based Numbers and Bit Operators."

block A set of one or more procedure statements enclosed by opening and closing braces. In the listing below, `/*1*/` and `/*4*/` indicate the beginning and end of a block of code, which is all of the code of a function. Points `/*2*/` and `/*3*/` designate an inner block of code.

```
func(x)
int x;
{                       /*1*/
    if( x == 0)
        {               /*2*/
        x = 1;
        return(x);
        }               /*3*/
}                       /*4*/
```

carriage return See *CR.*

compiler A program that takes a source code file, processes it, and generates a translated version of the source code that the computer can understand. This translation is called an object and is usually saved in an object file.

CR The ASCII name for a carriage return character. This has a value of 13 (hexadecimal 0D) and causes terminals and printers to move the cursor or print head to the far left column of the display or page.

CR-LF A carriage return and line feed pair (see *CR* and *LF*). These characters are used to end a line of text in a text file on an MS-DOS computer. They are also the standard response of a cursor or print head at the end of a line.

declaration A description of a variable or a function in a program that names the variable or function and describes its data type, scope, and other attributes. A declaration may only describe a variable without allocating space for it.

The following declaration states that a variable named `a_value` is an array of integers and exists somewhere else in the program.

```
extern int a_value[];
```

See *prototype* for an example of a function declaration.

default A condition, value, or action that is executed or set up without having to be asked for. For example, the default initialization of a global integer is zero:

```
int a_value;
is equivalent to
int a_value = 0;
```

because 0 is the default value supplied by the compiler.

See also *implicit* and *explicit.*

definition A declaration for a variable or function that also indicates that the compiler and linker must create space for it.

The following definition is a declaration that creates an array of 5 integers named values.

```
int values[5];
```

element An individual variable in an array of the same type of variable, or an individual variable in a structure which may contain dissimilar variables.

executable A file containing a runnable program that has been created by linking one or more objects. See Appendix A, "Program Development."

explicit Describes a condition, value, or action that is specifically requested by some action. For example, C functions are given a return value type of integer, unless an explicit return type is given to the function. The following code

```
long a_func()
{
}
```

forces the compiler to see `a_func()` as a function returning a long value whereas

```
a_func()
{
}
```

will be seen by the compiler as a function returning an integer.

See also *implicit* and *default.*

`extern` A storage class used to declare a variable that is either defined later in the current source code file, or defined elsewhere in some other part of the program. In the following listing, `user_name` is a variable created in some other module in the program.

```
extern char user_name[];
print_user_name()
{
    printf("User is %s\n",user_name);
}
```

function A block of self-contained code designed to handle a specific task. All C programs require one function named `main()`.

global A variable or function that can be seen or accessed by every part of the program.

header file The C language allows a file to copy or include another file at compile time. In the listing below, for dummy.c, stdio.h is copied into the source code file when the file is compiled.

```
/* dummy.c */
#include <stdio.h>
char *str = NULL;
main()
{
    /* some code here */
}
```

The file stdio.h might contain information for compiling the program, such as:

```
#define    NULL    0
```

The stdio.h file is the standard I/O header file.

hexadecimal A base-16 numbering system using 16 digits: 0–9, A, B, C, D, E, and F. See Chapter 13, "Based Numbers and Bit Operators."

hierarchy of operators See *precedence.*

implicit Describes a condition, value, or action that is implied by context. For example, the implicit return value of a function is an integer data type:

```
a_func()
{
}
```

is equivalent to

```
int a_func()
{
}
```

because the compiler establishes an implicit return type of `int` for any function.

See also *default* and *explicit.*

ISAM Indexed Sequential Access Method. Originally a specific method of creating and accessing indexed files that allowed record storage and retrieval by a key value in the record. The term now tends to be used loosely to refer to any method of storing and retrieving indexed records. See Appendix E, "Screen Handling and Indexed Files."

LF The ASCII name for a line feed character. This has a value of 10 (hex 0A) and causes terminals and printers to move the cursor of print head to the next line on the display or page.

library A file containing one or more object files (see *object file*). It is a convenient way of combining objects for later use. A library may contain a variety of different objects that may not even be related. When a linker (see *linker*) processes a library file, it extracts only those objects that it needs. See Appendix A, "Program Development."

line feed See *LF.*

linker A program that combines object files and object files extracted from library files into an executable program. See Appendix A, "Program Development."

member An element of a structure. The `string_holder` structure in the following code contains the members `length` and `string`.

```
struct string_holder{
    int length;
    char *string;
```

```
};
```

newline A line feed character (see *LF*) used in C as a text terminator and written as `\n`. A newline character causes different behavior depending on its context:

- A newline appearing in a program is stored as a line feed character (see *LF*).
- If a string containing a newline is sent to a terminal or a printer, it behaves as a CR-LF pair (see *CR-LF*).
- If written to a file, the newline is stored as the end of line terminator used by the target machine for a text file. Under UNIX this is a line feed character; under MS-DOS this is a carriage return and line feed pair.

NUL The ASCII name for the character that has a value of zero.

NULL A convention in C used to indicate a pointer to nothing. NULL is not a C reserved word, but is defined in the stdio.h header file with whatever value the target machine needs to signify a pointer to nothing (see *header file*).

object file A file containing codes that can be understood by a computer that has been created by compiling (see *compiler*) a source code file (see *source code*). See Appendix A, "Program Development."

octal A base-8 numbering system using 8 digits, 0–7. See Chapter 13, "Based Numbers and Bit Operators."

order of operators See *precedence.*

pass by address A method of passing a variable to a function by passing the address of the variable in memory. If the called function modifies the variable by using the address to locate the variable and changing the value, the value is changed in both the called and calling function. This is sometimes called *pass by reference.*

pass by copy See *pass by value.*

pass by reference See *pass by address.*

pass by value A method of passing a variable to a function by making a copy of the variable and giving it to the called function. If the called function changes the variable, it does not affect the value of the variable in the calling function. This is sometimes called *pass by copy.*

pointer In C programs, a variable that holds the address of another variable, or is considered to hold an address of a value when used in equations or function calls.

precedence The order in which operators are applied to an expression or a statement. Usually called *precedence of operators.* In the expression

```
x = 1 + 3 * 4;
```

the `*` operator has a higher precedence than the `+` operator. The expression is evaluated as

```
x = 1 + (3 * 4);
```

rather than

```
x = (1 + 3) * 4;
```

setting `x` to 13 instead of 16.

This is also sometimes called *order of operators* or *hierarchy of operators.*

prototype A C function declaration that describes the value returned by a function and the variable types expected by the function.

```
int strlen(char*);
```

declares `strlen()` to be a function that returns an integer, and is passed a pointer to a `char`.

```
char *strcpy(char*,char*);
```

declares `strcpy()` as a function that returns a pointer to `char` and expects to be passed two pointers to `char`.

register A storage class used for variables defined inside functions and for declarations of variables passed to functions. It indicates that the temporary variable associated with that storage class is to be placed in a machine register, or other fast access area to improve the speed of accessing and using the variable. In `fast_count()` below, the variable `x` will be placed in a register if one is available, which will speed up the time up the loop.

```
fast_count()
{
    register int x;
    for(x = 0; x < 32000; ++x)
        {
        /* do something */
```

```
        }
}
```

relational operator An operator that is used to compare two expressions usually used in an `if` statement. Some C relational operators are

```
if( x != y)    not equal
if( x == y)    is equal
if( x < y)     is less than
```

scope The range over which a variable or function is available to other functions in the final executable program. C has three scopes that are established by storage classes and by the location of the variable in the source code (see storage class). See Chapter 8, "Scope, Storage, and Prototyping."

- **global** Available to all parts of the program.
- **local** Available only within one source code file.
- **block** Available only within a block of code such as a single function.

source file A text file containing statements in a programming language. A file containing

```
#include <stdio.h>
main()
{
    printf("Hello world.");
}
```

named hello.c would be a C source code file. See Appendix A, "Program Development."

`static` A storage class that can be assigned to functions, variables within a function, or variables defined outside a function. Functions and variables outside of functions classed as `static` are only available within a particular source code file. Variables within a function classed as `static` are only available within the function, but retain their value between function calls and are not destroyed when the function exits. `static` variables within a function may be initialized, as shown in the following code:

```
error_msg(msg)
{
    static char emsg[]= "error";
    printf("%s:%s\n",emsg,msg);
}
```

In `error_msg()`, the string `emsg` is defined and initialized as a constant used only by the `error_msg()` function.

stdio.h The standard I/O header file (see *header file*).

storage class A keyword in C used to tell the compiler how to treat variables and functions at compile time. C storage classes are

- `auto`
- `register`
- `extern`
- `static`
- `typedef`

Each of these is described in this glossary. Also see Chapter 8, "Scope, Storage, and Prototyping."

string A combined C data type. This is actually an array of characters that is treated specially by the C compiler. A string contains one or more characters and is terminated by a 0 or an ASCII NUL.

structure A user-defined composite data type composed of other C data types.

In the following code, `string_holder` can be considered a single C data type containing an integer and a pointer to `char`. The elements of the structure are called members.

```
struct string_holder{
    int length;
    char *string;
};
```

structure tag The identifier in a structure declaration by which the structure becomes known. The tag can then be used to define instances of the structure.

In the following example, `_cust` is the structure tag.

```
struct _cust{
    int no;
    char name[31];
    };
```

Instances of this structure are defined by using the tag as in:

```
struct _cust customer;
```

subscript A number in brackets that identifies one element of an array. The `2` in the following code is a subscript identifying a single element of the data array.

```
int data[4]={10,20,30,40};
    data[2] = 15;
```

`typedef` A storage class used to create an alias for another C data type. In the following code, `LONG_INT` becomes an alias for the `long` data type.

```
typedef long LONG_INT;
func()
{
    LONG_INT one,two;
    /* do something */
}
```

INDEX

Symbols

A

C

D

E

F

G

H

I

J-K

L

M

N

O

P

Q-R

U

V

W

X-Z

Book ISBN 0-672-30327-2

Order Your Program Disk Today

You can save yourself hours of tedious typing by ordering the companion disk to *Moving from COBOL to C.* The disk contains the source code for all of the complete programs and many of the code samples in this book. You get code that shows you how to do screen input and output, build your own C libraries, and do file IO. Disks are available in 3 ½-inch or 5 ¼-inch format. The cost is $12.00 per disk.

Just make a copy of this page, fill in the blanks, and mail it with your check or postal money order to:

Mo Budlong, COBOL to C Disk
PO Box 728
Tujunga, CA 91043-0728

Please print the following information:

Number of 3 ½ disks:________________________ @ $12.00 = __________

Number of 5 ¼ disks:________________________ @ $12.00 = __________

Name: ____

Street Address: __________________________________

City: ____________________________State: __________

ZIP: ____

Checks and money orders should be made payable to Mo Budlong.

Foreign orders:

Please use a separate page to give your mailing address in the format required by your post office. Add $5.00 for shipping and handling. Make payment by International Money Order in U.S. dollars.

(This offer is made by Mo Budlong, not by Sams Publishing.)